THINKING skills

ages 9-11

CREDITS

Author
Georgie Beasley

Editor
Gaynor Spry

Assistant Editor
Helen Skelton

Series Designers
Rachael Hammond
Joy Monkhouse

Designer
Rachael Hammond

Illustrations
Robin Edmonds

Cover image
© Digital Vision and © Dynamic Graphics

Material from The National Curriculum © Crown copyright. Reproduced with the permission of the Controller of HMSO and the Queen's Printer for Scotland.

Material from the National Literacy Strategy *Framework for Teaching* and the National Numeracy Strategy *Framework for Teaching Mathematics* © Crown copyright. Reproduced under the terms or HMSO Guidance Note 8.

Published by Scholastic Ltd,
Villiers House,
Clarendon Avenue,
Leamington Spa,
Warwickshire CV32 5PR

www.scholastic.co.uk

Text © 2004 Georgie Beasley
© 2004 Scholastic Ltd

Designed using Adobe Indesign

Printed by Bell & Bain Ltd, Glasgow

1 2 3 4 5 6 7 8 9 0   4 5 6 7 8 9 0 1 2 3

British Library Cataloguing-in-Publication Data
A catalogue record for this book is available from the British Library.

ISBN 0-439-98341-X

CONTENTS

 INTRODUCTION 5

INFORMATION-PROCESSING SKILLS 7

REASONING SKILLS 32

 ENQUIRY SKILLS 59

 CREATIVE THINKING SKILLS 84

 EVALUATION SKILLS 107

 CROSS-CURRICULAR PROJECTS 132

INTRODUCTION

Thinking Skills is a series of books which outlines detailed lesson plans for developing children's thinking and helping them to develop key skills of learning. The series gives ideas on how to incorporate the teaching of thinking skills into current curriculum teaching by making changes to the way activities are presented and, in particular, matching tasks to the different ways that children learn.

There are five thinking skills identified in the National Curriculum 2000 document:
- information-processing skills
- reasoning skills
- enquiry skills
- creative thinking skills
- evaluation skills.

Teachers are probably most familiar with information-processing skills and are used to planning activities to develop these skills in maths and science. Similarly, evaluative thinking skills are usually developed well in gymnastics, dance, music and design and technology lessons, when children are encouraged to evaluate the quality of their own and other's performances, or the quality of their models and other artefacts and to consider ways to make any improvements. The aim of this series of books is to find contexts in all subjects in which to develop all types of thinking skills.

ABOUT THE BOOK

Where appropriate, this book follows the National Literacy and Numeracy strategy objectives and the QCA Schemes of Work for all National Curriculum subjects.

The activities in this book identify exactly how to develop each thinking skill within specific units of work. They also show how to adapt familiar activities to make sure that suitable emphasis is given to developing children's thinking. Sometimes an activity which follows one identified in a QCA

unit of work is planned with a specific focus on its organisation so that it will support the development of children's thinking. Sometimes activities rely on specific questions which will encourage the children to identify why a particular activity is being done.

There are many specific learning styles and strategies that encourage children's thinking, including those to develop memory, thought sharing, concept mapping and exchanging ideas. Very often a lesson activity can be organised in a different way to allow children to organise their own thoughts and work. This will encourage thinking rather than having knowledge over-directed. For example, the activity in the Enquiry skills chapter 'Fairground rides' (page 65) encourages the children to think of their own questions to plan their research. This helps them to define the problems they are likely to meet whilst researching, and to decide whether the information they collect is relevant to their studies. In this way they are becoming independent learners and will have the necessary skills to plan and carry out independent research into other topics and themes. Too often children are told how to present their findings with too little opportunity to understand why.

QUESTIONING

Asking questions of children is a dangerous sport. We all think in a different way and the first thing to remember about asking questions is that children of this age are most definitely not thinking the same things, or in the same way, as the teacher. Questions which encourage children to guess what the teacher is thinking are the worst kind to ask. Instead, open-ended questions not only help the teacher to find out what the children are thinking, but also what they already know. This helps the teacher to understand where the children are in their thinking processes and to gain an insight into their conceptual

6

understanding. This early assessment will help the teacher form the next set of questions to challenge and build on the children's understanding.

There are different kinds of questions that can be asked to encourage and actively develop children's thinking. The skill of questioning isn't always getting the question right but being able to respond to the children's answers with another suitable question. This way the teacher is not giving the children a right or wrong answer but using questioning to direct their thinking to the correct answer. This will enable children to think their way to the correct answer by themselves and iron out any misconceptions that they may have. There are suggestions to get teachers started on this process and these can be used as prompts to help direct the children's thinking towards the required answer for the purpose of the activity.

THE ORGANISATION OF THE BOOK

There are six chapters in this book. The first five focus on developing each of the five types of thinking. Chapter 6 includes two thinking-skills projects and in order to complete them children will be required to work over a longer period of time than is required for the other activities in the book. These projects, entitled 'Italy' and 'Planning a school trip', are suitable for the end of the summer term after SATs. They are intended to develop all the thinking skills in a themed cross-curricular way.

Each chapter begins with a short explanation of the thinking skill being focused on and is followed by two sections of activities – to introduce then extend skills – each section covering most if not all of the curriculum subjects. Each section has a quick-reference grid for teachers to see what the activities contain and quickly evaluate which fit easily into their own schemes of work.

The first section introduces thinking in short activities. These contain a learning objective specific to the activity and related to QCA Schemes of Work or the Literacy or Numeracy Strategies. A 'Thinking objective' outlines the particular thinking skill that the children will be developing in the activity. This is expanded under 'Thinking skills', which detail how the activity will bring out the thinking skills in line with the learning objective. A useful resource list is provided along with a detailed explanation of how to conduct the activity. These detailed activities have been designed to encourage and develop the children's thinking skills through practical investigation and enquiry. They are structured to encourage the children to ask why that particular activity is being carried out. Particular emphasis is placed on 'how' the children will learn – the way the learning is organised and the involvement of the children in this process – rather than the 'what'. Suggestions for questions to spark discussion and encourage the children to pose questions for investigation themselves are a focus of the activities.

The second section contains extended activities which, in addition to those sections outlined above, also contain a differentiation section with suggestions for how lower attaining children can be supported and the thinking of higher attaining children can be extended. The 'Where next' section gives ideas on how teachers can consolidate, practise, reintroduce or extend the particular activity and thinking skill. There is assessment advice on how to gauge the children's success in thinking through a problem or planning an investigation. 'Learning outcomes' relate to the 'Thinking objectives', expanding on them to describe what the children have achieved and can now do as a result of the lesson.

INFORMATION-PROCESSING SKILLS

INTRODUCTION

Information processing is about being able to collect, sort, organise and interpret a range of information to support learning in all subjects. By learning to process information in different ways, children make sense of the world in which they live. The process is more than presenting data in different forms. It also involves deciding whether information is useful for a particular purpose. Organising information in certain ways can support memory development, and help to make links and identify pattern and relationships between different pieces of information.

Information can be found in the form of data, facts and knowledge. Data is collected in maths, science, history, geography, ICT and design and technology. Most data is recorded in graphical form through tables, pictograms, bar charts and sets. Facts are found to support learning in most subjects, including history, geography, music, art and design and RE. In history, for instance, timelines are a useful way to sequence facts to allow understanding of chronology and the passing of time. In geography, collecting, measuring and comparing weather statistics help children identify pattern and relationships in climate and give an insight into how climate changes affect where and how people live. Knowledge is collected to support work in English, maths and PE and helps children develop the key skill of identifying what they need to do to improve their own performance. ICT is used throughout to sort and present data in a range of different forms, as well as being used as a source for research activities. The activities in this chapter show how computers and other ICT equipment can be used to support learning in a range of subjects.

Information processing helps children to develop the learning process and equips them with skills which can be applied throughout their school career. By allowing the children to process information more and more independently, you enable thinking to be developed.

The key to information processing is opening the children's inquisitive minds. *What are we trying to find out and for what purpose?* is the usual question, but we need to take the children beyond that for them to realise that information will give us more than one answer, and often raises further questions. By adjusting the organisation of existing lessons and planned activities, and identifying suitable questions which will require the children to consider carefully what they are doing and why, they will process the information as a natural part of learning. This means that we must learn to step back and give the children time to organise the learning themselves, develop their ideas and refrain from directing them towards the lessons' objectives. By allowing children this freedom, they will begin to notice when they can use the processes in other learning. This will accelerate learning in the long term.

The lessons in this chapter require you to let the children explain what they are doing so that their thinking can be assessed. You can then move things forward by asking relevant and open questions to shift the direction of the work or consolidate the children's ideas.

Skills in the following areas all form a part of information processing:
- sequencing
- pattern and relationship
- sorting and classifying
- matching
- locating and collecting
- comparing and measuring
- analysing.

INTRODUCING INFORMATION-PROCESSING SKILLS

Subject and QCA unit, NLS or NNS objective	Activity title	Thinking objective	Activity	Page
English NLS objective: To explore onomatopoeia; to understand terms which describe different kinds of poems and to identify typical features; to recognise how poets manipulate words; to investigate humorous verse	Limericks and all that	To analyse and collect	Analysing the structure and poetic devices of different types and styles of poetry to note what each has in common	9
Maths NNS objective: To solve a problem by representing, extracting and interpreting data in tables, graphs, charts and diagrams	Football divisions	To collect data	Keeping football tables up to date and relating this to team points, and any other sporting positional table	9
Science QCA unit: 5A Keeping healthy	Healthy lifestyles	To collect and sort information	Sorting substances into good and bad, and foods into different groups, classifying them by the essentials they provide	10
History QCA unit: 13 How has life in Britain changed since 1948?	Teenage revolution	To locate and collect information	Looking at the changes brought about by the teenage revolution following World War II	11
Geography QCA unit: 11 Water	Saving water	To measure and compare	Carrying out a survey of the amount of water used in school over a week and identifying ways to reduce this level	11
Design and technology QCA unit: 5C Moving toys	Nodding animals	To sort and analyse information	Analysing the mechanism to inform a design for a nodding toy	12
ICT QCA unit: 5E Controlling devices; 6C Control and monitoring – What happens when ...?	Lights, camera, action	To sort and classify information	Sorting everyday devices according to whether they are controlled by instructions, a timing device or by a sensor	13
Art and design QCA unit: 6A People in action	Expressive faces	To identify pattern and relationships	Identifying and analysing the pattern and relationships between a range of faces	14
Music QCA unit: 15 Ongoing skills	Staccato and legato	To locate and match techniques	Matching staccato or legato techniques to create singing effects	15
RE QCA unit: 5C Where did the Christian Bible come from?	Bible facts	To analyse and sort	Analysing the books contained in the Bible and sorting them into types	15
PE QCA unit: 5 Gymnastics activities	Forward roll	To analyse and sequence	Analysing the start, middle and end of different gymnastic rolls and tumbles	16

LIMERICKS AND ALL THAT

SUBJECT: ENGLISH. NLS OBJECTIVES: TO EXPLORE ONOMATOPOEIA; TO UNDERSTAND TERMS WHICH DESCRIBE DIFFERENT KINDS OF POEMS AND TO IDENTIFY TYPICAL FEATURES; TO RECOGNISE HOW POETS MANIPULATE WORDS; TO INVESTIGATE HUMOROUS VERSE.

LEARNING OBJECTIVES
To recognise different kinds of poetry; to understand some of the ways poets communicate their intention.

THINKING OBJECTIVE
To analyse and collect.

THINKING SKILLS
The children will analyse poems in two ways. First, they will classify the poem based on an analysis of rhythm, rhyming pattern, number of syllables and lines, and whether it contains humour or narrative. Then they will look at poetic devices and features used by poets to convey moods and feelings, and use these to analyse how poets manipulate words to communicate their intention to the reader.

WHAT YOU NEED
Several poetry anthologies containing similar and different styles (include anthologies by the same author, such as Roger McGough, Allan Ahlberg, Edward Lear and Christina Rossetti); poems from different cultures and countries; Post-it Notes.

WHAT TO DO
Set up a classification system for the children to follow when they are introduced to a new kind of poem. First, look at the poetry books in your collection and revisit the poets. Look in the index and locate some of the children's favourite poems. Pass the books around and ask pairs to find one they like. Ask, *What type of poem it is?* Invite one or two children to say which poem they have chosen and what kind of poem it is. Ask, *How do you know?* Discuss the content (narrative, humour, ballad), the poem's rhythm and rhyme (limerick, sonnet), the number of syllables and lines (haiku, tanka). Ask, *How do you know this is a limerick? How is it structured? Which lines rhyme? What about the syllable pattern? How is this structured? Are they always the same? Are any lines repeated?*

Compare a suitable sonnet by William Shakespeare, such as numbers 17 or 23, to 'Soccer Sonnet' by Allan Ahlberg, and compare the rhyming scheme. Ask, *How do you know this is a sonnet? How many lines does it have?* Invite the children to select a favourite poem and to analyse the structure and the poetic device used. Present the findings to the class orally or in writing for a display.

Choose an engaging poem such as 'The Sound Collector' by Roger Mc Gough or 'Team Talk' by Allan Ahlberg. Read the poem and discuss the structure: number of verses, lines in each verse, the rhythm and rhyme. Analyse the number of syllables and stanza, the rhythmic pattern and rhyming lines. Look closely at the language used. Annotate the devices the poet uses such as alliteration, imagery, onomatopoeia, similes and metaphors using Post-it Notes.

Share the children's discoveries. Discuss how the poets depict humour, suspense and imagery, and how they manipulate words. Ask, *What devices do they use? How are different poems structured? What does this tell you about the kind of poems they are?* Display the analysed poems and invite the children to add others of the same kind or that use the same devices.

FOOTBALL DIVISIONS

SUBJECT: MATHS. NNS OBJECTIVE: TO SOLVE A PROBLEM BY REPRESENTING, EXTRACTING AND INTERPRETING DATA IN TABLES, GRAPHS, CHARTS AND DIAGRAMS.

LEARNING OBJECTIVE
To present data in tables to help extract useful information and solve problems.

THINKING OBJECTIVE
To collect data.

THINKING SKILLS
The children will collect the current football results and record these as tables and graphs. The activity could be adapted for any context which provides mathematical information that can be interpreted and represented in a variety of ways.

WHAT YOU NEED
A set of football scores for the current season; names of the football teams in your chosen division; paper and writing materials.

WHAT TO DO
Ask the children to keep the football results for the Premier division or the division in which their favourite team plays. They should tally the number of times each team wins, draws or loses, and award the correct number of points: three for a win, one for a draw, zero for a lost match. Ask them to compile a league table to show each team's position each week, with the team names on labels that can be moved around according to their performance. Ask, *How can you keep track of the number of goals each team scores each week?* (Individuals could pick one team in the league and keep a running total of the number of goals they score each week.)

Using the tally chart, ask the children to represent the information as a graph, showing how many times the teams score nil, one, two, three, four or five goals as the season progresses. (One football symbol could represent four goals.) Challenge the children to glean as much information as they can about each match, such as the player formation used, shirt numbers worn, the size of the pitch in length, width, perimeter and area, crowd attendance, crowd capacity, and ticket-pricing structure. Towards the end of the season, challenge the children to predict who can still win the league by calculating the total number of points each team could win. Ask, *What would happen if this team won or lost?* Challenge the children to find ways to represent this probability score. Find the mode, mean and median scores for each team.

Ask the children to take any object and record all the mathematical facts they can about it. For example, look at different-sized chocolate bars and record the size, volume, weight and content of each ingredient, and calculate these as percentages per bar. As a graph and/or a pie chart, record the children's favourites (one symbol could represent five bars). Ask, *Can you work out how many bars would*

be needed to stretch around the perimeter of the classroom, placed edge-to-edge?

HEALTHY LIFESTYLES
SUBJECT: SCIENCE. QCA UNIT: 5A KEEPING HEALTHY.

LEARNING OBJECTIVES
To learn that some foods give energy, some are necessary for growth and others provide other essential properties; to learn that fats, sugars and starches provide energy; to learn that some substances are harmful.

THINKING OBJECTIVE
To collect and sort information.

THINKING SKILLS
The children will collect pictures of different foods, and substances such as tobacco, alcohol, drugs and medicines, and consider whether they are good or bad for their health. They will classify the items into those which are essential, desirable, necessary for growth, or energy-giving. They will also use the information they gather during the activity to realise that some foods provide more than one essential property.

WHAT YOU NEED
Pictures of foods and drinks, and harmful substances; large sheets of paper and glue.

WHAT TO DO
Look at the pictures and ask, *Is this food/drink/ substance essential or harmful to your health?* Discuss the reasons why. For example, tobacco is a drug and has been linked with cancer, most recreational drugs are dangerous and an overdose can be fatal, fish is essential as it provides for the growth of healthy cells. Look at the remaining pictures and decide why they have not been categorised as essential or harmful. Discuss how medicines can be harmful if taken at certain times but can be essential at other times. Talk about how fats, sugar and starch are all necessary but in small quantities. Be sensitive to those children who may be overweight.

Challenge the children to draw conclusions and write these as statements at the bottom of each list. For example, 'These things are harmful to your health', 'These things are necessary in small quantities to give energy, or cure ailments', and 'These things are essential for growth'.

Ask groups to divide a large sheet of paper into three columns with the headings: 'Energy-giving foods', 'Foods necessary for growth', 'Other essentials including fibre, minerals and vitamins to keep the body healthy'. Ask them to classify each food item according to the essential it provides. If an item gives more than one essential they should put it into more than one column. Draw conclusions from each grouping and write these at the bottom of each column. For example, 'Foods which are energy-giving are starches, sugars or fats', 'Foods which provide for growth are dairy, meat and fish products', 'Foods which provide fibre, minerals and vitamins include grains, fruit and vegetables'. Ring all those foods that appear in more than one list and discuss these.

At the end of the lesson, compare each group's classifications, noting any differences. Ask, *Are both groups right? Why? Why not?*

TEENAGE REVOLUTION

SUBJECT: HISTORY. QCA UNIT: 13 HOW HAS LIFE IN BRITAIN CHANGED SINCE 1948?

LEARNING OBJECTIVE
To carry out personal research about the recent past by locating and collecting information about life after World War II.

THINKING OBJECTIVE
To locate and collect information.

THINKING SKILLS
The children will research what life was like immediately after World War II for young people and women, in particular the impact of pop music and new technology. Groups will research different elements of that period and identify areas for further exploration, then consider how these factors impacted on social attitudes during the 1960s.

WHAT YOU NEED
Accessibility to reference materials, including music of the 1950s in vinyl and CD form, news reports, magazines, photographs, records and videos of pop artists (such as Bill Haley); Internet access.

WHAT TO DO
Look at photographs of people in the 1950s and talk about the state of the world at this time. Reflect on the impact of World War II on the lives of ordinary people. Talk about the teenage revolution, the coming of rock'n'roll via TV, radio and record players, and consider what parents may have thought about teddy boys, swirly skirts and the latest pop music. Watch a video of Bill Haley singing 'Rock Around the Clock' and note the differences between his hairstyle, clothes and music style to that of people in Britain immediately after World War II. Ask, *Which fashion/ style of music do you prefer? Why?*

Explain that you want the children to research different aspects of teenage life in the 1950s and '60s. List all the possible reference sources, and talk about how to use each one. (Check suitable websites beforehand and give the children a restricted list.)

Organise groups to research 1950s' fashions, pop music, technology (including TV and films), means of transport, everyday home appliances, and famous people. Ask the children to list the information and the source on one side of a large sheet of paper. Then ask them to find a fact which explains the impact of each item on ordinary people, on social attitudes, and on changes it brought to everyday activities.

As a class, share the lists of facts and the relating reference material. Discuss which sources the children found most useful and why, linking the activity briefly to evaluation skills. Use the list to identify ways to research the aspects in more detail, identifying links to enquiry skills.

SAVING WATER

SUBJECT: GEOGRAPHY. QCA UNIT: 11 WATER.

LEARNING OBJECTIVE
To learn about the uses of water and consider ways to conserve it when used for non-essential activities.

THINKING OBJECTIVE
To measure and compare.

THINKING SKILLS
The children will carry out a survey to find out how water is used by different classes. They will collect information about the uses and the amount of water used for each type of activity and collate the information. They will measure the quantity of water used for some activities and compare the results across classes. They will use the information to suggest ways of conserving water for non-essential activities. They will also suggest more effcient ways of using water for hand washing and flushing the toilet.

WHAT YOU NEED
A spreadsheet; measuring jugs; survey sheets.

WHAT TO DO
Tell the class that they are going to carry out a survey to find out how much water is used by each class every day. They will record how much water is used for different activities then compare the information to see if one class uses more or less water than other classes for the same activity. The information will be recorded on a large picture of a sea lion pool where the amount of water used every week is removed. The aim is to reduce the amount of non-essential water used, but not at the expense of essential activities such as drinking and hand washing. Organise pairs to visit each classroom in advance to explain what they will be doing and why. (You will need cooperation from other teachers, and give thought to what class work the observers will be missing when they are absent from their own class. Alternatively, each class might like to record their own data for your class to collate at the end of each week.)

For each class, provide a chart with five columns headed 'Monday' to 'Friday'. Discuss which classroom activities use water and list these down the left-hand side of the chart: drinking, hand washing, filling the water tray, flushing the toilet, washing paint pots.

Set up an observation rota for these activities, with pairs recording how much water is used. The observers should also note answers to the following: *Are the paint pots washed in a bowl so that the water can be used for several pots, or are they washed out under a running tap? To wash their hands, do the children fill the washbasin or run their hands under a tap? Measure how much water is used each time to flush the toilet? Is this amount of water necessary? Can the job be done as efficiently with less water? What can we do to reduce the amount of water used?*

At the end of the week, collate how much water is used in each class for the different activities. Compare the amounts and talk about why some classes use more water than others. This could be related to the age of the children or the method used for the different activities. For each activity, discuss which method uses just the right amount necessary to do the job properly. Talk about how best to present these findings at an assembly. (It is important to emphasise that drinking a good amount of water every day is essential, though.)

Continue the observations over a few weeks and note whether the amount of water being used has reduced, and whether the children are thinking about how to save water. Each week, record the reduction in the use of water on your picture – leaving more water for the sea lions to enjoy!

Relate this work to the use of water in different countries where, through absolute necessity, water is used for essential activities only. Research how these hot countries use irrigation systems to preserve water.

NODDING ANIMALS

SUBJECT: DESIGN AND TECHNOLOGY. QCA UNIT: 5C MOVING TOYS.

LEARNING OBJECTIVES
To recognise the movement of a mechanism within a model; to understand that a cam will change rotary motion into linear motion.

THINKING OBJECTIVE
To sort and analyse information.

THINKING SKILLS
The children will begin by looking closely at a range of toys which move. They will sort them according to the type of movement and the way the parts are made to move. They will analyse those with a cam mechanism to understand how rotary motion can be changed to linear motion. They will then adapt this idea to think about how it can be used to make a moving model.

WHAT YOU NEED
A nodding dog or similar toy; a collection of toys that move in different ways, including those with spring, pneumatic, lever and wheel mechanisms; prototypes and/or toys that have a cam mechanism (there are few newer toys available which show the cam mechanism clearly, but Technic Lego is one kit the children can use to make their own mechanisms).

WHAT TO DO

Pass the toys around for the children to look at. Talk about the parts that move and ask, *Do any have parts which move freely but rely on other mechanisms to make them work? Are there any that work with cogs?*

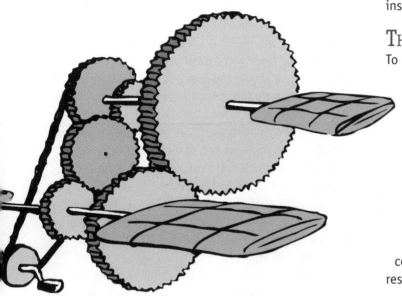

What do you notice about the way the direction of turn can be changed when the cogs turn? Why are cogs used? Is it to guide a particular part into place? Ask the children to sort the collection into sets according to their mechanism. Look at the toys that move with wheels and discuss how they move along. Note also that some of these toys have a moving part that goes up and down or backwards and forwards. Ask, *How do these work?* Explain that these toys have 'cams' – a mechanism that allows the rotary motion (the turn) to change the movement of some parts into linear motion (moving up and down, or forwards and backwards).

Show the children the toys that use cams and analyse these together. Discuss the kinds of toys that could make use of this mechanism, such as animals with nodding heads, cars containing bouncing passengers, and frogs that jump on and off lily pads. With higher attaining children, talk about how to make a cam from a worm cog mechanism. This allows the wheel to move along while changing rotary into linear motion. This mechanism would be particularly useful for making a toy that moves along as well as up and down, such as dolphins jumping out of water.

The children can use commercial kits such as Lego and K-Nex to make models which use cams to change rotary to linear motion.

LIGHTS, CAMERA, ACTION

SUBJECT: ICT. QCA UNIT: 5E CONTROLLING DEVICES; 6C CONTROL AND MONITORING – WHAT HAPPENS WHEN ... ?

LEARNING OBJECTIVE

To learn that devices are controlled through direct instructions or physical change.

THINKING OBJECTIVE

To sort and classify information.

THINKING SKILLS

The children will consider the range of everyday devices which are controlled by instructions (traffic lights and pedestrian crossings, timers such as central heating systems, lights and alarm clocks) or by physical change (thermostats in heating systems and refrigerators, and light sensors). They will sort and classify these according to whether they are controlled through a set of instructions, or as a result of physical change.

WHAT YOU NEED

Pictures and/or small models of things that are controlled by instructions, timers, changes in light, temperature and sound, including refrigerators, video recorders, washing machines, microwaves, outside lights, burglar alarms, traffic lights, car park barriers (light, ticket and money operated), escalators (those which move constantly and those that operate when someone stands on them), automatic doors and sound-activated key fobs; paper; writing materials.

WHAT TO DO

Show the children a toy which dances or sings when a button is pressed, and which works for so long and then stops. Discuss how it operates through a set of instructions which start when the switch is on and stops after the sequence of instructions is finished. Brainstorm other items that work in the same way and list them.

Next think about devices that operate through timers plus a set of instructions, such as video recorders and microwaves, and agree that these belong to the first set because the timer is part of the instruction. Refine the first list to include those devices which include a time element in their instruction sequence.

Look at a model that works when a light sensor is broken – frogs that croak when something moves in front of the sensor work well. Ask, *How is this object different to the ones in the earlier set?* Agree that the frog is controlled by a sensor which operates the noise when a change occurs – when somethng interrupts the light. Brainstorm other items that work in the same way and list them.

Give groups pictures of devices that are controlled by a timer, a set of instructions or a sensor which monitors physical change. Ask the children to sort the pictures into these three sets, discussing their criteria as they do so. Ask higher attaining children to consider whether the items in the set controlled by instructions need one or a sequence of instructions to operate.

EXPRESSIVE FACES

SUBJECT: ART AND DESIGN. QCA UNIT: 6A PEOPLE IN ACTION.

LEARNING OBJECTIVE
To learn that the features on faces have relative positions and distances.

THINKING OBJECTIVE
To identify pattern and relationships.

THINKING SKILLS
The children will look in mirrors and find pattern and relationships in their own and other's faces. They will consider the relationship between the position and distance of facial features and use this information to draw portraits, note changes in their features when they make different expressions, collect a range of faces and describe how the features create different expressions. Finally, they will look at portraits by Picasso and think about how he has changed the relationship between the position and distance between features to create a unique way of presenting faces. (Be sensitive to any Muslim children for whom it is not acceptable to reproduce the human body.)

WHAT YOU NEED
Portraits by Picasso; mirrors; photographs and pictures of peoples' and animals' faces; paper; pastels; scissors; glue.

WHAT TO DO
Give each child a mirror and allow about two minutes for them to look at the position of their eyes, and their relative position and size to their nose, mouth, lips and ears.

Pass around the pictures of faces and discuss what makes these people look different from each other (the shape, size and colour of each of the features). Ask, *What do the faces have in common? What can you say about the comparative distance between each*

feature, for example the eyes and the ears? What about the comparative position of the eyes and nose? Note the comparative position and distance between other features on the faces. Ask, *Are they all the same or are they different in some way?*

Explain that you are going to draw a 'universal face'. Use pastels to draw a faint outline of a face on a large sheet of paper. Discuss how people have different-shaped faces but for the purpose of this activity you will use this shape today. Ask, *Which feature shall I add first? Which is the most prominent?* (Eyes.) *Where should the eyes go? Are they in the same position on every face?* Ask the children to look in the mirrors again and to describe the exact position of their eyes on their faces. (They will probably suggest about a third from the top of the face.) Using a picture of someone with a shaved head, measure the distance from top to bottom of the head and then the distance of the eyes from the top and bottom. You will discover that the eyes are in the centre of the head. Are the children surprised? Draw the eyes and eyebrows in.

Repeat the process with the other features. Talk about the relative position of the ears to the eyes by referring to spectacles. Ask, *Where are the tops of the ears in relation to the eyes? How do you know the tops of the ears are in line with the eyes? How do you know the bridge of the nose is in line with the eyes? What would glasses look like if this were not the case?* Continue drawing the other features, noting their relative position and distance from each other.

Invite the children to pull faces in the mirrors, and ask, *How did your features change when you made a surprised expression? How did your eyes look when you were cross or angry? What happened to the eyes and mouth when you smiled? Did the ears and hair change or stay the same? Did the position of any features move? Which ones? How?*

As a class, make a faces board by collecting faces from magazines, photographs, comic books and those that the children draw themselves. Include portraits from famous artists. Label the faces with the different shapes of heads, faces and features, and note the pattern and relationships that exist between them. Write descriptions of the different expressions shown, and how changing the shape, size and/or position of some or all of the features does this.

Now look at how Picasso changes the pattern and relationships of features in his paintings. Consider the angular effect he creates and the way he positions the eyes to create the uniqueness in his work. Ask, *Can you find any pattern or relationship between the features? What are the expressions of the people in these paintings?*

STACCATO AND LEGATO

SUBJECT: MUSIC. QCA UNIT: 15 ONGOING SKILLS.

LEARNING OBJECTIVE
To improve performance skills in singing and production quality by using diction, staccato and legato singing techniques.

THINKING OBJECTIVE
To locate and match techniques.

THINKING SKILLS
The children will learn to locate long (legato) and short (staccato) notes in different pieces of music, and consider how these create certain moods and effects. They will use these to perform songs, and to improve their singing skills and performance techniques. The children will listen carefully to the natural pauses or phrase demarcations in a song and match these to the breathing opportunities.

WHAT YOU NEED
A collection of familiar songs that use legato and staccato singing, such as 'Ghost of Tom' (from *Jolly Herring*, A&C Black), 'Drunken Sailor' (from *Flying Around*, A&C Black), 'Ghost Train' (from *The Multi-coloured Music Bus*, Collins).

WHAT TO DO
Sing together one of the children's favourite songs which lends itself to staccato or legato treatment to improve the quality of performance. Ask a small group to sing the song again while everyone else listens carefully to the words and decides whether they are long words or should be sung short. Ask, *Why should some words be sung long and some short? Is it to make the words clearer to the listener? Is it to*

create a different mood? What is the song about? What sort of mood should it have? Would staccato or legato techniques improve the mood? Sing the song again, using staccato notes and then legato notes and agree which is the best way.

Give groups tapes of songs with which they are familiar. Ask them to listen to each song and to say whether staccato or legato notes should be used to create the desired mood and effect the song portrays. Ask them to match the technique to the words and style of the song. Share the groups' opinions and sing through a selection of songs, applying either the matching staccato or legato techniques.

Extend the activity by asking each group to add a matching percussion accompaniment to one of the songs. Perform the songs at the end of the lesson and discuss the matching accompaniment that has been added.

BIBLE FACTS

SUBJECT: RE. QCA UNIT: 5C WHERE DID THE CHRISTIAN BIBLE COME FROM?

LEARNING OBJECTIVE
To know that the Bible contains many different literary genres.

THINKING OBJECTIVE
To analyse and sort.

THINKING SKILLS
In Years 3 and 4 the children learned how and where to locate the books in the Old and New Testaments. This lesson builds on that learning. The children will extend this thinking by analysing the range of genres in which the books are written and relate this to the different people who told the stories at different times in different ways. They will sort the genres and identify the range covered, and think about how these relate to the style and way the stories were told.

WHAT YOU NEED
A selection of Bibles with contents pages, which the children can read; large sheets of paper divided into sections, one for each genre.

WHAT TO DO
Look at the books of the Bible and talk about how they were written over a long period of time by different people. Explain that each book was written for a particular purpose. Some were written to tell the history at that time, to teach us about the way we should behave, to suggest ways to praise God, and

some are in the form of proverbs, letters and stories which detail the lives of people and some of the things that they did. List these genres in the sections of your large sheet of paper.

Ask each group to analyse a different part of the Bible. Ask them to locate the book, read a section and to say in which genre it is written. They should write the title of the book in the corresponding section. Collate the information, and ask, *How many books tell the history? How many tell a story in poetic form? How many tell a moral or give guidance on how we should behave?* Identify each genre through similar questions.

Provide the groups with Bible extracts with which they are familiar. Ask them to read, locate and analyse each one and to say in which genre it is written. Encourage the children to debate and discuss their opinions. Ask the groups to present their opinions to the rest of the class and agree on which genres have been used.

FORWARD ROLL

SUBJECT: PE. QCA UNIT: 5 GYMNASTIC ACTIVITIES.

LEARNING OBJECTIVE
To perform rolls in a fluent and controlled way.

THINKING OBJECTIVE
To analyse and sequence.

THINKING SKILLS
The children will learn to perform a forward roll, analyse the sequence to aid memory of its execution and make sure this is done safely and in a controlled and fluent way. They will use this knowledge to improve the quality of the performance by identifying the evaluation process before, during and after the roll is performed. This approach to learning a gymnastic technique or skill can be applied to learning other types of moves such as a cartwheel, handspring and tumble.

WHAT YOU NEED
A large space and enough mats for the children to work in pairs or threes.

WHAT TO DO
Talk to the children before the lesson about how to perform a forward roll. Identify the beginning, middle and end and explain this is a general balance-roll-balance sequence.

Consider why the roll starts and ends with a balance and relate this to the need to control the roll to keep the children safe from injury.

For each section of the sequence, break the actions into smaller, precise sequences. For example, talk about where to stand, how to stand and the first part of the movement from the balance down into the roll. Identify the sequence for rolling forward, focusing on the quality and safety of the action, and finish with how to move from the roll into the final balance, identifying the length of time this should be to establish control and prevent falling over.

Organise the children into groups and ask them to analyse the sequence in the same way for different types of roll. Include backward, side and V rolls. Record the sequences and discuss and agree the analysis to make sure all aspects are included in the recorded sequences.

In the hall, ask the children to follow the sequences to perform a range of controlled rolls. Help them to follow the usual pattern of evaluation to improve the quality of the moves and refine the sequences. Encourage them to try out symmetric and asymmetric actions and to develop the rolls into a sequence of balances and moves.

EXTENDING INFORMATION-PROCESSING SKILLS

Subject and QCA unit, NLS or NNS objective	Activity title	Thinking objective	Activity	Page
English NLS objective: To identify and classify the features of myths, legends and fables	Mythical beasts	To locate and classify	Classifying features of myths, legends and fables	18
Maths NNS objectives: To describe and visualise properties of solid shapes, such as parallel, perpendicular, faces or edges; to recognise where a shape will be after reflection in a mirror line parallel to one side	Rotating patterns	To classify, compare and match	Matching shapes and nets to make identical patterns and models	19
Science QCA unit: 5B Life cycles	Keys	To sort and match	Using keys to classify organisms or substances	20
History QCA unit: Any	Where can I look?	To locate and collect	Locating the range of information available, and collecting for a stimulus display	22
Geography QCA unit: 14 Investigating rivers	Rivers of the world	To locate, collect and sequence	Locating rivers on a world map, and collecting statistics about these to compare and sequence, finding similarities and differences	23
Design and Technology QCA unit: 5A Musical instruments	Sounds like	To sort and classify	Classifying musical instruments by their country of origin and consequent sound quality and production (ICT link)	24
ICT QCA unit: 5E Controlling devices	Picture lotto	To match correct procedures to designs	Matching the correct set of written instructions to the correct Logo design, and relating this to controlling devices	26
Art and design QCA unit: 5A Objects and meaning	Still life	To collect and match	Making different arrangements of vases and bottles, taking photographs and choosing a composition to paint	27
Music QCA unit: 15 Ongoing skills	Big dipper	To analyse structure and how elements are used to create effect	Analysing the musical elements that create the sound picture of a big dipper	28
RE QCA unit: 5B How do Muslims express their beliefs through practices?	Hajj	To sequence the preparation and journey of the Hajj	Interviewing a Muslim to find out about the preparations and journey of Hajj, and using this to write an account of this pilgrimage, including the symbolism and significance of this event	29
PE QCA unit: 5 Dance activities	Dance steps	To analyse and collect	Analysing and collecting dance step and motifs from traditional Irish dancing to build into sequences	30

MYTHICAL BEASTS

SUBJECT: ENGLISH. NLS OBJECTIVE: TO IDENTIFY AND CLASSIFY THE FEATURES OF MYTHS, LEGENDS AND FABLES.

LEARNING OBJECTIVE
To learn that morals, legends and myths have different types of characters and beasts.

THINKING OBJECTIVE
To locate and classify.

THINKING SKILLS
The children will look at the content of a range of fables, myths and legends and classify these according to whether they have a moral, contain actual or fantastical characters and beasts, imaginary events or other features. They will use the classification system to draw conclusions about these different types of stories: fables always have a moral; legends are usually stories about people who could have existed, and contain facts that could have happened; myths usually contain imaginary and fantastical beasts, characters and events.

WHAT YOU NEED
A collection of fables such as Aesop; legends such as Robin Hood, Buffalo Bill and King Arthur; myths such as Norse, Roman and Greek mythology stories; video extracts of some of these (Disney is usually a good source); large sheets of paper; writing materials.

WHAT TO DO
As a homework activity, ask the children to locate and collect the names of as many fables, legends and myths as they can. During the week, ask them to write these on a large sheet of paper, organised into three columns, one for each genre.

At the end of the week, look at the range of legends, myths and fables the children have found and recall some that the children are familiar with. Ask the children to suggest some characteristics that stories in each genre have in common and note their ideas.

Read two short fables to the children and analyse each one for its content. Classify the type of characters used by the author and note how they both end with a moral. Listen to a third fable and note whether this one too uses animals to tell a story of a moral nature. Look at the class list of fables and ask the children to predict whether they have animal characters and always tell a moral story. Ask, *Can you think of any other features that fables might have in common?*

Organise the children into groups and provide them with stories to classify by their content. Ask pairs to read one of these stories and to note any characteristics. Then, with another pair who are reading a story of the same genre, ask the children to disuss whether the stories have any characteristics in common. Challenge them to find general classification criteria for each genre, for example, myths usually contain imaginary or fantastical beasts, characters and events; legends are tall stories about people who *could* have existed, doing things that *could* have happened even though there is little or no actual evidence. Share these general classification criteria and use them to check whether the list collated from the homework research is accurate.

DIFFERENTIATION
Introduce one type of story at a time to lower attaining children, and draw their attention to the features discussed above. Check the classification criteria for a number of fables, first using the questions, *Does the story use animals as characters? Does it have a moral?* to show the children that all fables have morals and usually animal characters. Higher attaining children should be encouraged to look at the different events and to classify these according to their content. For example, in fables the weaker animal characters usually win in the end, the events in myths are usually not real and totally unbelievable, while legends tell of brave and spectacular encounters between good people and villains, and usually involve some kind of battle. Include fairy stories in the genre classification.

WHERE NEXT
When reading fairy tales and other traditional and modern stories with groups or the class, discuss and classify them according the criteria.

Look at a range of poetry and classify these in terms of their style and structure.

ASSESSMENT
Assess which children understand the categories and can sort and classify the information correctly, helping them understand and remember the content of each style of text. Note those who are able to locate the information from the index or contents page, and, in particular, the children who can skim and scan for the relevant information.

LEARNING OUTCOMES

Most children will be able to locate the information they need and classify this according to the given criteria. Some will need help with this to draw generalisations from the information they have located and classified.

FURTHER ENGLISH CHALLENGES

Greek Odyssey

After reading and watching video extracts of some of the stories in Homer's *Odyssey*, ask the children to classify the characters, beasts and other mythical creatures and Gods into actual or fantastical groups. Challenge higher attaining children to refine their classification system according to the type of event such as dangerous, dramatic, imaginary or loving. Invite them to ask questions to identify which character, beast or event appears the most often throughout the stories and book.

The Hobbit

Read extracts of JRR Tolkien's *The Hobbit*, or watch a film extract, and note the characters, places and events involved. Using the classification criteria identified in the main activity, ask the children to classify this story according to the genre they think it fits best.

ROTATING PATTERNS

SUBJECT: MATHS. NNS OBJECTIVES: TO DESCRIBE AND VISUALISE PROPERTIES OF SOLID SHAPES, SUCH AS PARALLEL, PERPENDICULAR, FACES OR EDGES; TO RECOGNISE WHERE A SHAPE WILL BE AFTER REFLECTION IN A MIRROR LINE PARALLEL TO ONE SIDE.

LEARNING OBJECTIVE

To describe and visualise the properties of solid 3-D shapes.

THINKING OBJECTIVE

To classify, compare and match.

THINKING SKILLS

The children will look at different 2-D nets of solid shapes, and try to match these to the correct 3-D shapes before constructing each net to check whether they were right.

WHAT YOU NEED

A set of nets for solid shapes, including cubes, cuboids, cones and cylinders, made from card or plastic linkable shapes; matching solid 3-D shapes.

WHAT TO DO

Revisit what the children know about the properties of cubes, cuboids, cones and cylinders from Years 3 and 4 of the NNS, and talk about the nets of these solid shapes. Look at the net of a cube, and ask, *Which solid shape does this net match with? How do you know this is the matching solid shape? Can you describe its properties? Do the properties of the net match the properties of the cube?* If the children do not use mathematical vocabulary as they describe the properties, model this and encourage them to use the correct mathematical terms as the activity progresses.

Repeat the task for cuboids, but this time introduce the terms 'parallel', 'perpendicular', 'faces', 'vertices' and 'edges' when describing the nets. Ask the children to find the matching solid shape in response to the identification of these properties.

Look at a net of a shape that the children are not familiar with. Challenge them to suggest which is its matching shape from the collection. Ask, *Why do you think this shape matches this net? Does it have the same properties? How can you check if you are right?*

Organise the children into groups and work with them to match the correct solid shapes to the correct nets. Ask them to record the net and shape, and to say why they have matched the two. Encourage them to consider the following questions as they explain their thinking: *What clues are there to tell you which solid shape this net will make? What shape are the faces? How many of each shape are there? How many edges are there? How many vertices? Are any edges perpendicular to each other? Are any edges parallel? Are there any right angles? Are there any shapes with acute angles?*

Share the results as a class during the plenary, discuss any reasoning, and creat each shape as you go to check whether the children matched the nets to the shapes correctly.

DIFFERENTIATION

Analyse the solid shapes in your collection with the less able children first, revisiting the various properties: number of edges and vertices, whether there are perpendicular or parallel edges, how many and whether any angles are right angles or acute. Discuss these terms in relation to the nets first, then see if the children can correctly match the nets to the solid shapes without the need to construct the nets. Give higher attaining children solid shapes (and corresponding nets) with which they are less familiar. Encourage them to analyse the properties of the solid shapes first before trying to match them to the correct nets.

WHERE NEXT

Set up an interactive display of nets and encourage the children to try to visualise each net in its 3-D form before matching it to the correct solid shape. Include some unfamiliar nets and shapes.

Challenge the children to make nets for their friends to visualise and/or match to its solid shape.

ASSESSMENT

Assess which children are able to visualise the solid shape from its net by using their understanding of the properties of numbers of edges, vertices and shape of faces. Note those who can match the net to its solid shape but are not yet able to visualise this. Provide more, similar work for these children, to develop their understanding of the properties of shape, helping them to realise that this knowledge and understanding is essential in completing the task.

LEARNING OUTCOMES

Most children will learn to describe shapes using the correct mathematical language of properties of solid shapes. Most will learn the nets of different solid shapes, either by visualising the shape from its net, or by matching the net to the finished shape.

FURTHER MATHS CHALLENGES

Matching towers

Sit a pair of children on either side of a screen, or with their backs to each other. Ask one of the pair to make a model by joining four 3-D shapes together. Challenge him or her to describe the shape they have made, using the correct mathematical vocabulary for shape and position, to their friend. The second child should follow the oral instructions, place the shapes in the correct position and orientation, and create a matching model. Compare the two models and ask the class to say whether the shapes are identical and, if so, why this has happened. If they are not identical, identify as a class how the first child could improve his or her description in order to ensure the two models are identical. Repeat the activity with everyone in pairs, evaluating the success, or not, of each pair's efforts as a class.

Repeat the activity over a number of weeks, using either the same four shapes or four different shapes, depending on which shapes you would like the children to learn about and describe.

Procedures

Write a procedure for rotating a square or a triangle in Logo. Ask the children to try to draw these without taking the pencil off the paper, following the same pattern as the turtle on the computer.

KEYS

SUBJECT: SCIENCE. QCA UNIT: 5B LIFE CYCLES

LEARNING OBJECTIVE

To learn that all plants produce seeds to enable them to reproduce their own kind.

THINKING OBJECTIVE

To sort and match.

THINKING SKILLS

The children will look at and sort a collection of fruits and seeds. They will sort these according to different attributes: whether they are fruits with seeds or not; whether they provide food for animals and humans; which method of dispersal they use. They will also match the fruits and seeds to their parent plant.

WHAT YOU NEED

A collection of fruits and seeds (following the guidelines from your LEA, and those in the *Be Safe* booklet; avoid nuts and check for children who may suffer from hay fever); matching parent plants (or pictures).

WHAT TO DO

Remind the children of the importance of not tasting unfamiliar fruits and seeds and why. Look closely at the collection and identify those that the children know. Tell them the names of the ones they don't know, and the plant which produces them. Show the children pictures of the parent plants, and ask, *How can you recognise which plant produces which fruit and seed?*

Ask the children to sort the fruits and seeds into their two sets. Look at those the children have identified as fruits, and ask, *How do you know these are fruits?* Define a fruit as a seedpod or container. Ask, *Are they all seedpods or containers?* Check that this is the case. Now look at the seeds. Decide together whether they are all, in fact, seeds, checking whether there are seeds attached to or inside the cases, in which case they are fruits. Look at any seeds or fruits that have not been sorted and discuss the reasons why. Check whether they are fruits or seeds, using the following definition to help the children make a decision. Explain that a fruit is the seed with its case, while the seed has no case. You may wish to discuss which are dry and succulent fruits with the more able children.

Wonder with the children how the seeds are dispersed. Invite their suggestions and listen carefully as this will allow you to assess what they

obscure fruits and seeds, which they will need to research to find the matching plant.

WHERE NEXT

Sort all the fruits that are eaten by humans into one set and all those that are not into another. Sort these into subsets of whether the fruits have the seeds on the inside of the fruits or the outside. Match the fruits and seeds to the parent plant and suggest all the ways the seeds may be dispersed.

Adapt this format to sort solids, liquids and gases and match them with their uses, for example carbon dioxide with fizzy drinks, air with breathing and helium with inflating balloons.

ASSESSMENT

Note the different ways in which the children sort the fruits and seeds. Note those who successfully sort the seeds according to the way they are dispersed. Assess how well the children use the features of the parent plant and other research methods to match the correct fruit and seed to its parent plant.

LEARNING OUTCOMES

Most children will learn the difference between fruits and seeds, and will be able to sort these according to the way they are dispersed. They will use a range of methods to match the fruits and seeds to their parent plant.

FURTHER SCIENCE CHALLENGES

Seed supper

Ask the children to sort the seeds into sets according to whether we eat them or not. Note those that are eaten raw and those that are processed into some other type of food, such as cereals and flour. Ask, *Can you think of other ways to sort the seeds? How many sets have you made? What criteria have you used? Have you considered those seeds that could belong to more than one set?* (For example, peas are planted and eaten by humans, and can be dispersed by animals and explosion.) Invite them to use Carroll diagrams to refine the sorting activity, including criteria such as 'eaten raw'/'not eaten raw', and 'processed'/'not processed'.

Vegetable stew

Look at a range of vegetables and encourage the children to sort them into sets according to the part of the plant they come from. For example, the cauliflower is the flower, peas are the seeds, mange tout are the fruits, carrots are the roots and cabbages are the leaves. Let the children decide on their own sorting criteria. Challenge them to think of 'are'/'are not' criteria to sort the vegetables using a Carroll diagram.

understand about the way seeds manage to grow into plants. Think about the success rate of the seeds growing into plants. How many will succeed?

Write the children's suggestions about seed dispersal onto cards and add any that they have not thought of. The methods of dispersal are water, wind, explosion and animals.

Give groups collections of seeds and fruits, and invite the children to sort them according to the method of dispersal. Ask, *Are there any seeds that are dispersed in more than one way, for example, the wind and animals, or water and animals?* Invite each group to feed back, explaining why they think the different seeds are dispersed in particular ways. Ask, *Do you all agree?* Discuss whether the dispersal of any seeds or fruits require further investigation.

Focus on the seeds that are dispersed by animals, and think about how this is done. Ask, *Are all of these seeds eaten by animals? Are some dispersed in some other way? If animals eat the seeds, how then are they dispersed?* (Wait for the giggles!) Talk about how humans disperse seeds by planting them to grow fruits and vegetables.

Finally, provide the children with pictures of parent plants and challenge groups to use the features of these plants plus what they have learned about fruits and seeds to match the seeds with the fruits and the parent plants. Use reference material if necessary to research what matches to what.

DIFFERENTIATION

With less able children, match the seeds with the correct fruit and help them to identify which is the fruit and which is the seed in particular plants. Higher attaining children should be given more

WHERE CAN I LOOK?

SUBJECT: HISTORY. QCA UNIT: ANY.

LEARNING OBJECTIVE
To identify a range of suitable resources for a display.

THINKING OBJECTIVE
To locate and collect.

THINKING SKILLS
The children will list everything they have learned so far about their current history topic, and note which reference materials and historical artefacts provided this information. This will provide the starting point for a stimulus display to help the next year group to study this topic. The children will think about questions to inspire initial interest, developing the enquiry skill of asking questions. They will discuss each other's ideas and decide what to include in the stimulus display, evaluating any gaps in the range of reference material in their collection. Many pupils will be developing independent planning and working skills by the end of Year 6 because they will be in the habit of thinking things through for themselves.

WHAT YOU NEED
Access to a range of historical resources including books, CDs, pictures, photographs, copies of documents, musical extracts, artefacts; internet access; a large box in which to collect the resources; access to a photocopier; paper; writing materials.

WHAT TO DO
As a class, discuss what the children have learned about the current history topic so far, and any sources of information that they have used. Tell the children that they will be putting together a stimulus display to inspire interest in the same topic for the following Year group. Later, they will need to decide which aspects they found the most interesting, and why, and identify the sources of evidence used for these particular sections.

Ask groups to draw three columns on a large sheet of paper. Then they should brainstorm again what they have learned about the topic and note these in the left-hand column. In the middle column, they should note the sources of evidence which provided the information.

Then ask the groups to note down in the right-hand column which particular activities they found most interesting and why, for example, the *Who Wants to be a Millionaire?* quiz where the 'phone a friend' had access to reference material to find answers to a question. Collect the sheets of paper

together and look at them as a class. Discuss any overlap of aspects covered, sources used and activities enjoyed. Identify if any aspects of the topic have been forgotten and fill these in, together with the relevant historical sources.

Using the lists, allocate a different aspect or activity to each group, and ask them to locate the sources of evidence listed, for inclusion in the stimulus display. The children should collect these sources in a form that can be easily included in the display box, for example, in relation to books: photocopied sections of large books, the books themselves if available, a list of library books. They could write stimulating questions to spark interest on one side of pieces of card, with sources that will help to answer the questions suggested on the back. Devise a system to identify what the box contains, to help future groups locate quickly what sources they need for each of the topic aspects.

DIFFERENTIATION
Challenge higher attaining children to be more precise and to provide the location of particular book extracts, CDs and websites which they found most useful, or particular pictures or maps. Lower attaining children should think about the activities they liked and why, and locate and collect the sources that they used.

WHERE NEXT
Identify further questions to inspire lines of enquiry.

ASSESSMENT
Use the children's lists to identify which groups successfully located and collected a wide range of historical sources to support learning of historical knowledge, concepts and skills. Note those who located particular bits of information from within these sources to make certain sections of information easier to locate and collect.

LEARNING OUTCOMES
All children will locate and collect relevant reference material to support historical enquiry. They will think about how this supports learning in particular aspects of history and how the collection can be

classified to help others locate the information they need quickly.

FURTHER HISTORY CHALLENGES
Museum pieces
At some time during the year, ask the children to think of all the history themes they have studied since Year 3. Brainstorm all the historical artefacts they have looked at and used, and identify the ones they found most interesting and why. Together, make a list and sort these into themes, for example the Victorians, the Romans or the Ancient Greeks. Ask the children to locate these sources around the school and collect them to make a 'museum' for other groups of children to use when they are studying these particular topics. Ask them to label each artefact with its age and the decade to which it belongs, and display them in an accessible place. They can devise a classification system, presented as a booklet, to help other children locate what they need to support a particular enquiry.

RIVERS OF THE WORLD

SUBJECT: GEOGRAPHY.
QCA UNIT: 14
INVESTIGATING RIVERS.

LEARNING OBJECTIVE
To learn that rivers have attributes that are the same, and attributes that are different.

THINKING OBJECTIVE
To locate, collect and sequence.

THINKING SKILLS
The children will locate famous rivers of the British Isles, Europe and the rest of the world on a world map, and groups will collect statistics and other information about one river. They will sequence the rivers according to any chosen criteria before comparing the data they have collected to find similarities and differences between the rivers. Finally, they will note where their local rivers and streams would be placed on the 'information line' to enable them to note any similarities and differences between the local stream they studied earlier in the QCA unit and the larger rivers of the world.

WHAT YOU NEED
Resources to locate and find statistics about the rivers of the world, including atlases, maps, books, CDs and internet access; paper and writing materials.

WHAT TO DO
As a class, brainstorm all the rivers the children already know. Then ask pairs to look at maps and atlases of the British Isles, Europe and/or the world and to locate as many major rivers as they can. If necessary, give the children clues, for example, *Which river flows through London? Paris? Dublin? Which river is found in Egypt?* Join pairs together and ask each new group to look at a particular area of the world and to spend five minutes locating more names. Make sure that the major cities of the world and all the continents are covered.

Collate all the names of rivers found as a list on the board or large sheet of paper. Allocate a different river to pairs of children and ask them to find out as many statistics as they can about this river. Identify the kind of things the children should look for, including the length, width, main country and other countries through which it flows, any major towns or cities it passes through, the number and names of any tributaries. Ask the children to note these things on a sheet of A4 paper.

As a class, check each pair's information to make sure it includes data on all the required aspects, then photocopy enough of the sheets so that groups of six have one sheet to share.

Ask these groups to sequence the rivers in order, using a range of criteria. The group should choose the criteria, for example, they might order the rivers by length first, then by the number of tributaries, the number of towns through which it flows, and so on, each time creating an ordered list, or an 'information line'. Help the children to process their findings by asking, *Each time you sequence the rivers using new criteria, do they stay in the same relative place on your 'information line'? Does the longest river have the largest number of tributaries? Does one continent have more longer rivers than another? Is the longest river the widest?* Decide where the local stream or river should be placed on each of the 'information lines'.

As a class, compare the data found on each river and note what attributes they have in common: they all have tributaries, they all flow into the sea, they all pass through at least one town or city. Note the differences too: they are all different lengths, they have different numbers of tributaries, some flow through more than one country.

If time permits, continue investigating one of these rivers, researching its importance to transport, irrigation, industry, and any settlements along its banks. Compare this research to the information the children collected about the local streams and rivers in previous fieldwork studies. Ask the children, *What do you notice about the shape and direction in which the rivers flow? Do any of the rivers suffer from erosion? Do they change in depth and width as they meander through the countryside?*

DIFFERENTIATION

Pair lower attaining children with other children so that they are fully involved in the research. Ensure they can locate the country of their chosen river, and understand where it is in relation to their own locality. Encourage the children to record facts about their chosen river and the local stream, and to think about similarities and differences. Invite higher attaining children to investigate the type of formation the rivers have when they flow into the sea, for example a delta, isthmus or estuary.

WHERE NEXT

Consider river pollution and what may cause this.

Make a large display, showing how your most local river meanders and flows to the sea. Label the tributaries, towns and rivers it passes through on its course, and any interesting features such as weirs and floodplains.

ASSESSMENT

Note how well the children locate the rivers of the world and whether they start at the sea to track them back (applying a secure understanding that all rivers flow into the sea), or whether they look for these at random. Note those who process the information by comparing the statistics and facts they have collected to find similarities and differences between the different rivers they have researched.

LEARNING OUTCOMES

All children will locate and collect facts about at least one river. Some will go on to find information about its importance to local settlements and industry. They will process the information by finding similarities and differences and use the information to sequence the rivers in different orders.

FURTHER GEOGRAPHY CHALLENGES
River facts

Ask groups to select one river and research all the groups of people and animals who rely on this river for food, shelter, industry, irrigation, transport and other activity. They can use the information to write a group description of the river's journey, and should consider the cause and effect that a particular activity at one point along the river might have on a

settlement further along its course. For example, the effect of too much use of the river water for industry on the irrigation of crops further along.

Terminology

Brainstorm words that describe certain parts of a river's course, and ask the children to locate and label these on a map.

Challenge them to find more than one place for some of these, for example erosion, pollution, floodplain and tributary.

SOUNDS LIKE

SUBJECT: DESIGN AND TECHNOLOGY. QCA UNIT: 5A MUSICAL INSTRUMENTS.

LEARNING OBJECTIVE

To learn that the way instruments are played and the material from which they are made inform the type of sound they produce.

THINKING OBJECTIVE

To sort and classify.

THINKING SKILLS

The children will consider a variety of instruments and think about how these are played and the sound quality each one produces. They will link this to the materials from which each is made and the way it is constructed. They will play the different instruments and consider how their construction informs the

sound quality. They will use the information to classify the instruments according to the types of sounds each one produces and link it to the way it is produced.

WHAT YOU NEED
A range of tuned and untuned percussion and stringed instruments, which are simply made and produce a range of sounds: cabasa, maraca, wind chimes, drums, cymbals, guiro, Indian bells, castanets, wood blocks, sand blocks, guitar, violin.

WHAT TO DO
Pass the drums around the class and invite the children to say how they are played. Ask, *Are they struck, scraped, blown, shaken or plucked? How is the sound produced? What happens when the skin of the drum is struck?* Demonstrate this by placing rice on top of the drum and watch it move as the drum skin vibrates. Talk about the way the drum is constructed. Ask, *What components does it have? Why is the drum skin tight? How does this improve the quality of sound?* If possible, show the children what happens to the sound when the drum skin is tightened or loosened, and how it sounds differently when struck at the edge and in the middle.

Look at a violin together and note the same things. Ask, *How is it played? What components are there? What is the purpose of the bridge? Why are there keys at the end of the stem? Why are there holes in the box? What happens to the quality of sound when the strings are loosened? Tightened? Scraped? Plucked?*

Put all the instruments whose sound is produced by striking together in a set. Look at the remaining instruments and ask the children to think about how their sounds are made. Ask, *Can these instruments be sorted according to the way they are played?* Encourage them to offer the terms plucked, scraped or shaken independently, and to then sort the instruments into these sets.

Explain that you have not included instruments whose sound is produced by blowing for hygiene reasons, but do think of some together and include the names in another set.

Look at the range of instruments in each set. Ask the children a series of questions: *Are there some instruents which are in more than one set? What does this tell us about the versatility of the instruments? What about the construction? Are some a particular shape or have different parts for specific reasons? Do these affect the sound type or quality?* Talk about the materials from which each instrument is made. Ask, *Can this instrument be made from a different material?* (For example, flutes and recorders are made from wood, plastic and metal.) *How do you think the material affects the sound quality? Do you think it will make a different tone of sound?*

Look at the maracas and note the different materials from which they are made. Listen to each one in turn as it is shaken, and ask the children to consider whether the sound quality is the same or different each time. Ask, *What might be making the sound different: the material from which the maracas are made or the contents within each one?*

Together, sort the collection of instruments again, this time according to the sound that each one makes: the tone of the sound, whether it is closed (short and dull) or open (bright and resonant). Ask, *How are the closed and open sounds played? From which material are the instruments made that make these types of sounds? Can we draw any conclusions about the type of sound produced and the materials from which the instruments are made, or the way in which they are played?* Ask groups to record what they have found out about the way different instruments are played and made, and then link this to the sound each one produces.

DIFFERENTIATION
Give lower attaining children the criteria for sorting, such as 'Find all the instruments whose sound is made by plucking'. Higher attaining children should tackle the work in the latter part of the activity, and work as a group to sort the instruments by the sound that they make. When the other groups are busy on the recording task, check their thinking by asking them to give reasons for their sorting decisions. Process the information together and link the way the instruments are constructed and played to the sound quality that is produced.

WHERE NEXT
Ask the children to sort and classify a range of instruments from different countries and cultures. They should note similarities and differences, and how the sound quality relates to the way they are played, the way they are constructed and the materials from which they are made. Does the country of origin have some bearing on the choice of materials?

Let the children use the information to design and make their own instruments from a range of materials.

ASSESSMENT
Note the children who use the classification system to identify how the sound quality is affected by the way the instruments are constructed, played and the materials from which they are made.

LEARNING OUTCOMES

Most children will learn that they can draw conclusions about the quality of sound different instruments produce through sorting and classifying them according to the way they are constructed, played and the materials from which they are made. Some will do this with support while others will start to use the information to think about their own instruments.

FURTHER DESIGN AND TECHNOLOGY CHALLENGES

Musical keys

Set up a way of sorting and classifying instruments using keys. Start by sorting according to the way they are played, then by the material from which they are made, the way they are constructed or components they have, and finally by the sound quality. Challenge the children to find the instrument that has a sound that is made by scraping, made from wood, has a sound box and produces a long sound – a guiro; an instrument which is made from wood, has a sound produced by striking, has a sound box and produces a short sound – a wood block, and so on.

PICTURE LOTTO

SUBJECT: ICT. QCA UNIT: 5E CONTROLLING DEVICES.

LEARNING OBJECTIVE

To recognise which written procedures control which events.

THINKING OBJECTIVE

To match correct procedures to designs.

THINKING SKILLS

The children will reinforce their knowledge and understanding of writing procedures through this simple matching game. This activity should be used as a starting point for future learning (see Thinking challenges) about how to write a sequence to control devices using a control box.

WHAT YOU NEED

A collection of designs produced on Logo which show rotating shapes produced by writing a repeating procedure; matching procedures for each one, written on labels and put into a file on a computer; computer with Logo running; white board or paper; writing materials.

WHAT TO DO

Look at a simple design which is made from rotating a square (six times), either produced on a large sheet of paper or on a whiteboard linked to the computer. Ask, *What can you see? What shapes can you see? Can anyone work out how the shape was made?* Agree that the shape was made by drawing a square six times, turning it 60° each time to make a rotating pattern. (Link the measurement of turn to the degrees in a circle, if you wish – for six squares, divide 360° by six to work out the angle of turn.)

Run the computer program and produce this pattern on screen. Again, use a whiteboard if you have one. When the design has been reproduced, invite the children to suggest how the computer knew to make this picture. Talk through the procedure at this point, noting the sequence of events.

Look at another design and ask the children to count the number of squares. Show them two procedures, and ask, *Which one do you think made this design?* Link the number of squares to the number of 'repeat' commands and measurement of turn, asking, *How many times does the degree of turn go*

into 360? Produce the designs from both procedures and compare them to find the matching one. Were the children correct?

Finally, show the children two more designs made from triangles and rectangles and find their matching procedure from two choices. Produce the designs on screen to compare and ask them to check whether the match is correct.

Organise the children into pairs. Give each pair a sheet of designs using different numbers of squares, triangles and rectangles plus their matching procedures. Challenge the children to match the designs to the correct procedure. Show the children how to check out their matches by running the procedure and reproducing the design on screen for comparison.

Share the children's ideas at the end of the lesson, asking them to explain why they chose a particular procedure for a particular design. Ask, *Did they know by the number of repeats in the procedure, or did they work it out by the angle of turn each time?*

DIFFERENTIATION

Give lower attaining pupils one square, triangle and rectangle to begin with so that they can note the different number of rotations in order to inform their match. They may need to find the match by trial and error, by running each procedure and finding the matching design by comparison on screen. Give higher attaining children more complex designs, made of two or more shapes, and more complicated shapes, such as pentagons, hexagons and octagons.

WHERE NEXT

Challenge the children to write procedures and print out the matching designs for others to use in an independent activity on the classroom computer.

ASSESSMENT

Note how well the children match the procedures to the designs by noting the sequence of instructions.

LEARNING OUTCOMES

The children will learn to identify which procedures operate or control which sequence of events.

FURTHER ICT CHALLENGES

Procedural matters

Give the children a set of written procedures which control a sequence of bulbs lighting up in a certain order. Invite them to watch one sequence then ask them to describe what happened in terms of the bulb number that lit up first, second, third and so on. Ask them to find the matching written instructions for the sequence they have just watched. Start with

simple sequences, which light up two bulbs in order before turning them off again, before moving on to more complicated sequences, which vary the length of time different bulbs are alight. For example:
N 'Switch on 1, wait 10, switch off 1, switch on 2, wait 6, switch off 2'
N 'Switch on 1, wait 6, switch on 2, wait 2, switch off 1, wait 10, switch off 2'

STILL LIFE

SUBJECT: ART AND DESIGN. QCA UNIT: 5A OBJECTS AND MEANINGS.

LEARNING OBJECTIVES
To collect visual information to help develop ideas; to select and record from first-hand observation.

THINKING OBJECTIVE
To collect and match.

THINKING SKILLS
The children will collect different vases and bottles and arrange them in different ways to make interesting still-life compositions. They will record the different arrangements by taking photographs of each one before selecting the one they like best to paint a matching picture. They will consider families of colours when composing their arrangements and use these to add colour to their drawings.

WHAT YOU NEED
A collection of bottles and vases of different shapes and sizes, and in different colours; large sheets of paper and paint; a digital camera.

WHAT TO DO
Collect a range of vases and bottles of different colours and shapes, and ask small groups of children to make different arrangements to create still-life compositions. Photograph each composition from different angles and print the pictures out for the children's consideration. Encourage them to think about the shape and form the finished compositions will create, and to combine vases and bottles from the same family of colours to make complementary and contrasting arrangements.

With the children, identify the good points of each arrangement before they select the one they like best. Encourage them to work on different aspects and viewpoints in their sketchbooks, and to think about how line, shape and form create the image, before recreating the composition to draw from first-hand. Try to manipulate the children's choices so that a group works on the same composition. Challenge the children to look carefully at the photographs taken from different viewpoints to make sure they have reproduced their chosen composition in exactly the same arrangement. Invite the children to draw the composition from their preferred point of view, and to colour or shade those things that have colour. They should also show the reflection of light and dark areas.

DIFFERENTIATION
Encourage less able artists to use simple shapes in their compositions, and to concentrate on getting the line, shapes and sizes accurate. Higher attaining children should consider using objects of the same colour to develop their understanding of tints and tones of colour.

WHERE NEXT
Extend the activity to other objects and items with interesting shapes.

ASSESSMENT
Watch the children as they work and note whether they are using particular artistic elements to match the arrangement accurately. Make particular note of how well the children collect the things they need to make creative compositions.

LEARNING OUTCOMES
Most children will learn to collect things to compose different visual arrangements. They will select the one they want to draw and recreate this by matching the positions of the objects to create identical viewpoints.

FURTHER ART AND DESIGN CHALLENGES
Match me
Create compositions using interesting objects, and take photographs of these from different viewpoints. Give groups of children a set of photographs showing the same composition from different viewpoints, and ask them to recreate the arrangement by collecting the matching items and placing them in their correct positions. Match the photographs to their correct viewpoint to check whether they have recreated the composition accurately.

BIG DIPPER

SUBJECT: MUSIC. QCA UNIT: 15 ONGOING SKILLS.

LEARNING OBJECTIVE
To improve the children's singing performance by enhancing mood and effect by applying different musical elements.

THINKING OBJECTIVE
To analyse structure and how elements are used to create effect.

THINKING SKILLS
The children will learn a new song and decide how different musical elements are used to create the movement of the Big Dipper as it climbs slowly to the top of the ride before falling, getting faster and faster as it picks up speed. They will consider how the structure of the song depicts this movement and gives the song a clear beginning, middle and end. They will consider how changes in tempo, crescendo and diminuendo are used in other familiar songs and music, to create the movement of a particular object.

WHAT YOU NEED
A copy of the song 'Big Dipper' by Peter Caldwell (from *The Multi-coloured Music Bus*, Collins); 'The Little Train of Caipiri' by Villa Lobos (from *Classics for Kids*, RCA Victor music); paper; paints.

WHAT TO DO
Learn the song 'Big Dipper' and make sure the children are very familiar with the rise and fall of the tune. Ask, *Why do you think the tune goes up and down in the places that it does? Is this to match the rise and fall of the ride?*

Next, think about the words of the song. Ask, *Why are the words 'faster and faster and faster' used as they are? How do the words 'the kids scream with delight' depict the excitement of the ride? What do the words 'speed of sound' tell you about the speed of the ride? What is happening as the ride goes on? How do we know when the ride has come to an end?*

Next, think about the musical effects that are used in addition to the tune. Ask, *How does the tune speed up in the middle? Why is this? Why does the tempo start more slowly? How does it end, slowly or abruptly? How does this give the song structure? Are there any other musical elements used, such as crescendo and diminuendo? Why do we sing certain parts louder than others? How does this help to create the movement? The different speeds of the ride?*

Invite the children to name other songs that use, or could use, different musical elements to create mood and effect or depict the content of the song.

Listen to 'The Little Train of Caipiri' and identify how tempo and crescendo and diminuendo are used to depict the movement of the train. Encourage the children to paint pictures of some of the scenery it passes by and through.

DIFFERENTIATION
Challenge higher attaining children to record the

changes in tempo, dynamics and textures using musical terms and symbols. Invite them to add written accompaniments to a musical score. Lower attaining children should concentrate on pitch and dynamics to begin with before trying to alter the tempo of the song. Work with them to write the words of the song in the corresponding places on a picture of a big dipper. For example, the opening of the song up to 'slowly goes up to the top' should be written on the track going up on the big dipper, 'and then accelerates' on the first downward piece of track, while the 'faster and faster' words up to the end should be on the rest of the track.

WHERE NEXT
Analyse other songs in the children's repertoire and use the analysis to inform suitable accompaniments to enhance the intended mood and feelings of the song.

ASSESSMENT
Assess how well the children use the analysis of the song to add particular effects to create the intended mood and feelings of the song.

LEARNING OUTCOMES
The children will learn to analyse a song for structure, and the way that some musical elements are used to create musical mood and effects.

FURTHER MUSIC CHALLENGES
Expressive voices
Think about the structure and way musical elements are used in songwriting, and ask groups of children to compose vocal percussion to add to the structure of the 'Big Dipper'. Challenge the groups to give the vocal accompaniment a structure for the rest of the class to analyse when they perform to each other.
Match and mix
Listen to music from different countries and analyse what features gives each piece its particular mood

and style. Challenge the children to identify the different musical elements or instruments used and how these are used to create different musical features. For example, Spanish music uses rich harmonies and staccato strummed rhythms to depict an exciting mood; Indian music uses instruments and tunes which move in very small steps to create its style. Provide the children with a tape of music from different countries and invite them to match the music to the country. Ask them to give reasons for their choices in terms of the analysis of musical elements or instruments used.

HAJJ

SUBJECT: RE. QCA UNIT: 5B HOW DO MUSLIMS EXPRESS THEIR BELIEFS THROUGH PRACTICES?

LEARNING OBJECTIVE
To recount the events, and understand the purpose and meaning to Muslims, of the Hajj.

THINKING OBJECTIVE
To sequence the preparation and journey of the Hajj.

THINKING SKILLS
The children will learn that sequencing can help us remember important facts, and develop an understanding of the purpose and meaning of different religious practices. They will identify a series of questions to ask a visitor about their personal experiences of Hajj, then identify the sequence of events which lead up to, take place during and after the pilgrimage to Mecca. The children or visitor will identify questions which will lead the discussions towards the purpose and meaning of this event and to explain why it is important to Muslims. The answers to the questions will be sequenced to provide a structure that will recount accurately the pilgrimage and explain the significance of Hajj to Muslims.

WHAT YOU NEED
A practising Muslim who has been on Hajj to Mecca; a list of questions to ask the visitor which follows the structure of the sequencing task below; a space to display pictures, photographs and accounts; paper; writing materials.

WHAT TO DO

In advance, as a class, identify questions to ask your visitor about the Hajj. Ask the children to think about the preparations and their importance, the journey that is undertaken to complete the Hajj, what Hajj means, the significance of this event and why all Muslims go at least once in their lives to Mecca. Allocate questions to different children and send a copy of the questions to your visitor in advance so they can prepare their answers. Invite the visitor to add further questions to the list to make sure that the meaning and significance of this event is clearly communicated to the children. Ask the higher attaining children to take notes, and, at the end of the session, to take one question and answer to write up in full.

After the visit, review the answers to the questions. Display the questions and answers down the side of a large board and ask the children to recall what the Muslims do first in preparation for Hajj. Find the corresponding question and answer and place this at the top of the board. Continue until you have the questions and answers in the correct sequence. Ask the children, *Does this sequence give an accurate account of Hajj?* Read the answers to the questions and evaluate whether the practical journey and the purpose, meaning and significance are all explained.

DIFFERENTIATION

Focus on the factual recounting of the sequence of events with lower attaining children to begin with, to make sure that this information is understood before moving on to discuss the significance of the whole event. Discuss the significance of the different parts of the sequence with higher attaining children, and encourage appreciation of the purpose and meaning of planning the Hajj in the correct manner.

WHERE NEXT

If appropriate, ask the children to use the sequence to write an accurate personal account of Hajj. Complete a similar exercise for Sawm.

ASSESSMENT

Note whether the children sequence the event correctly in response to the information they have collected. Note those who understand how to apply these sequencing skills to recount an event accurately, and to identify the significance and meaning and purpose (symbolism) of this event to Muslims.

LEARNING OUTCOMES

Most children will learn about the event and significance of Hajj by sequencing what happens in the planning, preparation and following of this important journey.

FURTHER PE CHALLENGES

Planning a pilgrimage

Consider the journeys that people of different religions make and the places they visit. Locate these on a map and work out which route would be taken and think about possible means of transport. Consider how long the journey would take and all the elements the pilgrims would need to organise. Plan a pilgrimage to include these elements and consider the significance of the event to the people concerned. Sequence the pilgrimage to include the preparation, consideration of meaning and purpose, the journey to the place of pilgrimage and the events that take place. Use the sequence to write an accurate account of the pilgrimage, including known facts and the significance or symbolism of this event.

DANCE STEPS

SUBJECT: PE. QCA UNIT: 5 DANCE ACTIVITIES.

LEARNING OBJECTIVE

To explore and improvise ideas for dances in different styles.

THINKING OBJECTIVE

To analyse and collect.

THINKING SKILLS

The children will watch an extract from your chosen dance style and together analyse the type of steps and body actions used by the dances. They will analyse closely how the dance steps match and reflect the music and whether any are built into a repeating sequence. They will use the information to collect a range of dance steps to include in their own composition in the same style.

WHAT YOU NEED

Videos or visitors performing a traditional or cultural dance of your choice, for example Irish dancing; paper; writing materials.

WHAT TO DO

As a class, match the dance extract of your chosen dance style, for example Irish dancing. Look at the way the dancers move, the jumps, leg movements, the position of the body and the journeys they take. Analyse together the types of steps, the body positions and whether the dancers dance as a group or individually. Ask, *Can you identify how some dance steps have been built into motifs?*

Organise the children into three groups:

• Ask one group to work in pairs to collect the different steps they have seen in the extract and to give each one a name. They should perform the steps, refining the performance to make sure it is precise in terms of the shape and position of the legs, feet and rest of the body, and whether it includes a jump or hop. For each step they should write a short description.

• Another group should analyse the structure of the dance sequences by looking at the journeys the dancers take, and whether they are repeated in a structured sequence. They should also analyse how the dancers are organised – the groups in which the dancers perform. Ask, *Do they move in a line, in a circle or some other way? Do they cross over, work individually, in pairs or small groups? Are any of the movements or journeys repeated?* Ask the children to think of a way to collect the range of journeys and the way the dance is structured.

• The third group should analyse the structure of the whole dance. Ask, *Is it built up of different sequences which are clearly demarcated in some way? How does the dance start? How does it finish? What motifs are there? Are they built into sequences? Are these sequences repeated?* (See Differentiation below.)

Share the dance steps collected and the structure of the dance. Describe how the dancers look and think about the picture they create. Talk about how well the dance steps match the music and how the rhythmic aspect of the dance is reinforced through the journeys and body shape and positions.

DIFFERENTIATION

Work alongside higher attaining children to help them break down the dance steps into smaller precise parts which, when put together, make the whole. Analyse closely the shape of the feet, legs and toes and how they are positioned for each step, how they move and in which direction. Ask them to define the steps used as they compose their own dance. Lower attaining children should analyse the structure of the whole dance, looking for whether the dance repeats itself and when. They should be encouraged to look for particular sequences, which can be given a name, to identify the number of different sequences, and the order in which they are danced for each repetition.

WHERE NEXT

Encourage the children to use the collection of dance steps and sequences to compose their own Irish dance. Incorporate the analysis of the whole dance structure carried out by the lower attaining group.

Analyse other traditional dances for dance steps, and the structure of the whole dance.

ASSESSMENT

Note how well the children analyse the dance steps and structure by breaking the steps or dance into smaller parts, and note how well they collect these to make a repertoire from which to compose a dance in the same style.

LEARNING OUTCOMES

Some children will learn to analyse the precise moves in Irish dance steps to help them improve the quality of their own dance steps. Some children will learn how the dancers work together to build up the precision of the dance, and others will learn how the whole dance is structured by identifying the sequences.

FURHTER PE CHALLENGES

Irish dancing

Choose a different piece of Irish music and challenge the children to analyse the music in terms of which of their collected dance motifs will fit where. Give them time to arrange their motifs into different sequences to fit the music, which, when performed, completes a suitable dance with repeating sequences.

REASONING SKILLS

INTRODUCTION

Reasoning skills enable children to make considered decisions and give reasons for those decisions. Asking the children to explain what they are thinking or to talk through how they reached a particular conclusion, for example, will develop their reasoning skills. Eleven-year-old children have usually learned to link different pieces of information. This requires them to make judgements, interpret evidence and to use inference and deduction skills to work out who carried out a particular action, how something happened or why. Identifying links and predicting what may happen, and giving reasons for their opinions, is the basis of the children's abilities to solve a problem. By the age of eleven, with regular practice, many children have started to use these skills independently to question what is happening and why. This is certainly an expectation of higher attainers whose learning is being extended and is another way of differentiating work.

One strategy for developing the children's emerging reasoning skills is concept mapping, or mind mapping, as it allows you to identify whether children are beginning or already making links between different ideas. Many teachers use this to establish children's current knowledge and understanding of a concept or a new process, before planning work matched at a suitable level for groups and individuals. A version of this strategy is used in the activity 'Floating rocks', which asks the children to link ideas and to give reasons for their choices.

Although this strategy is used especially effectively in science, where new scientific concepts can be explored with the children and used as a basis for discussion, the same idea can be used in other subjects to find out what the children already know and understand before planning the unit of work. It is also useful at the end of a unit to find out what they have learned. Making links between ideas allows you to assess the children's understanding of these concepts and ideas.

As well as concept mapping, children will need to develop their reasoning skills using other strategies. In English the children will be developing their reasoning skills when they are trying to find a solution for a character in a story, looking at pictures to try to predict the ending of a story or by explaining why something happened the way it did. In maths, solving number problems and explaining the strategies used to find an answer, immediately springs to mind, while in PE pupils are constantly thinking about tactics and rules for their games. Art and design and design and technology require the children to overcome particular problems of colour mixing or making moving parts work, and in music the children decide which element is most suitable to create a particular effect in developing their listening, appraising and composition skills.

The following skills all form part of the reasoning process:
⊙ explaining
⊙ forming opinions
⊙ making judgements
⊙ making decisions
⊙ interpreting
⊙ inferring
⊙ deducing
⊙ giving reasons.

INTRODUCING REASONING SKILLS

Subject and QCA unit, NLS or NNS objective	Activity title	Thinking objective	Activity	Page
English NLS objectives: To explore spelling patterns of consonants; to formulate rules	Hard or soft	To use deduction and reasoning skills	Identifying whether a c or g is hard or soft	34
Maths NNS objective: To relate fractions to their decimal representations: that is, to recognise the equivalence between the decimal and fraction forms of one half, one quarter, three quarters ... and tenths and hundredths; to begin to understand percentage as the number of parts in every 100	Fractions, decimals or percentages?	To use skills of deduction	Exchanging totals in equivalent fractions, decimals and percentages	34
Science QCA unit: 6E Balanced and unbalanced forces	Floating rocks	To explain ideas and give reasons	Making a rock float	35
History QCA unit: 11 What was it like for children living in Victorian Britain?	Victorian children	To use skills of inference	Role-play activity, inferring how Victorian children might have felt in different situations	36
Geography QCA unit: 23 Investigating coasts	A day out	To interpret evidence and form opinions	Interpreting evidence to form opinions about different coastal features	37
Design and technology QCA unit: 6D Controllable vehicles	Remote-controlled vehicles	To use skills of deduction and to explain	Changing speed and direction of working models using construction kits and remote-controlled vehicles	37
ICT QCA unit: 5D Introduction to spreadsheets; 6B Spreadsheet modelling	Charity biscuits	To make decisions	Calculating the cost of ingredients to find out how much to charge per charity biscuit	38
Art and design QCA unit: 6C A sense of place	Moody pictures	To infer feelings	Inferring the mood and feelings from different landscape paintings	39
Music QCA unit: 19 Songwriter	Words	To use skills of interpretation	Agreeing on the intentions of song lyrics	40
RE QCA unit: 5C Where did the Christian Bible come from?	What is the moral?	To use skills of inference	Looking at different stories from the Bible and inferring other possible meanings apart from the literal facts presented	40
PE QCA unit: 3 Outdoor and adventurous activities	Where am I going?	To use the skills of deduction	Finding a way around the school grounds using map and compass	41

HARD OR SOFT

SUBJECT: ENGLISH. NLS OBJECTIVES: TO EXPLORE SPELLING PATTERNS OF CONSONANTS; TO FORMULATE RULES.

LEARNING OBJECTIVE

To learn that *c* is usually soft when followed by *i*, *y* or *e*.

THINKING OBJECTIVE

To use deduction and reasoning skills.

THINKING SKILLS

The children will collect a number of words which contain the letter *c*, some familiar and some unfamiliar. They will deduce whether the sound the *c* represents is hard or soft, using their knowledge of letter strings to help them make their deductions. They will give reasons for their thinking by formulating a rule which they can apply to other unfamiliar words. Some children can be encouraged to research French words to see if the same rule applies.

WHAT YOU NEED

Dictionaries; a list of words containing hard and soft *c*, some familiar and some unfamiliar to the children, written on a whiteboard or large sheet of paper.

WHAT TO DO

Using a whiteboard or large sheet of paper, show the children several words which contain the letter *c*, some of which sound hard and some soft. Ask them to read the words and note that some are hard and some are soft.

Say another word aloud, for example *concept*, and invite someone to spell it. If necessary, give the clue that the word contains two *c*s, one hard and one soft. Repeat this as often as you need to until the children begin to realise that the *s* phoneme is made by the *c* grapheme each time. Look at these words and the earlier list and ask, *Can you think of a rule which gives a clue to whether the* c *is hard or soft?* Note all the children's suggestions, discuss them and agree on which one is correct.

Organise the children into groups and, using dictionaries, ask them to find as many words as they can which contain a hard and soft *c*. Ask higher attaining children to collect words which contain the *s* phoneme, including those represented by double *ss*. Challenge these children to think of a rule which will tell them whether the grapheme is a *c* or an *s*. Ask, *What do you notice about the* s *phonemes in the words you have found? When the* s *phoneme is represented by the* s *grapheme, are one or two* ss *used?*

Extend the activity by testing out the rule for the letter *k*, writing new rules for whether a *c*, *k* or *ck* grapheme is used to represent the *k* phoneme. The rule is: a short vowel is followed by *ck* while a long vowel is followed by *k* or hard *c*. Therefore *spick* is *ck* while *spike* is *k* (because it follows an *i*).

FRACTIONS, DECIMALS OR PERCENTAGES?

SUBJECT: MATHS. NNS OBJECTIVE: TO RELATE FRACTIONS TO THEIR DECIMAL REPRESENTATIONS: THAT IS, TO RECOGNISE THE EQUIVALENCE BETWEEN THE DECIMAL AND FRACTION FORMS OF ONE HALF, ONE QUARTER, THREE QUARTERS ... AND TENTHS AND HUNDREDTHS; TO BEGIN TO UNDERSTAND PERCENTAGE AS THE NUMBER OF PARTS IN EVERY 100.

LEARNING OBJECTIVE

To understand that decimals, some fractions and percentages are equivalent.

THINKING OBJECTIVE

To use skills of deduction.

THINKING SKILLS

The children will play a familiar game to make tenths. They will convert these into decimals and percentages to deduce the equivalence between tenths, decimals and percentages.

WHAT YOU NEED

A die; a large sheet and smaller pieces of paper; cubes, longs and flats in base ten.

WHAT TO DO

Revise the number of thousandths in one-hundredth, hundredths in tenths and tenths in whole ones as a mental oral starter activity. If necessary, play the game outlined below using 1000ths, 100ths, 10ths and whole one as the exchanging columns, with each dot of the die representing one thousandth, to revisit and consolidate the children's understanding of these fractions and their equivalence. Ten thousandths = one hundredth, ten hundredths = one tenth and ten tenths = one whole.

1 whole	10ths

Divide the large sheet of paper into five columns, labelled 'hundredths', 'tenths', '20 per cent', '0.5' and 'one whole'. Explain to the children that you will throw the die and that the number of spots shown is equivalent to one hundredth, or a unit cube. When there are enough hundredths (ten) to make a tenth, the children can exchange these for a long. When you have two longs these can be placed in the 20 per cent column and a pair of these two longs, plus one from the tenth column will make 0.5. Two lots of five longs or two 0.5 make a flat. Through the game, deduce the following equivalences:

five tenths = 50 per cent or 0.5

20 per cent = two tenths or 0.2

0.5 = 20 per cent + 20 per cent + one tenth

ten hundredths make one tenth.

Consolidate the children's learning of equivalence as mental oral starters in other numeracy lessons. For example, ask the children, *How many tenths are there in 30 per cent? How can 0.6 be presented as a percentage or a fraction?*

Label the columns with different amounts, depending on the ability of the children. Some may work on equivalence between tenths and decimals, and decimals and percentages before combining all three.

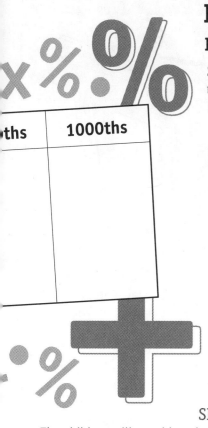

FLOATING ROCKS

SUBJECT: SCIENCE. QCA UNIT: 6E BALANCED AND UNBALANCED FORCES.

LEARNING OBJECTIVE

To understand that an object floats when the upthrust from the water balances its weight pushing downwards.

THINKING OBJECTIVE

To explain ideas and give reasons.

THINKING SKILLS

The children will consider what they already know about balanced and imbalanced forces and be invited to use this knowledge and understanding to find a way to make a rock float. They will consider the properties of the rock and the water, and the forces acting upon them, before suggesting and trying out ideas for balancing these forces. They will find a way to make the rock float and explain in scientific terms how they did this and why their ideas worked.

WHAT YOU NEED

Large sheets of paper; writing materials; rocks of different sizes; water trays which are deep enough to hold increasing levels of water.

WHAT TO DO

Use this activity to consolidate and assess the children's understanding of balanced and unbalanced forces at the end of the unit of work.

Revisit what the children know and understand about balanced and unbalanced forces by carrying out a mind mapping exercise in small groups according to ability. Brainstorm all the words that the children can think of relating to balanced and unbalanced forces. Accept all their suggestions. Examples could include: push, pull, upthrust, downthrust, float, sink. Write these at random places on the board and ask the children to link two or three with a line. Write the reasons for linking them on the line. For example, 'Sink links with downthrust because when this is greater than the upthrust, the object sinks.' 'Upthrust links with push, because upthrust is a pushing force.' Use this information to provide challenges to extend their learning further.

Note which children are able to explain that when an object is stationary or moves at a constant speed, the forces acting upon it are balanced; that when an object floats, the upthrust of water balances out its weight pushing downwards.

Challenge the children to make a rock float. Give lower attaining children a smaller rock and higher attaining children a heavier rock to begin with. Ask, *Why does the rock sink? What do you need to do to make the rock float?* Encourage the children to explain that the rock sinks because there is more weight acting downwards than there is upthrust from the water. To make the rock float, they must find a way to balance the forces acting upon the rock.

List the the children's suggestions for what they could do to make the rock float. For example, spreading the weight of the rock so that there is a greater surface area for the upthrust to balance against; increasing the amount of water to provide more upthrust; reducing the weight of the rock. Ask, *Why can't the weight of the rock be reduced? How could you increase the upthrust of the water? How can you spread the weight of the rock?* Allow groups to explore their ideas until they have managed to get the rock to float. Gather the groups back together and ask each one to describe how they managed to get their rock to float, encouraging them to use scientific terms to explain their reasoning.

Give each group a bigger and heavier rock to test out their conclusions.

VICTORIAN CHILDREN

SUBJECT: HISTORY. QCA UNIT: 11 WHAT WAS IT LIKE FOR CHILDREN LIVING IN VICTORIAN BRITAIN?

LEARNING OBJECTIVE
To learn what life was like for children in the Victorian era.

THINKING OBJECTIVE
To use skills of inference.

THINKING SKILLS
The children will consider the activities that formed the everyday lives of rich and poor Victorian children. They will put together short plays to show how different groups of children spent their time. They will go beyond factual representation by inferring what the children may have been thinking or feeling as they went about their lessons, work or everyday lives.

WHAT YOU NEED
Access to research information on the everyday activities of Victorian children; paper; writing materials.

WHAT TO DO
Introduce the activity to the children by explaining that they will be developing plays about a particular group of children, showing their everyday activities. Organise the class into three groups, to represent those children who were required to work, those who went to school and those who came from rich families and therefore spent much of their time learning how to be responsible adults. Tell the class that as well as depicting what these children actually did every day, you also want them to think of a way to portray what they were feeling or thinking.

Choose one of the groups and brainstorm some ideas as a class. For example, think about the kinds

of things the children may have done at school. Ask, *Where could you find this information?* The children may have carried out research into this aspect already. If they have, refer them to this; if not, provide them with reference material and ask, *What do you think school was like for girls and boys at this time? What subjects did they learn? What were they allowed to do? How were they treated by their teachers? How might they have felt about this treatment?* Brainstorm all the feelings these children might have had at different times and for different types of activity. Note what they could have been thinking during certain activities.

Briefly discuss how the groups could show these feelings and thoughts in their plays.

Provide each group with a large sheet of paper on which to plan the content of their play. Refer them to their research for information on what activities the Victorian children will be engaged in. They should write a list of the characters, and plan what they might say or think at particular times during the play to show how they are feeling about the activities in which they are involved.

Ask all three groups to perform their plays, then ask the audience how they think the different Victorian children felt about their activities and their lives. Discuss how well each group portrayed these feelings.

A DAY OUT

SUBJECT: GEOGRAPHY. QCA UNIT: 23 INVESTIGATING COASTS.

LEARNING OBJECTIVE
To learn that waves shape coastal environments.

THINKING OBJECTIVE
To interpret evidence and form opinions.

THINKING SKILLS
The children will interpret what they see on photographs and maps of different coastal regions and form opinions about the way these shapes were formed. They will consider the evidence and form opinions about how the beauty of some of these spots could be sustained through the use of natural materials, and by reducing the impact of human erosion.

WHAT YOU NEED
Photographs of different coastal regions around the coast of Britain which have different types of beaches, bays, ports, cliffs and arches. Suitable places include Lulworth Cove, Durdle Dor, Brighton and Woolacombe beaches, Beachey Head and Dover; matching maps for each photograph.

WHAT TO DO
Introduce the activity by talking about the different types of beaches and the distinguishing features of each one. Note the types of materials that are found there and where this may have come from. Explain that some beaches are 'deposited' – they have been made by people importing sand from another place. Talk about how some of the beaches have been formed by erosion, by the cliffs being washed away by the waves. Discuss the possible consequences of this continuing to happen if it was not halted by people taking remedial steps. Tell the children about Holbeck Hotel in Scarborough, and relate this to the family on the South Coast, and the National Trust, who have moved buildings away from the edge of the cliffs on the South Downs.

Look at a photograph of Lulworth Cove and ask the children to identify some of the features of this bay. They should use the evidence in the photographs to form opinions about how the bay was formed and why the cave is positioned where it is. Ask, *What evidence does the photograph show to support this opinion? How did you interpret the evidence to form this opinion?* Agree that the children's interpretation that the bay and cave were formed by the waves breaking against the rocks and cliffs in a certain way and from a certain direction is one possible theory. Look at the beach and agree the material that it is made from. Ask, *Is it a natural or deposited beach? What evidence is there to suggest that it is a natural beach?*

Next, look at photographs of Brighton and Woolacombe beaches. Encourage the children to interpret this photographic evidence and to form opinions about the type of beach shown, the surrounding features, and any clues that indicate how the beach was formed. Ask, *What steps have been taken to stop the beach being washed away? What other features of the coastline immediately adjacent to the beaches can be seen?*

Look at a photograph of Durdle Dor and consider how this feature was formed. Ask, *What evidence is there to suggest that it was shaped and formed by the waves? Can you think of any other features you have seen that were formed in the same way?*

In groups, ask the children to interpret photographs of different coastal areas in the same way to form opinions about how the coast was created and shaped, giving particular thought to features such as bays, caves, arches and cliffs. Encourage the children to interpret the evidence to form opinions about whether local people have acted to prevent further natural or human erosion and protect the coast.

Again in groups, ask the children to find evidence which, when interpreted, indicates that the council around Lulworth is keen to protect the environment, the steps taken to protect the sand dunes in Woolacombe, and how the buildings on the edge of the cliffs near Beachey Head are protected.

REMOTE-CONTROLLED VEHICLES

SUBJECT: DESIGN AND TECHNLOGY. QCA UNIT: 6D CONTROLLABLE VEHICLES.

LEARNING OBJECTIVE
To learn that vehicles can be controlled by remote control.

THINKING OBJECTIVE
To use skills of deduction and to explain.

THINKING SKILLS
The children will control different kinds of models and explain what makes these work and how. They will consider how to make the vehicle change direction and speed by moving the controls in different ways. They will use these explanations to write precise instructions on how to control the models. They will think about the detail of the instructions, and consider how precise the instructions should be. They will also write a computer program to control a model.

WHAT YOU NEED
Several models and vehicles that move by remote control, including cars and cranes.

WHAT TO DO
Go into the hall or another large space and explore with the children all the different ways that the remote-controlled vehicle will move. Look at how to change speed and direction by moving the joysticks or whatever means of control is being used. Invite the children to explain what is happening and to link this with what you are doing with the controls. Ask, *Why is this way of moving the vehicle called 'remote control'?* (The vehicle is being controlled via radio signals between the handset and the vehicle aerial by remote from a distance.) Invite the children to explain precisely what is happening to move the vehicle. Next, define the explanation further by describing exactly what you are doing with the controls and how this is changing the speed and direction of the vehicle.

Agree with the children a route that they would like the vehicle to follow. Work out beforehand what you need to do to make the vehicle move through this route. Ask, *What is the first move on the control box?* Invite the children to think of the first precise instruction, then the next and so on, until the sequence of instructions has been worked out. Follow the children's instructions, explaining as you go what you are doing. Alternatively, ask a child to control the vehicle following the other children's instructions, and to explain afterwards precisely what he or she did to control the vehicle in this way. Return to the classroom and model how to write the children's explanations of the precise control moves as a set of instructions.

Organise the children into groups and let them explore different types of remote-controlled vehicles. Ask, *Can you explain how the vehicles move? What are they doing to make this happen?* Put together

different routes through which to control the vehicles by remote and work out how to present this as instructions to guide to others.

Challenge the children to build remote-controlled vehicles from commercial construction kits such as Lego, Meccano and K-Nex. They should attach these to the computer and write precise sets of instructions to make them move in different ways and through different routes.

CHARITY BISCUITS

SUBJECT: ICT. QCA UNITS: 5D INTRODUCTION TO SPREADSHEETS; 6B SPREADSHEET MODELLING.

LEARNING OBJECTIVE
To learn that computers can calculate costs.

THINKING OBJECTIVE
To make decisions.

THINKING SKILLS
The children will identify the amount of ingredients they need to make a batch of biscuits to sell for charity. They will estimate the cost of each ingredient and put this information into a spreadsheet format and use it to work out how much it will cost to produce different numbers of batches. They will research the cost of the ingredients at different supermarkets and use the formula to work out the different costs. They will use the information to make decisions about where to shop and how much to charge per biscuit to make a profit.

WHAT YOU NEED
A simple biscuit recipe; recipe ingredients; cooking utensils; spreadsheet software.

WHAT TO DO
As a class, make a batch of biscuits to find out how many biscuits can be made from a certain amount of ingredients.

Tell children they are going to work out the cost of making the biscuits to sell for charity. They will put this information into a spreadsheet so they can decide on a realistic price.

Ask small groups to enter some example prices of the different ingredients into a spreadsheet, and to write a formula to calculate the total cost. They will then need to write another formula to divide the total cost by the total number of biscuits in each batch, thus giving them a price per biscuit.

They could then research the cost of the ingredients in different shops and change the prices accordingly. This should automatically change the final cost per biscuit.

Ask the children to make a decision about the best place to shop. Ask, *How much is the cheapest biscuit you can make? Do you need to go to more than one shop to buy the ingredients? How do you know?*

MOODY PICTURES

SUBJECT: ART AND DESIGN. QCA UNIT: 6C A SENSE OF PLACE.

LEARNING OBJECTIVE

To identify different artistic ideas and approaches, and to explain any feelings evoked.

THINKING OBJECTIVE

To infer feelings.

THINKING SKILLS

The children will look at landscape paintings by different artists and explain any feelings these pictures evoke. They will talk about how the artists communicate these feelings through their paintings,
inferring this from the way colour, shape and form are used. They will then look at a photograph they took on a recent visit, or of the local environment, and give reasons for why they took this particular view. They will link this scene to the way they felt, and think of a way of reproducing this feeling to evoke similar feelings in others.

WHAT YOU NEED

Photographs taken by the children of interesting features in the local environment or on a visit; paintings by different artists of people and landscapes, including a landscape by Constable; paper; writing materials.

WHAT TO DO

In a previous lesson, take photographs of features the children find interesting. Look at any landscape by Constable and talk about the way it makes the children feel. Record their ideas on the board. Ask, *Why do you feel like this? What has the artist done to make us infer these feelings? Is it because of a particular object, the way the objects are positioned, the expression on the face of any people, the colours used or some other technique? Is there a sense of urgency in the painting or does it portray a very calm picture? How is this mood created?* Talk about the use of line, colour, shape and form and how these elements are combined and used to create certain effects.

Repeat the questions for a contrasting painting.

Ask the children to think about these elements when planning their own composition. Ask them to look at the photographs they took in an earlier lesson and to think about why they chose this particular feature or view. Ask, *What feelings did you have when you looked at this feature/view? What was it that attracted it to your eye? How can you show this in your own composition? What techniques and elements will help you depict the feelings you had when you chose to photograph this particular feature/view?* Encourage the children to think about and plan how they might create the same feelings in a painting, so an observer might feel the same emotions when looking at the painting. The children should stick their photograph to a sheet of paper and label the elements and techniques they intend to use. Prompt the children to paint pictures of the scene and to evaluate each others' pictures in terms of how well they evoke the intended feeling.

WORDS

SUBJECT: MUSIC. QCA UNIT: 19 SONGWRITER.

LEARNING OBJECTIVES

To learn the term 'lyrics'; to understand how lyrics can reflect mood and feeling in a song, convey a message or tell a story.

THINKING OBJECTIVE

To use skills of interpretation.

THINKING SKILLS

The children will listen to different lyrics in a variety of songs and interpret how songwriters use words to reflect the intended emotional response to a song. They will identify how the songwriter chooses the words carefully to affect some kind of personal emotional response from the listener. This may be to evoke a particular mood or feeling, to put over a particular message or to tell a story. They will think about songs that they know and interpret the lyrics to decide what emotional response the songwriter wishes to affect from the listener.

WHAT YOU NEED

Copies of the words of three pop songs which include lyrics that reflect a mood or feeling, convey a message or tell a story. (Ensure that the words are suitable.) Examples of songs that tell a story include 'Eleanor Rigby' by the Beatles, and many country and western songs. Suggestions for songs conveying a message include 'Hand Bags and Glad Rags' by Rod Stewart or The Stereophonics, while songs which evoke some kind of mood or feeling include 'Bridge Over Troubled Water' by Simon and Garfunkel and 'Angels' by Robbie Williams.

WHAT TO DO

Tell the children that you are going to consider how songwriters use the words of a song, the lyrics, to convey a feeling or mood, get across a message or tell a story.

Listen to one of the songs and let the children join in if they know it. Ask, *Do you like this song? Why or why not?* After several suggestions, focus on any reasons given that refer to the words and what they are saying. Talk about how the words convey particular moods or feelings. Ask, for example, *How does 'Bridge over Troubled Water' make you feel by the end of the song? What is the song about? Does it convey a positive mood by the end of the song? What feelings are conveyed at the beginning of the song? What does he or she say they will do when their friend is not feeling happy? Is it a song about helping a friend and, if so, how is that communicated in the words?* Ask the children to identify all the words that convey a mood or particular feeling. Interpret the last verse of the song (or other appropriate section of a different song) and identify the words that reflect a more positive mood: 'sail on silver girl' and 'your time has come to shine'.

Next, listen to 'Hand Bags and Glad Rags' (the children might be more familiar with the more recent version by The Stereophonics). Ask, *What are the words saying?* Interpret the intended meaning of the words 'that your poor old granddad had to sweat to buy them' means. One interpretation is that people in the past were forced to work very hard to buy what they needed, material goods that we take for granted today. Ask, *Are the words saying that it is easier to buy or get hold of everything we need today and, if so, what is it that has changed over the years to make this possible?* Refer the children to the lyrics 'They told me you missed school today' and 'Now you've gone and thrown it all away'. Ask, *What do these words mean? What message or moral is the songwriter trying to convey about the importance of education?*

Continue to interpret the lyrics of other songs. Ask the children to identify for themselves songs that contain words that convey a mood, feeling or particular message before considering those which tell a story or reflect the time or place in which they were composed.

WHAT IS THE MORAL?

SUBJECT: RE. QCA UNIT: 5C WHERE DID THE CHRISTIAN BIBLE COME FROM?

LEARNING OBJECTIVE

To learn that stories in the Bible include literal and non-literal meanings.

THINKING OBJECTIVE

To use skills of inference.

THINKING SKILLS

The children will look at different stories from the Bible and infer other possible meanings in addition to the literal facts presented.

WHAT YOU NEED
Copies of stories from the Bible, written for children (suitable stories to include are Noah, Jonah, Samson, and David and Goliath).

WHAT TO DO
Remind the children of the story of David and Goliath and talk about the facts presented. Ask, *What was happening at that time? Why?* Think about the other non-literal messages the story might be trying to convey. Ask, *What can we infer from the story's content, from what was said by either side?* Explain that some people interpret the story beyond the literal, suggesting that the story gives guidance on how people should lead their lives. (Be careful not to infer that the children in the class are all Christians by avoiding the use of 'we'. You might like to use the phrase 'Some people believe that …' instead.) Collect the children's inferences on what the different parts of the story might be trying to teach people. From these inferences write the moral of the story with the children.

Give groups of children different Bible stories to read and ask them to infer possible meaning beyond the literal. Ask them to consider the following questions: *What might the story be trying to teach people about how to lead their lives? What is the moral of the story?* Challenge the children to write the possible moral of the story from their collected ideas. Look at the story of Adam and Eve in some detail and brainstorm all the issues that this story infers.

WHERE AM I GOING?

SUBJECT: PE. QCA UNIT: OUTDOOR AND ADVENTUROUS ACTIVITIES UNIT 3.

LEARNING OBJECTIVE
To follow a route using a map and compass.

THINKING OBJECTIVE
To use the skills of deduction.

THINKING SKILLS
The children will learn how to use a compass to deduce the angle of turn, then use it to locate different features and places on a map. They will deduce the angle of turn in order to deduce the direction in which they need to go and the distance in which they need to travel to reach their intended position. They will collect clues at different destinations and draw the route they followed on a map.

WHAT YOU NEED
A map of the school grounds; compass bearings for, and distances between, the different features and places in the school grounds; preprepared clues (see below); writing materials; circular protractor.

WHAT TO DO
Play a game where the children (standing facing north) find the compass bearing for different features in the school grounds.

Challenge individuals to give their friend a compass bearing for them to work out which feature is in that position. For example, *What is at 60° west?*

Ask the children to turn, from facing north, by, for example, 45°, 210° and so on. Assess whether they have turned in the right direction and whether the size of turn was correct. Relate the direction of turn to compass points.

Ask the children to find different features and places from their position. For example, ask, *Can you find the feature that is 60° west at a distance of 10 metres?* Continue with this activity until you are sure the children can locate where they are, and deduce from the instructions (the angle of turn, direction and distance) which feature is described.

Set up a trail for the children to follow, where they find clues describing a pathway around the school grounds or perhaps the local park. Post clues at each point which tell the children in which direction to go next. (Make sure the children are in groups and that you can see them at all times. Organise additional adults to help with the supervision of this activity.)

Back in class, ask the children to draw the route they took. Check that they visited each place in the correct order.

Challenge the children to use a circular protractor to match the eight points of a compass to the correct number of degrees. They can use the protractor to draw and measure different-sized angles.

EXTENDING REASONING SKILLS

Subject and QCA unit, NLS or NNS objective	Activity title	Thinking objective	Activity	Page
English NLS objectives: To analyse the success of texts and writers in evoking particular responses in the reader; to prepare a short section of story as a script; to explore the challenge and appeal of older literature through: listening to older literature being read aloud; reading accessible poems, stories and extracts; reading extracts from classic serials shown on television; discussing differences in language used	Little creatures	To use skills of inference	Looking at different extracts from *The Hobbit* and inferring from the text how different characters might be feeling	43
Maths NNS objectives: To reason and generalise about numbers or shapes; to explain methods and reasoning, orally and in writing	Windowpanes	To explain reasons	Finding how many rectangles and triangles there are in windows with different panes of glass	44
Science QCA unit: 6A Interdependence and adaptation	Depend on me	To use reasoning skills	Identifying how animals and plants are interdependent	45
History QCA unit: 14 Who were the Ancient Greeks?	A Greek legacy	To interpret information and make judgements	Looking at evidence and interpreting what can be learned from it about the Ancient Greeks	47
Geography QCA unit: 12 Should the high street be closed to traffic?	Welcome back	To make decisions	Reaching decisions about a local environmental issue	48
Design and technology QCA unit: 6C Fairgrounds	Carousel and big wheels	To explain	Explaining how different fairground rides work	49
ICT QCA unit: 5A Graphical modelling	Pleasure park	To make judgements, form opinions and make decisions	Creating a plan for a theme park, using symbols to represent rides and other facilities	50
Art and design QCA unit: 5C Talking textiles	Stories from pictures	To interpret pictures	Interpreting stories through different media	52
Music QCA unit: 17 Roundabout	Roundabout	To form opinions	Identifying when harmonies are concordant or discordant and using this to compose two or more note accompaniments to a familiar song	53
RE QCA unit: 6E What can we learn from Christian religious buildings?	Christian churches	To explain and infer	Comparing religious buildings and artefacts, and explaining why these are important to Christian worship and beliefs	55
PE QCA unit: 3 Invasion games	To pass or not to pass	To make decisions and judgements	Deciding when to keep possession and when to pass a ball in a game	57

LITTLE CREATURES

SUBJECT: ENGLISH. NLS OBJECTIVES: TO ANALYSE THE SUCCESS OF TEXTS AND WRITERS IN EVOKING PARTICULAR RESPONSES IN THE READER; TO PREPARE A SHORT SECTION OF STORY AS A SCRIPT; TO EXPLORE THE CHALLENGE AND APPEAL OF OLDER LITERATURE THROUGH: LISTENING TO OLDER LITERATURE BEING READ ALOUD; READING ACCESSIBLE POEMS, STORIES AND EXTRACTS; READING EXTRACTS FROM CLASSIC SERIALS SHOWN ON TELEVISION; DISCUSSING DIFFERENCES IN LANGUAGE USED.

LEARNING OBJECTIVE
To begin to understand how authors evoke particular feelings in their characters.

THINKING OBJECTIVE
To use skills of inference.

THINKING SKILLS
The children will watch an extract from *Lord of the Rings* and consider how the film-makers create the mood and effect. They will then consider how this mood evokes feelings in the characters concerned. They will brainstorm all the possible feelings, then consider those that haven't been mentioned. They will then read a section from *The Hobbit* and identify the devices used by the author to imply how the characters are feeling. Finally, the children will decide whether it is easier for them to infer the feelings of characters through film or text. (This activity also links to analysing, an information-processing skill.)

WHAT YOU NEED
A copy if the video version of *Lord of the Rings*; a copy of *The Hobbit* by JRR Tolkien (HarperCollins).

WHAT TO DO
Watch the opening scenes from *The Lord of the Rings*, up to the point where the rings are dispatched. Make sure you stop the film before the Dark Lord appears, just after we see the map showing Mordor. Discuss how the opening scenes make the children feel. Ask, *What feelings does the image of the gold rings being forged create? How does the music contribute to the mood and effect? What about the vocal introduction? How does the choice of words add to the drama and suspense?* Discuss how the film-maker creates suspense and the feelings and mood discussed through the choice of words, music and images.

Watch a later extract, for example, when Gollum appears for the first time, or when Gandalf meets young Bilbo Baggins (to the point when Bilbo Baggins gives Gandalf some tea). Discuss the mood and feelings created and how the film-maker has conveyed these. Ask, *How does the colour change? What scene is portrayed? Why has such a green and peaceful setting been chosen?* List all the children's feelings and together note some that have not yet been mentioned. Ask, *Have any of the extracts you have seen implied these feelings?*

Read the section in *The Hobbit* where Bilbo Baggins meets Gollum (look around page 68), starting with 'Deep down here in the dark water lived Old Gollum' to the part where the first riddle starts. Talk about how the text shows how Bilbo is feeling and how it implies this. Ask, *What devices has the author used? How has he set the scene? How has he put the message across? How do authors imply feelings in comparison to film-makers? Do film-makers have other devices at their disposal?* Compare the devices used in the text to those used in the film extract to depict the setting, and to describe the traits of the characters. Invite the children to close their eyes and to listen to the section of the book where Bilbo enters the mountain (look around page 200) to 'The glow of Smaug!'. Afterwards, allow them two minutes to talk with a partner about all the feelings that the extract implies and the way the author conveys these. Share the suggestions in a class discussion.

Ask groups of children to scan different chapters to find extracts of literal and implied text which shows how the characters are feeling. Use some of these for the thinking challenges below.

Watch suitable extracts from the film or, if in doubt, watch the cartoon version produced by Warner Brothers.

DIFFERENTIATION
Work alongside lower attaining children, encouraging them to contribute in their group discussion by referring them to the text and asking direct questions to help them identify the words used by the author.

Challenge higher attaining children to find their own extracts. They should try to infer possible content from the chapter titles and scanning the text for clues.

THINKING SKILLS: AGES 9–11

WHERE NEXT
Ask the children to look out for literal and implied text as they read their individual reading books. They could share these with the class or record them in their reading diaries.

ASSESSMENT
Note the children who can infer from the text how the different characters are feeling. Assess how well they refer to the text and look at the vocabulary used by the author in communicating these feelings to the reader.

LEARNING OUTCOMES
Most children will find words to describe how the characters they are reading about are feeling. Most will begin to understand that authors make careful use of expressive vocabulary to imply feelings in their characters and to evoke particular responses in the reader.

FURTHER ENGLISH CHALLENGES
Read and write
Give different groups different extracts to read and ask them to infer from the text what they think the characters are feeling. Ask them to write the extract as a playscript, and to include stage directions for the actors to show clearly their feelings to the audience. Watch each group's short playlet during the plenary and identify how the actors show the way they are feeling. Read the extract from which the playlet was written and identify how the author conveys these feelings in the text. Suitable extracts include where Bilbo tries to rob the trolls (look around page 35), where the dwarves meet Smaug (look around page 204) and when Bilbo realises that Smaug is not really asleep (look around page 208).

WINDOWPANES

SUBJECT: MATHS. NNS OBJECTIVES: TO REASON AND GENERALISE ABOUT NUMBERS OR SHAPES; TO EXPLAIN METHODS AND REASONING, ORALLY AND IN WRITING.

LEARNING OBJECTIVE
To reason, in a logical way, the total possible number of rectangles in a window.

THINKING OBJECTIVE
To explain reasons.

THINKING SKILLS
The children will decide how to approach the investigation of finding the number of rectangles in the pane pattern of a particular window design. They will explain how they solved the problem and apply this to a bigger window with the same design. They will use the explanations to try to devise a rule for solving the investigation for any window of the same design before thinking about whether the same rule can be applied to windows of different designs.

WHAT YOU NEED
Pictures of Georgian windows with 6, 8, 10 and 20 panes and one which has two horizontal rectangluar panes; access to a photocopier; large sheets of paper; writing materials.

WHAT TO DO
Show the children a double Georgian window with 20 panes of glass. Ask the children to explain how they could find out how many rectangles there are in this window. Listen to the children's suggestions. When they have made their suggestions ask, *Would your method be the best method to work out how many rectangles there are in a window with 50 panes of glass?* Explain that the children should think of a way to find a mathematical rule which will help calculate the number using a mathematical formula.
Explain that it is best to break the problem down into smaller steps and to try to identify a pattern in the numbers. Ask the children to describe the smallest window design possible. Agree that this is one pane – one rectangle. Draw this for the children.

Next, look at the picture of the Georgian window, which has two rectangular windowpanes organised horizontally, and draw this.

Ask the children to say how many rectangles they can see. There are three – two small and one large, formed by the perimeter of the whole window. Draw another second window but this time with four panes.

Ask, *How many rectangles can you see?* Agree that there are nine rectangles, and ask the children to explain where these are. Shade the nine rectangles on several different pictures of windows of the same design to be sure everyone can see them.
Pin up window designs with six, eight and ten panes of glass. Look at each in turn, asking the children, *How many rectangles can you see now? Can you see a pattern in the numbers? What is the pattern? Is there a relationship between the number of panes and the number of rectangles you can see? Is there a pattern or relationship between the number of panes and the number of extra rectangles each time? Can you use this pattern to predict the number of rectangles in a window with 20 or 50 panes in the same design?*
Watch the children to see if they use a logical approach to investigate the number of rectangles. Ask them to explain their reasoning.

Share the children's reasoning during the plenary and try to write a rule for finding the number of rectangles that can be found in the windows. The rule is: n (the total number of rectangles) = the previous total + (1.5 x number of panes). For 16 panes $n = 84$ (the total number of rectangles in 14 panes) + (1.5 x 16). $N = 84 + 24$.

Differentiation

Provide lower attaining children with several pictures of the same window design so that they can colour in each rectangle as they find it and then count these individually. Lead them to look for a pattern in the way they find the rectangles rather than at random, for example, first find those made from single panes, then two panes, four panes and so on. Challenge higher attaining children to do this for themselves, asking them to explain the reasoning behind their systematic approach.

Where next

Carry out the 'How many squares on a chessboard' investigation in the same way, noting the children who understand how to break down the board into smaller pieces to help them find a rule to help their reasoning. Encourage the children to find how many squares in one square (one) then four (five) then nine and so on. Each time they need to add the square number to find the answer. For example, a 3 x 3 square made up of nine smaller squares contains 9 + 4 + 1, while a 5 x 5 square contains 25 + 16 + 9 + 4 + 1.

Assessment

Watch the children as they work and note those who work out a logical approach to solving the problem and can use this to explain their strategies. Challenge them to find a pattern in their results by drawing the next arrangement and working out the total number of rectangles.

Learning outcomes

All children will offer some explanation of how they solved the problem. Some will explain their reasoning more logically.

Further maths challenges

Windows I can see

Ask the children to look at the windowpane arrangements in windows around the school and count the number of rectangles in each one. Challenge them to find pattern and relationships between those of the same design, and try to find a rule to predict the number in larger window designs, with a greater number of panes.

Leaded windows

Look at leaded windows and explain the way the panes of glass are organised. Find a way of finding out how many triangles or diamonds there are in each windowpane. The children will need to work with small windows to begin with, to break down the problem into bite-sized pieces and help them to identify the pattern or rule for this challenge.

Depend on me

SUBJECT: SCIENCE. QCA UNIT: 6A INTERDEPENDENCE AND ADAPTATION.

Learning objective

To learn that animals and plants in a local habitat are interdependent.

Thinking objective

To use reasoning skills.

Thinking skills

The children will use a concept map to link ideas about interdependence and give reasons for joining those terms and concepts. They will base their reasons on their knowledge and understanding of what living things need to survive and remain healthy. They will use this information to learn about food chains and to consider the role of the sun in this process. (The context for this activity can also be set within Unit 5C Gases around us and Unit 5B Life cycles.)

What you need

Large sheets of paper; writing materials; pictures of creatures, animals and plants found in local and other habitats.

What to do

Look at a local habitat and identify all the plants and creatures that depend on this habitat to survive. Ask the children, *Why do you think the animals and plants have decided to live in this place? Was it by accident or design?* Gather the children's responses. Ask the children to give reasons why the plants and creatures are there by design. (Because they depend on each other to survive.)

Look at pictures of all the animals and plants that live in a particular habitat with which the children are familiar, for example, a section of the school field with trees, birds, insects including bees, pollen bearing flowers and humans. Glue the pictures randomly around a large sheet of paper. Invite the children to say whether any of these items is dependent on another for survival. For example, the bird relies on the tree for shelter. Link these two items with a line and write how the bird is dependent on the tree along the line. Ask the children to suggest whether the tree is dependent on the birds, for example, to eat the insects which may feed off the tree and keep them down to an acceptable level. Agree that the two things are 'interdependent' because they provide each other with services to help them both keep healthy and to survive. Continue until you have linked several pairs of living things and given reasons to explain their interdependence.

Provide the children with a set of pictures showing plants and animals from another habitat, and ask them to investigate the interdependence of these plants and creatures. This time, invite them to draw or stick simple pictures of the plants and animals to a large sheet of paper, and, discussing their decisions as a group, to join and record the reasons why they have linked things together.

Take care not to use arrows on the ends of the lines as this may confuse the children when they come to draw food chains (when the arrow should point to the feeder not the food source).

Ask the children to add a picture of the sun. Ask, *Which plants and animals are dependent on the sun? Why? Is the sun dependent on any of the plants and creatures or is this relationship a one-way route?* Agree that the sun is a provider for all living things and that the world's survival is dependent upon it. However, because the sun does not rely on us to survive, it is a dependent relationship we have with the sun rather than an interdependent one.

DIFFERENTIATION
Ask higher attaining children to investigate habitats found further afield, such as desert or ocean environments. Lower attaining children should consider groups of plants and animals with which they are familiar. This will help their reasoning, as they will know something about the living needs of this group of living things.

WHERE NEXT
Ask the children to use their new knowledge to construct food chains. Encourage them to say why they have chosen the plants and animals they have, and note whether the groups chosen belong to one type of habitat.

ASSESSMENT
Use the children's completed sheets as evidence for their ability to give logical and relevant reasons for the links they have made. Do this by noting whether the reasons are based on knowledge and understanding of the conditions living things need to survive and to grow in a healthy way.

LEARNING OUTCOMES
All children will learn to give reasons for why pairs of living things are interdependent. Some will set this within a familiar context while others will apply their reasoning to more obscure and unfamiliar habitats.

FURTHER SCIENCE CHALLENGES
Crossing habitats
Investigate those occasions when interdependency crosses more than one habitat. For example, how humans have invaded the rest of the earth by fishing the oceans and removing the trees from rainforests. Talk about the interdependence of these habitats on humans and vice versa. Ask the children to give reasons why humans are interdependent with oceans and rainforests and why we need to care for the environment and our world.

A GREEK LEGACY

SUBJECT: HISTORY. QCA UNIT: 14 WHO WERE THE ANCIENT GREEKS?

LEARNING OBJECTIVES
To learn about some of the activities in which Ancient Greeks took part, and to understand that these activities were often connected to their religious beliefs.

THINKING OBJECTIVE
To interpret information and make judgements.

THINKING SKILLS
The children will look at a range of historical sources and brainstorm the information gained from these. They will interpret pictures on vases, writing on documents, paintings and drawings, and extracts from myths and legends to learn about the Ancient Greeks and some of their legacies.

What you need

Greek vases and urns and/or pictures of these; a copy of Greek legends and myths, such as those found in *The Odyssey* by Homer; pictures, paintings and photographs of Greek statues and ruined buildings; large sheets of paper; writing materials.

What to do

Choose one source of evidence which gives information about the buildings, daily tasks, leisure activities, transport or clothes of Ancient Greeks, for example a reproduction amphora (a vase depicting events), postcards from travel magazines and brochures that show the remains of ancient buildings, or a book containing Greek myths with pictures. As a class, note as much information as you can from the source. For example, you could challenge the children to interpret what any figures on the amphora are doing and hypothesise why. Note what this tells you about the activities of the Ancient Greeks. Ask, *What evidence is there that tells us about the clothes they wore? Can you see any tools, weapons or sporting equipment? What does this tell us about the games they played? Why did the Ancient Greeks take part in the Games?* Explain that it was a religious celebration.

Look at the pictures of Ancient Greek buildings. Ask, *What do you think these buildings were used for? How do you know? What evidence remains to indicate how the Ancient Greeks lived their lives?* Again, relate the use of the building to their religious beliefs.

Move on to the Greek legends and myths. Ask, *What do these stories tell us about the beliefs of the Ancient Greeks, the way the travelled the world, the wars they fought, the places they visited?* Note with the children how much information can be discovered by interpreting the evidence given by the sources, and how this helps you to make judgements about their way of life.

Organise the children into groups, and give each group a large sheet of paper divided into the headings 'Beliefs', 'Leisure activities', 'Clothes', 'Buildings' and any others you can think of. Give each group a range of evidence sources and ask them to interpret what each one tells them about one or more of these aspects. For each piece of information gained from their interpretation, ask the children to make judgements about what it tells us about the Ancient Greeks' way of life and their beliefs. Share the range of information you have found together at the end of the lesson and identify further aspects to research in more detail. Have the children uncovered an area of particular interest they would like to pursue to see if their judgements are accurate?

Differentiation

Point out the figures in pictures or on vases and ask, *What do you think these figures are doing?* Link this to the activities of the people at that time, such as the Olympic Games and other sporting events, and training for war. Continue by interpreting the pictures that show what the people wore and the items they used in their everyday lives. Higher attaining children should be given the buildings to interpret and to make judgements about the way they were used. (Pictures of the Acropolis in Athens are suitable for this.) Allow them to research these buildings in reference books to help them in their interpretations.

Where next

Help the children to interpret words with Greek prefixes and suffixes and learn what these words mean today.

Assessment

Assess how well the children interpret the sources of evidence to find information about the Ancient Greeks. Note those who use this information to make judgements about the way the Ancient Greeks lived, what they believed, what they wore and how they spent their leisure time. Check that they all make at least one interpretation and make at least one judgement about the Ancient Greeks.

LEARNING OUTCOMES

All children will make at least one interpretation from the evidence, and make at least one judgement about an aspect of the way of life of the Ancient Greeks. Some will look at the legacies left behind and use this as evidence to interpret and make judgements about how ordinary people lived their lives.

FURTHER HISTORY CHALLENGES

The Olympic Games

Ask the children to list all the sports in the original Olympic Games. They can link these to their equivalent today. Ask them to work out where the name *Olympics* came from and to note which games remain the same and which have changed. Look at the modern Olympic flag and interpret together what the rings may represent. Use what the children have found out about the games that the Ancient Greeks played in the original Games and link this with the number of rings.

Greek production

Put together a Greek playlet which tells the story of one of Odysseus' adventures on his return journey to Ithaca after the Trojan wars. Challenge the children to interpret the evidence in the story to re-enact the event, and to make judgements about the kind of costumes the people would be wearing and what weapons they would be carrying.

WELCOME BACK

SUBJECT: GEOGRAPHY. QCA UNIT: 12 SHOULD THE HIGH STREET BE CLOSED TO TRAFFIC?

LEARNING OBJECTIVE

To conduct a survey into how to make the local high street accessible to shoppers.

THINKING OBJECTIVE

To make decisions.

THINKING SKILLS

Out-of-town shopping complexes are thought by some to be responsible for the death of local town centres. The children will consider the advantages and disadvantages for keeping an out-of-town shopping area against increasing the popularity of the local High Street in order to entice shoppers back. They will collect evidence and use this to decide the best way forward in terms of closing the local high street to traffic to increase pedestrian access, or developing a park-and-ride scheme. At the same time they will consider how to avoid alienating the out-of-town businesses. They will consider issues such as car parking and easy access to shops.

WHAT YOU NEED

A map of the local high street and town centre, access roads and out-of-town shopping and recreation areas; large sheets of paper; clipboards; paper; writing materials.

WHAT TO DO

Talk to the children about why people travel into their local town centre and list their ideas. Consider how out-of-town shopping and recreation centres have impacted on the number of people visiting town centres. Ask, *Do you think out-of-town shopping facilities have reduced or increased the number of people visiting town centres? What do you think shopkeepers in town centres think of this?* Discuss any local issues or any local impact that has been felt from the development of new facilities. Think about how local shoppers could be attracted back into the town centres.

Organise the children to conduct surveys on the use of land in the town centre, and list the people who use different types of buildings, such as shops, offices and council offices. Look at car parking facilities and at how easy or difficult it is to get in and out of the places that people want to visit quickly. Consider public transport access and whether this is helpful to local traders. Use the outcomes of the surveys to put together a questionnaire to collect people's views about traffic issues, car parking difficulties and getting in and out of town. Ask the children, *Are any of these issues preventing people from coming into the town centre? Would they prefer the high street to be closed to traffic? If the high street was more accessible, would people shop in the town centre more often? Why would this entice them back?* Also collect the children's views on providing a park-and-ride facility or closing the high street to traffic at certain times of the day.

Use all these responses to identify a list of possible questions to ask town shopkeepers, businesses both in and out of the town centre, shoppers, office staff and other workers, and local residents on the following issues:

◉ Would it be useful to organise a park-and-ride scheme from the local out-of-town shopping and recreation area to the town centre?

Possible questions to ask on this issue: Would people travel into town to shop? Would buses be frequent enough? How easy would it be to store purchases? What if you forgot to lock the car? Would this scheme decrease the amount of traffic using the roads around the town? Would it reduce the cost of upkeep of the roads?

◉ Would it be useful if the high street was made into a pedestrian-only access permanently, or between the hours of 8am and 6pm?

Possible questions to ask on this issue: How would residents get to the bank cash points? Would shops need to be open at night to receive deliveries? Is there an easy way to drive around the town centre? Would the high street still have access to buses? How can we get to our favourite restaurant or pub? Where can taxis drop off passengers? How easy is it to park the car and how much would it cost?

Consider both of the above issues, looking at all the questions in turn, and as a class make a list of the advantages and disadvantages for each issue. Then consider whether the suggestions of park-and-ride and pedestrianisation are good ones or not.

Look again at the list of disadvantages and, again as a class, try to find solutions to the difficulties that these new developments might have for different people, such as improving car parking and ensuring easy access to cash point machines. Challenge the children to consider the advantages and disadvantages of their suggested solutions, focusing on whether their ideas will entice people back into the town centre. Encourage the children to make further suggestions for improving shopping in the local high street and to attract shoppers.

DIFFERENTIATION

Challenge higher attaining children to reach decisions about a particular plan of action and to devise leaflets for enticing different groups of people back into the town centre. Focus on shoppers and shopkeepers with the lower attaining children.

WHERE NEXT

Adapt the activity to address any current local issue which affects the local residents or other people who come to the area, for example the building of a new housing estate and the impact this will have on local services, a new shopping complex outside town, a new night club and recreation centre in the middle of town, developing a new airport or runway or the development of a football stadium.

Set up a debate to argue for and against a reduction of traffic in the town centre.

ASSESSMENT

Use the lists created above to assess how well the children have reached decisions on how they can entice people back to the town centres. Note those who have considered a range of options and thought about the advantages and disadvantages of each one when deciding which ideas would be worth developing.

LEARNING OUTCOMES

The children will learn to base their decisions on the opinions of other people and to consider carefully the impact decisions of this kind will have on the different people who use the town centre.

FURTHER GEOGRAPHY CHALLENGES

Sports complex

Look at a map of the local area and choose a possible suitable spot to build a sports complex. The children should think about the implications this decision will have on local people and make a 'for' and 'against' list to inform the decision.

Motorway

Tell the children that there is to be a new motorway built near to or through the middle of your town. Discuss the likely route and note the people who will be affected. Together, make a list of disadvantages and advantages for the proposal of the building of the new motorway.

CAROUSEL AND BIG WHEELS

SUBJECT: DESIGN AND TECHNOLOGY. QCA UNIT: 6C FAIRGROUNDS.

LEARNING OBJECTIVE

To learn how a belt and pulley system can transfer movement from one part of a model to another.

THINKING OBJECTIVE

To explain.

THINKING SKILLS

The children will build a model of a big wheel from a commercial construction kit and explain how they have made it move. They will incorporate a belt and pulley system into the model and explain how this transfers movement from one part of the model – the motor wheel – to another – the big wheel.

WHAT YOU NEED

Videos or pictures of working big wheels; commercial construction kits suitable for this activity, for example Meccano and K-Nex.

WHAT TO DO

Look at videos of big wheels and talk about how they move. Encourage the children to use the terms 'rotate', 'vertical rotation', 'faster', 'slower' and 'stop'. Talk about what is making the ride turn (the power system) and the way this is transferred from one part of the ride to another to make it move in a circle or rotate.

Look at the commercial kits that the children are going to use to build a working model of a big wheel. Allow them time to build a group model before talking about the power source and how they can make it move. Collect their ideas first before suggesting they use a simple motor driven by batteries. Revise how to make an electrical circuit using a battery, wire and motor. Ask, *How are you going to attach the power source to your model to make it go round?* Show the class how to make a simple belt and pulley system, attached to the centre of the wheel and motor. Challenge the children to explain how the model works and how the belt and pulley system transfers the movement from the motor to the model.

DIFFERENTIATION

With higher attaining children apply the same system to a roundabout, encouraging them to explain how the belt and pulley system works in a similar way. Explain what happens when the belt is put on the pulley in a figure-of-eight configuration.

WHERE NEXT

Ask the children to design and make individual models of big wheels. Talk to the children as they work and ask them to explain what equipment they are using and why. Encourage them to apply their knowledge and understanding to make other rides which move in rotation. Ask them to explain the power system and movement of their models.

ASSESSMENT

Listen carefully to the children's explanation to see if they have a secure understanding of the way their model works and the systems they have used. Note those who are ready to work independently on their own models and those who need further input from you.

LEARNING OUTCOMES

The children will work together to make a working model of a big wheel and help each other explain what they have used, how they have joined components and the power source which drives the movement. They will explain how a pulley system works to transfer power from one place to another.

FURTHER DESIGN AND TECHNOLOGY CHALLENGES

Theme park rides
Look at modern rides at theme parks and ask the children to work in groups to agree an explanation of how their chosen ride works. They need to consider the mechanics and what powers the ride. Rides from Alton Towers, Disney and Universal Studios are a good resource for this activity, and the children will probably talk about these rides with great excitement. Disney provides useful alternatives for discussion with higher attaining children as some rides are solar powered.
Looping cars
Watch toy cars travelling at speed on tracks that loop to send them upside down without falling off. Ask the children to explain what is happening and to reason why the cars are not falling from the track when they turn upside down.

PLEASURE PARK

SUBJECT: ICT. QCA UNIT: 5A GRAPHICAL MODELLING.

LEARNING OBJECTIVE
To use an object-based graphics package to produce and explore a graphical model.

THINKING OBJECTIVE
To make judgements, form opinions and make decisions.

THINKING SKILLS
The children will consider how to create objects from lines and geometric shapes to design a plan for a theme park. They will create their own key to show which shapes and lines represent which rides and facilities. When placing the objects around the plan, they will make judgements about the size and colour of their objects, and decide where to put them and their orientation. They will form opinions about whether the toilets need to be near the food outlets, whether types of rides need to be in the same area and whether ice-cream outlets need to be at various points around the park rather than in one place.

WHAT YOU NEED
A suitable object-based drawing package; internet access.

WHAT TO DO
Explain to the children that they are going to create a plan of a theme park which will show a range of rides, attractions and other facilities using symbols and objects to represent the rides and facilities. Visit the Alton Towers website at www.alton-towers.co.uk, go to 'See the park' and choose the 'full screen view' option so children can see the map and how the grounds are laid out. Talk about the symbols that have been used, the organisation of the rides into different areas and how the toilet facilities are located at various points around the park but especially next to food outlets. Ask, *Why did the designer of the park locate the items where he or she did? What judgements and decisions did he or she make about which rides to put next to each other? Where are the food outlets located? How many there are? What different types of food can you buy? Why is this? How are the food outlets represented on the plan and in the key? Why are the drinks and ice-cream kiosks scattered about the park? Is this to keep the people spread out and to reduce queuing?* Encourage the children to form opinions based on their responses to these questions.

Remind the children how to use the graphic modelling programme so they can design their own symbols and shapes to represent the rides and facilities. List the rides that the children would like to include and the other facilities that are needed to complete the park and optimise its services.

Organise the children into pairs, and allow them time to create their own shapes and symbols to represent the rides and facilities, and to make decisions and judgements about the best places for the rides to go in the park. Encourage the children to form opinions about whether toilets need to be close to food outlets and why, and whether ice-cream and drinks kiosks need to be scattered around the park. Ask the children to make a key to explain the meaning of their symbols and to decide where to place this on the plan. Ask them to give reasons for why they have put the key where they have, thus forming opinions about the best place for it.

Ask the children to explain their plans and to justify their decisions to another pair and to discuss the similarities and differences of each other's plans. Ask, *Is one plan better than another and, if so/not, why?*

DIFFERENTIATION
Ask higher attaining children to make judgements and decisions about whether to include water fountains for visitors' comfort. Ask them to form opinions about the best place for these. Ask, *Why do they need to be located near a water source? Where might these be?* Organise the other children into mixed-ability pairings, but question any lower attaining children directly to ensure they have a chance to give their reasons for any joint judgements and decisions, and to ensure that they are involved in the decision-making process. This will help them to form opinions about the positioning of any rides, attractions and facilities.

WHERE NEXT
Print out the plans and display them for the class to evaluate in terms of the judgements and decisions that have been made. Ask them to form opinions about the positions of certain facilities on each other's plans, and whether these have been placed in suitable positions based on the reasons and explanations given for the choices.

ASSESSMENT
Question the children as they work, to probe the reasons for their judgements and decisions. Note those who base these on practical reasons, such as fitting the rides into a particular space, deciding that toilets are best next to food outlets, that ice-cream and drinks kiosks are best scattered about to cut down on queuing and having too many people in one place at a time.

LEARNING OUTCOMES

The children will learn to create symbols using a graphic modelling package, and make judgements and decisions about the size, colour and position of these symbols on a plan. They will form opinions about why they have placed certain rides, attractions and facilities where they have and give reasons for their choices.

FURTHER ICT CHALLENGES

Graphical scoring

Challenge the children to create symbols to represent sound effects to accompany a favourite poem, or to represent chords for an accompaniment to a song. Organise the screen into grids to represent bars of music and ask the children to make judgements about the shape and colour of the symbols to represent certain sounds. The children could then make decisions about how these could be arranged on the grid to show the accompaniment. Ask the children to form opinions about whether the symbols support the performance of the song or whether they need to be positioned in a different way.

Art class

Use graphic elements to draw symbols and shapes to create pictures in the style of Russian art, for example artists such as Kandinsky and Kasimir Malevich. Look at El Lissitsky's poster 'Beat the Whites with the Red Wedge' which uses abstract geometric designs to convey a message after the Russian revolution. Ask the children to make judgements about the size, shape and colour of their symbols and designs, and to decide how to copy, layer and reposition them in different ways to make their pictures. Ask them to form opinions about whether to include more shapes with straight or curved lines and the effect that this creates.

STORIES FROM PICTURES

SUBJECT: ART AND DESIGN. QCA UNIT: 5C TALKING TEXTILES.

LEARNING OBJECTIVE

To investigate and combine visual and tactile qualities of materials.

THINKING OBJECTIVE

To interpret pictures.

THINKING SKILLS

The children will look at the way different artists tell a story through their art. They will interpret how they have conveyed particular moods and feelings through the range of materials that have been combined to create the whole effect. They will interpret not only the detail of the story but also the feelings of the characters, the sounds that can be heard and other sensual qualities of the piece of work.

WHAT YOU NEED

Paintings, pottery, textiles and tapestries (or photographs of these) from a range of countries and cultures, including Aborigine art.

WHAT TO DO

As a class, look at an Aborigine painting and note the different artistic elements that have been used. Talk about the colour of the background and paints, and ask, *Why have these colours been used?* Explain that these colours are used because the paints are made from natural materials available to the Aborigine people who live in the deserts in Australia. Note the creatures that are depicted either by an actual drawing or by their footprints. Ask, *How are these painted?* Talk about how the Aborigine people paint in dots of colour. Note the direction of these dots and the way they face. Interpret the journey that the creatures are making and tell the story together. Explain to the children that the Aborigines often use art to depict the stories of their Dreamtime (a mythical age of the past) as a way of telling younger generations about their beliefs. Interpret the painting again with this in mind, thinking about the story that this could be telling the observer. Ask, *How does the style of painting and the use of colour depict the feelings and mood of the story?*

Explain to the children that people have been telling stories through art for centuries, and pass round the pictures and photographs for the children to look at briefly. After a few minutes, give pairs a picture or photograph and ask them to interpret the story. Allow five minutes for the children to discuss what they can see, and how the artist has told the story. They should think about the items that have been drawn, the way they are drawn and their position, the colours and techniques used, and the way the pictures are laid out – vertically, horizontally or in a circle. Invite a few pairs of children to show their pictures and to tell the story, incorporating the content, mood and feelings it depicts. Explore the reasons for this interpretation by asking, *What made you interpret the story in this way? Was it because of the techniques and/or the elements used?*

Organise the children into groups and, giving each group a picture showing a different style of visual storytelling, ask them to list the materials and techniques that the artist has used to convey the content, feelings and mood of the story being depicted. Link each technique with a particular mood or feeling and note how this is achieved, for example the facial expressions, the way the body is arched, the darker tones of the colour or the way the lines have been made less distinct. Ask, *What techniques have the artists used? How does this convey a certain mood or feeling? What element of art has the artist used? How effective is it?*

To finish, share the children's ideas and ask them to say if they could clarify the interpretation of the story by adding or changing a particular technique.

DIFFERENTIATION

Give lower attaining children a piece of art which clearly tells a story, for example a photograph of the Bayeux tapestry. Ask, *Can you interpret the story? How are the people in the picture feeling? What techniques did the artist use to inform their interpretation?* Give higher attaining children more obscure art examples, such as Picasso's Guernica, and talk about how he depicts the Spanish Civil War through this famous painting. If you don't think the children in your class are mature enough for this, look at examples of Renoir's street scenes instead, asking the children to interpret what is going on in them.

WHERE NEXT

Look at illustrations in books and interpret the moods and feelings they convey to the reader. Note how well they help us understand the author's intended message.

ASSESSMENT

Note the children's comments as they interpret the pictures and as they discuss what they have learned about how artists convey particular moods and feelings.

LEARNING OUTCOMES

The children will learn to interpret the story or tale told by a series of pictures, and to use this to inform their own work.

FURTHER ART AND DESIGN CHALLENGES

Picture storyboard

Organise the children into groups and ask them to act out a different part of the same short story or poem. Ask them to 'freeze frame' on the most important scenes. Put two groups together and ask the pairs of groups to act out the story to each other and to interpret what they think each frame is depicting in terms of action, mood and feelings. When the acting group freezes the frame, the other group should take a photograph. Choose four photographs to form the basis of a storyboard. Pairs of groups can then depict the whole story in picture form, drawing illustrations to fill the gaps in the narrative between the photographs.

Picture magic

Look at a comic strip story and ask the children to interpret the content, mood and feelings in the story. Challenge them to label the strip with the different techniques they would use to make the effects clearer to an observer.

ROUNDABOUT

SUBJECT: MUSIC. QCA UNIT: 17 ROUNDABOUT.

LEARNING OBJECTIVE

To identify when harmonies are concordant or discordant.

THINKING OBJECTIVE

To form opinions.

THINKING SKILLS

The children will combine and listen to pairs of notes and decide whether they are concordant or discordant. They will learn, by describing the effects these notes create, that there are discordant and concordant intervals in music. The children will sing a familiar song and add first one- and then two-note accompaniments to this. They will listen to each other's compositions and form opinions about the effects the accompaniments create and why.

What you need

Tuned percussion instruments that have an eight-note octave, including chime bars, xylophones, glockenspiels and keyboards; a song with simple chordal harmonies with which the children are familiar; music with a simple harmonic accompaniment. (Most pop songs will do but 'When I'm Sixty-Four' or 'Yellow Submarine' by the Beatles are suitable.)

What to do

Listen to a pop song (with suitable words) and identify the tune and accompaniment. Agree that the tune has, depending on the song, one- or two-part melody and the accompaniment contains more than one note played together. Identify the instruments that produce the accompaniment. Again it will depend on the song you have chosen but is likely to be guitar or keyboard. Tell the children, if they do not already know, that when more than one note is played together we call this a 'harmony'. Ask, *Do you like the sound of the song?* Emphasise that you are not asking whether they *like* the song but whether the notes are combined in such as way to produce a pleasing sound. Explain that this is because the notes have been chosen because the composer thinks they go together well.

Tell the children that they are going to form an opinion about whether they like the harmony, or the combination, of certain notes. They will decide whether these form a concordant note (the notes go well together to create a relaxed and pleasing sound) or discordant note (the notes create a clashing or tense sound). There is no one right answer to this so the children will be expressing an opinion. This may be different to those of others, but is still a valid opinion!

Organise the children into groups and ask them to explore the sounds that the tuned percussion makes. Ask them to combine two sounds and to form opinions about whether they produce a bright and pleasant or tense and unpleasant sound. Ask them to think of adjectives to describe the effect the combination of notes creates, and to form an opinion about whether they are concordant or discordant. Remind the children that they are forming opinions and therefore these may be different from another group, or person in their group. Ask the children to find all the combination of notes in their octaves and to form opinions about whether they like the combinations and whether they are concordant or discordant.

Share the children's opinions after about ten minutes, or when the children have formed their opinions about each pair of notes in the octave.

Sing a familiar and simple song through together, for example 'My Grandfather's Clock' by Henry C Work (from *Ta-ra-ra Boom-de-ay*, A&C Black), and talk about how the children can add a tuned accompaniment to this. Ask them to work in groups or pairs to add first a single-note (the 'tick-tock') and then, if they are able, a two-note accompaniment. The children can decide whether to make this concordant or discordant depending on the effect they want to create. After ten minutes, invite each group to perform their composition and ask the rest of the class to form an opinion about the effect the accompaniment creates in terms of whether it is concordant or discordant. Ask, *What has made you form that opinion?*

Differentiation

Model the process of combining two notes with the lower attaining children, and talk to them about what each combination sounds like. Use their response first to identify whether they like the combination and why, and then to identify if the notes are concordant or discordant. Challenge higher attaining children to combine three notes to form opinions about the effects each combination creates. Ask them to write descriptions to help them form opinions about whether they like or dislike the combination and why, before saying whether they think it is concordant or discordant.

Where next

Sing rounds, taping these for the children to decide whether they are concordant or discordant. With those who are able, identify why they are concordant. Listen to music by different composers and encourage the children to form opinions about whether they like the music and why, and whether the harmonies are concordant or discordant.

Assessment

Note whether the children form opinions about their likes and dislikes of the sounds being produced and whether the sounds are concordant or discordant.

Learning outcomes

All children will be able to form an opinion about whether they like or dislike certain note combinations, and most will be able to say why; some will use this opinion to form other opinions about whether certain note combinations are concordant or discordant.

Further music challenges
Chords

Give the children a simple song to sing. In groups, they can then compose a three-note chordal

accompaniment.
Record the
performance on tape
so that the groups can
form opinions about
whether they like their
composition or not,
and make changes
based on review.
Invite each group to
perform their song
and accompaniment
to the rest of the
class. Encourage
the audience to
form opinions about
whether the harmonies
are concordant
or discordant and
whether they like it or
not. Suitable songs
include 'Jamaica
Farewell', and
'Favourite Things'
from *The Sound of
Music*.

Rap along
Ask groups of children to adapt a favourite song or
poem as a rap, putting in syncopated rhythms and
adding a one-, two- or three-note accompaniment.
They can perform it to the rest of the class,
evaluating what makes it successful and forming
opinions about whether they like the chordal
accompaniment, the rap rhythms and why.

CHRISTIAN CHURCHES

SUBJECT: RE. QCA UNIT: 6E WHAT CAN WE LEARN FROM
CHRISTIAN RELIGIOUS BUILDINGS?

LEARNING OBJECTIVE
To understand that religious symbols convey different
meanings to different people.

THINKING OBJECTIVE
To explain and infer.

THINKING SKILLS
The children will consider the artefacts and symbols
found in Christian churches and brainstorm the range
of possible meanings these bring to people. They
will base this work on visits, from visitors or from
pictures of the different kinds of Christian churches.
They will infer from these the different ways people
feel when they visit a Christian building.

WHAT YOU NEED
If possible, visit at least two different Christian
churches and encourage the class to look at all
the artefacts and symbols contained within them.
Arrange for a member of each congregation to explain
to the children how each artefact is used in services
and worship, or what religious signifiance they have,
and how these link to Christian beliefs. Alternatively,
provide pictures of the interiors of two different
Christian buildings for the children to identify the
range of religious artefacts and symbols. Large
sheets of paper; writing materials.

WHAT TO DO
Discuss what the children saw on their visit, or ask
them to identify in the pictures you have of the two
Christian buildings, the artefacts and symbols shown.
Choose one symbol or artefact to model what you
would like the children to do in groups. For example,
write 'cross' in the centre of the board or large
sheet of paper and around it write all the words
that the children associate with this symbol. Accept
all suggestions. Encourage the children to include
any feelings that the cross might evoke in Christian
believers, such as the crucifixion of Jesus and how
this reminds them of the reasons for his death.
Next, look at the collection of words you have
identified together and complete a simple mind

mapping activity by linking those that the children think have something in common. For example, 'Jesus' can be linked to 'cross'. Encourage the children to explain why they have linked these two things and write this along the linking line. Continue until you have linked all the words to at least one other. Note with the children how all the words link to the cross, a symbol of Christian belief. Note the range of meanings and feelings this symbol has evoked in them as a class and how this has the same effect on Christian believers when they visit their church.

Organise the children into groups and ask each one to develop another symbol in the same way. Symbols to use include water, candles, stained-glass windows, books, bell, music and altar table. Monitor the children as they work, reminding them to think about the feelings the artefacts or symbols evoke and to write their explanations and reasons for joining the words they have.

Share the children's explanations of how they have linked the words. Note the number of different meanings the artefacts and symbols convey as children
and, therefore, to believers who visit the Christian buildings.

DIFFERENTIATION

Give lower attaining children artefacts, such as an altar table, books or windows. Give higher attaining children symbols, including water, candles and music to consider.

WHERE NEXT

Use the words and links identified above as a basis for the children to write about any feelings they had on the visit to the Christian church. Relate these feelings to those they might have experienced when visiting buildings from other religions.

Discuss whether the same symbols are found in all religious buildings or whether some can only be found in Christian places of worship.

ASSESSMENT

Look carefully at the children's writing and note who has identified inferred feelings from the symbols and artefacts. Note those who have linked some words because of the way each one is used in worship and services and the different meaning each one can have for individuals.

LEARNING OUTCOMES

Most children will understand and explain that the many symbols found in Christian churches and buildings evoke different feelings and mean different things to different people.

FURTHER RE CHALLENGES

Religious metaphors

Provide the children with religious metaphors and ask them to explain what they mean and the inferred feelings of each one. Include simple ideas – ask them to describe another symbol as a different object, such as a candle as a person, or water as milk. Examples from the Bible include 'the land of milk and honey', 'the breath of God' and 'Jacob's ladder'.

Christingles

Make Christingles with the children by wrapping a red ribbon around the centre of an orange. Stick a candle in the top. Use cocktail sticks to spear raisins, sultanas, small sweets and stick these at 45 degrees to the candle and red ribbon and diagonally opposite below. Ask the children to explain what the items represent: the orange is the world, the red ribbon represents the blood of Jesus and how He reaches all around the world, the candle reminds us that Jesus

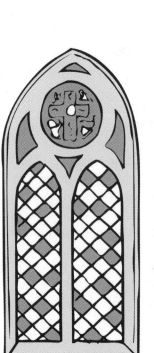

was the centre and the light of the world, the sweets represent the people of the world from different nations and these are stuck into the orange at the points of the compass to show that Jesus reaches all people. List all the inferred meanings the Christingles evoke.

TO PASS OR NOT TO PASS

SUBJECT: PE. QCA UNIT: 3 INVASION GAMES.

LEARNING OBJECTIVE
To consider when to pass and when to keep possession of a ball.

THINKING OBJECTIVE
To make decisions and judgements.

THINKING SKILLS
The children will play a small team game where the focus will be on the tactics of gaining or keeping possession of the ball. They will consider their role of defender or attacker by judging the space around them to find a place to best receive the ball, or how to mark the other team members who are free and prevent them from moving into a big enough space. They will make decisions based on this information on where to send the ball and how, or how to intercept and gain possession.

WHAT YOU NEED
Large balls; games area divided into small courts.

WHAT TO DO
Spend five minutes warming up and practising throwing and catching skills in pairs or threes. Play a quick game of 'Piggy in the middle' and discuss the strategies for keeping possession and intercepting the ball. Revisit the best places to stand to intercept, such as being able to see the sender, watching the receiver, giving yourself time to track the ball after it is sent so you have more time to plan the interception. Consider the judgements the 'piggy', or defender, makes when judging the speed and space to which the ball is being sent. Transfer this analysis to the senders. Make judgements about where the best place is to send the ball. Ask, *What decisions does the receiver need to make?* (When and how quickly to move into a space, keeping this secret from the defender, how they will signal this to the sender.) Consider the judgements the sender has to make, whether to throw or bounce the ball, the direction and speed on which to send it, noting where the receiver intends to move and the position of the defender.

Develop the game into a small group games situation where the teams score points by hitting a target. Place the target inside a particular area, which is bounded by another area, so that the teams do not defend the target by standing on or in front of it. This way, tactics will need to be developed before the attacking team gets near the target. Explain to the children that they need to get the ball into the opposing team's half and to hit the target to score as many point as they can to win. Give them five minutes to play the game. Note with them which team has won and why. Ask, *What tactics did you use? Did you manage to intercept the ball? How did you do this? On what did you base your decisions for where to move and how to gain possession? How did you make judgements about the direction and speed of the ball so that you could intercept more accurately and successfully? How did you manage to keep possession? How did you know where, how and to whom to pass? What did the other team members do? How did you judge where to run? Was it because there was a space? Was it because you could get a clear shot at the target? How did you judge the speed and direction to hit the target? What tactics did you use?*

Play the game again, encouraging the children to think tactically, to judge the speed, direction and space around them, and to note what the other team members are doing before deciding on a move. Ask, *Was the game closer this time? Was it more difficult to score a point?*

DIFFERENTIATION
Spend time working with those groups that include less able children. For the first few times they gain

possession, question them about to whom they can pass the ball, how they will do this and why.

Introduce the rule that when certain children gain possession, both teams must stand still. This will give the children in possession time to evaluate the positions of their team members, make judgements about where and how to send the ball and use this information on which to base the decision to whom they will send it. If you nominate all the children in turn for this privilege the less able will be included without feeling different.

Organise more able children as a group and give them a smaller space in which to work to make it more difficult to find a space and to keep possession. This will influence their judgements about speed and direction and decisions about where to move and when.

WHERE NEXT

Talk about games in which you can only keep possession for three seconds, or when you cannot run when in possession, for example netball and basketball. Talk about how this affects the decision and judgement of to whom to pass during a game. Ask, *How important is it to consider the position and space available of the player to whom you think it best to pass?*

Organise different types of small games such as hockey, football and tag rugby. Ask, *Do the same tactics apply? Do you still need to make judgements to make decisions about where to go and what to do to intercept the ball or to keep possession?*

ASSESSMENT

Towards the end of the lesson, watch the groups and note the children who are making judgements and decisions about where and to whom to pass the ball by looking around for the team member who has found the biggest space, or who has the best chance to score a point. Note those who judge the position of the opposing team to decide where to run to mark players and intercept the ball.

LEARNING OUTCOMES

The children will play a small team invasion game and concentrate specifically on when and to whom to pass the ball. They will consider space and speed when making their judgements and decisions.

FURTHER PE CHALLENGES

Short tennis

Set up a one-against-one competition, where competitors aim to score as many points as possible by bouncing a ball twice on their opponent's half of the court. After a five-minute match, judge who scored most points and why, evaluating how they managed to bounce the ball twice. Discuss how the winner made the decision to send the ball to a particular place, or to send it in a particular way. Ask questions to glean how the judgement was made and why the decision was taken. For example, *Was this because you hit the ball into a bigger space? How did you decide this was the best place to hit the ball? Was your opponent running in the opposite direction? Were you too far away? Were you able to hit the ball faster and thus stop your opponent reaching the ball?* Play the game again but this time assess how well the loser last time adjusts his or her game to outwit their opponent by making decisions and judgements about where to send the ball.

Who would you pass to and how?

Take photographs of the children as they play their small team games and display these in the classroom for the children to consider the teams' next moves. Encourage them to discuss the tactics of the team in possession, and to make decisions about who would be the best person to pass to next, how and why. Ask them to give reasons for their judgements. Next ask them to consider, judge and make a decision about where best to move to intercept the ball. Ask, *How can you use the information from the photograph to judge the people and places where the ball may be sent next? How can this help you decide which tactics to use in your game?*

ENQUIRY SKILLS

INTRODUCTION

The enquiry process is a means through which children can be fully involved in their own learning. This process gives them the opportunity to identify why they are learning something, as well as how and what. The ability to ask questions is fundamental to the development of children's independent enquiry skills. Once they are able to ask questions, the next step is to identify when they have asked the right questions to suit the needs of their research requirements. The questions can only be identified if the children can note what the problem is and what they need to find out in order to solve it. Only then can they begin to plan research into a topic or area.

Too often the children are presented with a ready-made set of questions and, therefore, play no part in developing the skill of asking questions themselves. The process undertaken with scientific enquiry can be applied to other subjects and is a good starting point through which to develop the children's enquiry skills. Often, teachers start with a question in science and yet rarely do so for other subjects. By identifying questions for each unit of work in all subjects, you will be setting up the enquiry process, allowing the children to find things out for themselves and to develop enquiry skills. This is the start of planning their own research. It involves them asking their own questions to start off an independent enquiry. While teachers generally model the asking of questions clearly in science to help identify a problem, enquiry or investigation (which gives the children the opportunity to plan their investigation and carry out a test), they tend not to revisit the investigation to improve ideas or refine the hypothesis, which may lead to a redefinition of the problem to make it more precise. This is the point at which children may begin

to ask more of their own questions to lead them into investigations and to conduct research, which takes their achievement beyond the average. Thinking becomes visible from this point forward.

The enquiry process is generally addressed as a whole, and the links between the range of skills are established easily. The activities in this chapter are planned to focus on particular aspects of the enquiry process, but at the same time recognise that these are probably set within a whole research project. It will, therefore, be difficult to see the skills on their own in all activities and the overlap between them. The enquiry process and skills are:

- asking questions
- defining the problem
- planning research
- predicting outcomes
- anticipating consequences
- testing conclusions
- improving ideas.

INTRODUCING ENQUIRY SKILLS

Subject and QCA unit, NLS or NNS objective	Activity title	Thinking objective	Activity	Page
English NLS objective: To distinguish between homophones i.e. words with common pronunciations but different spellings	Spelling check	To anticipate consequences	Predicting whether Word will highlight a word because of incorrect spelling or grammar	61
Maths NNS objectives: To discuss the chance or likelihood of particular events; to use language associated with probability to discuss events, including those with equally likely outcomes	Probability	To ask questions	Discussing the chance or likelihood of particular events, and using language associated with probability to discuss events, including those with equally likely outcomes	61
Science QCA unit: 5F Changing sounds	Sounding off	To anticipate consequences and test conclusions	Investigating what happens to pitch when the amount of material vibrating reduces in size	62
History QCA unit: 13 How has life changed in Britain since 1948?	The age of the car	To plan research and anticipate consequences	Planning how, and finding out how people carried out everyday activities in the 1950s and 1960 without the availability of a car	63
Geography QCA unit: 15 The mountain environment	Tired legs	To define the problem and plan research	Using mapping skills to answer questions about different mountains in the UK and abroad	64
Design and technology QCA unit: 6C Fairground	Fairground rides	To ask questions to inform research	Thinking about how fairground rides work and use this research to help in their own fairground model designs	65
ICT QCA unit: 6D Using the internet to search large databases and to interpret information	Location exercise	To plan research, predict outcomes, anticipate consequences and improve ideas	Using complex searches to locate information, working with others to interpret information	65
Art and design QCA unit: 5A Objects and meaning	Bright colours	To predict outcomes	Predicting how pictures will look with different colour mixes – contrasts, tone and tints	66
Music QCA unit: 21 Who knows?	Picture this	To improve ideas	Improving the sounds composed to depict an image or description	67
RE QCA unit: 6C Why are sacred texts important?	The Creation story	To ask questions	Comparing the stories of the Creation from different cultures and noting the similarities and differences between them	67
PE QCA unit: Dance activities link unit	Rock and roll	To plan research	Researching rock and roll steps	68

Spelling check

Subject: English. NLS objective: To distinguish between homophones i.e. words with common pronunciations but different spellings.

Learning objective

To learn the importance of checking spellings using different sources.

Thinking objective

To anticipate consequences.

Thinking skills

The children will think about how a computer highlights a word to show incorrect spelling or grammar. They will anticipate the consequences of what happens when the computer recognises that a word is misspelled. They will learn that they need to have a good understanding of spellings themselves to check the computer's spellchecker. They will learn that one way to do this is through the 'find and replace' tool.

What you need

A computer program with a paragraph already written with some words spelled incorrectly, and others where incorrect homophones or graphemes have been used.

What to do

As a group activity, look at a printed version of the paragraph that contains spelling mistakes. Make some of the mistakes the incorrect use of homophones and graphemes, for example *meat* and *meet*, *pair* and *pear* or *write* and *right*.

Ask the children to work in pairs to draw red or green wavy lines underneath the spellings and grammar they think the computer will highlight.

Load the version on the computer screen and compare the children's versions with that on screen. Ask, *Did you predict correctly which words the computer would highlight? Which incorrect words did it leave? What do these words have in common? Are they spelled correctly? Do they make sense?* Explain that the computer only highlights words that it doesn't recognise. It will look for incorrect spellings and grammar only. If the words are conventional spellings then it will not recognise them as incorrect because it has not been taught to understand the meaning. Therefore, if the sentence reads 'The children got all their spellings write in the test' the computer will not pick this up because although the wrong 'write' has been used it is spelled correctly. Explain to the children that this is why they cannot rely on computer spellcheckers but need to have some knowledge themselves of spelling conventions.

Show the children how to identify possible homonyms and to use the 'find and replace' tool to change those that have been used incorrectly.

Probability

Subject: Maths. NNS objectives: To discuss the chance or likelihood of particular events; to use language associated with probability to discuss events, including those with equally likely outcomes.

Learning objective

To understand the likelihood of something happening, including an equal chance.

Thinking objective

To ask questions.

Thinking skills

The children will identify questions which, when answered, will inform the probability of something happening in terms of likelihood and in terms of ratio.

What you need

A box of different coloured sweets; chart showing total of sunny days over a year in a holiday resort; large sheet of paper; writing materials.

What to do

Tip out the sweets and count how many there are of each colour. Write these down for the class to see. Ask the children, *Do you think there will always be the same number of each colour in each box? Why not?* Agree that this is because the boxes are filled by a machine with random numbers and not counted out individually. Ask, *How can you work out the probability of choosing a particular coloured sweet from the box?* Agree that this will depend on the number of different-coloured sweets in any given box.

Ask the children to give odds on picking out a particular coloured sweet based on the numbers you noted earlier. For example, if there are 30 sweets in the box and 10 of these are red, then this gives a 1 in 3 chance of choosing a red sweet from the box. The chance of choosing a rainbow coloured sweet are 0 (impossible). Continue until the children understand the language and process of working out probability.

Next, look at a chart showing the number of sunny days for different months of the year in a holiday resort. (Any holiday brochure should contain these.) Using 'not at all likely', 'quite likely', 'likely', 'very likely' or 'definitely', ask the children to suggest the probability of getting a sunny day in each month of the year. Discuss these phrases, then place each of them on a probability line of likelihood with 'not at all likely' at one end and 'definitely' at the other. Provide different groups with information on different resorts, and ask them to express the likelihood of having a sunny day or rain for each month of the year. During the plenary, share the information and use it to decide which is the best resort for guaranteeing the most sunny days at different times of the year. Note the resorts which provide an equal chance of sunshine and rain.

Extend the activity by looking at the form of different football teams and, using this information, work out the probability of whether each team is likely to win or lose their next match.

Ask the children to think of scenarios for each of the terms of likelihood ('not at all likely' through to 'definitely'), for example *It is not at all likely that I will dye my hair blue tomorrow, but it is very likely that I will get out of bed in the morning.* Encourage the children to use their imagination.

Talk about 'equal chance' or a 50/50 chance that something will happen. For example, there is an equal chance that a child would pick a red counter from a bag of ten red and ten blue counters.

SOUNDING OFF

SUBJECT: SCIENCE. QCA UNIT: 5F CHANGING SOUNDS.

LEARNING OBJECTIVE

To learn that when a vibrating material is reduced in size, the pitch of the sound gets higher.

THINKING OBJECTIVE

To anticipate consequences and test conclusions.

THINKING SKILLS

The children will explore what happens to the pitch when bottles containing varying amounts of water are tapped. They will make a link between the amount of water vibrating and the changes in pitch, then use this information to anticipate whether the same effect would happen when blowing across the top of the bottles to produce a sound. They will then test out whether their predictions were correct. The children will predict which of two chime bars produces the higher note, and relate this to the amount of material that vibrates.

WHAT YOU NEED

Enough sets of identical glass bottles containing different amounts of water for each group investigation; a set of chime bars; paper; writing materials.

WHAT TO DO

As a class, look at a set of bottles and talk about their contents. Note that the bottles are identical apart from the fact that they contain different amounts of water. (Revisit the fair testing concepts at this point if you wish.) Ask the children, *What do you think will happen when each bottle is tapped?* Some may have previous experience and know that they will sound different because there is a different amount of water in each one. Ask, *How is the pitch produced by the different bottles likely to change if we change the amount of water? Why?* Note that the pitch of the note gets higher as the amount of water decreases. Explain that this is because the amount of material vibrating (water) has been reduced.

Draw a table with two columns, one to record the children's predictions and the other to record the actual outcomes. Using one bottle, put in more water. Ask, *What will happen to the pitch of the note?* Record the children's predictions in the first column before testing this out. Repeat by tipping some water out of the bottle. (Take care when working with glass bottles. Remind the children the importance of not tapping them too hard and to handle them carefully.) Tell the children that they will be working in groups to find out what happens to the pitch of the note produced by blowing over the top of the bottle when the amount of water in the bottle is altered. Record all the children's ideas first, asking, *What do you think will happen when the amount of water is changed? Will the pitch will be higher or lower? Will the note be higher when there is more or less water in the bottle? Which material is vibrating? Has the amount of material vibrating been increased or decreased?* Invite them to say how they could test their conclusions. Ask, *How will you make the test fair? How will you structure the test? How will you record what you have found out? How will you measure what happens?*

Let the children carry out the test. Give each group a set of bottles and ask them to put them in order according to which they think will make the higher or lower sound each time. Encourage one child only to blow into each bottle to find out what happens. Ask, *Did you get the order right? Did the bottle with the most water make the highest or lowest sound when blown? Why is this different to the order when the bottles were tapped?* Explain that this is because a different material is vibrating, therefore,

the bottle with less air has a higher note when blown (the air is vibrating) but a lower note when tapped because it has more water (the water is vibrating). Ask, *Did you work out the right order of pitch?* Interpret the results and record the conclusion that the pitch is higher when the material vibrating is less.

Extend the activity by using what the children have found out about vibrating materials to anticipate which of two chime bars makes a higher note, which end of a xylophone will produce the lowest note, or whether a thicker or thinner string will make a lower or higher note when plucked. Ask the children to explain their predictions before testing out whether they were right.

THE AGE OF THE CAR

SUBJECT: HISTORY. QCA UNIT: 13 HOW HAS LIFE CHANGED IN BRITAIN SINCE 1948?

LEARNING OBJECTIVE
To learn how life changed for people in the 1950s and 1960s.

THINKING OBJECTIVE
To plan research and anticipate consequences.

THINKING SKILLS
The children will consider the ways that cars have changed the way people live today in comparison with the past. They will start by considering how cars are used today and how they were used in the past. They will think about the consequences of not having a car on the way people lived their lives in the 1950s and 1960s; how this would affect everyday activities such as going shopping, going to school or work, or going out for the evening. (Be sensitive to those children who do not have a car and talk about the possible reasons for this: affordability, choices, living in an urban area where public transport is good.)

WHAT YOU NEED
Large sheets of paper; writing materials.

WHAT TO DO
Talk about the number of cars and vans that are on the roads today. Organise the children into groups and ask one group to brainstorm the models and makes of all the cars they can think of, another to think of all the uses, another to list the kind of people who use cars, such as parents, delivery people, sales staff, teenagers, police officers, ambulance staff and so on. Allow about five minutes for this task.

Next, ask the groups to discuss the items on their list. Help them to conclude that cars play a very important part in most people's everyday lives. Explain to the children that there were fewer cars and other road vehicles about during the 1950s and 1960s. Ask them to consider why. Include in the discussion: cost, availability, need and other transport systems. Ask the groups to list the consequences of not using cars in the way we do today. Encourage them to consider the following questions: *How were goods delivered? How and where did people go to work? How and where did children get to school?*

Explain that it was taken for granted that you did not own a car in the 1950s and 1960s. Talk about how different groups of people travelled around, particularly those people who lived in rural areas. Ask, *Towns and cities provided buses and trains, but was this the case in rural areas? What other forms of transport were used? Were there more local buses and trains then than there are today? How can you find* out? Further questions to help focus the research include: *How did people do their shopping? How did they get to work? How did children get to school? How did people get to the cinema in the evening?* Explain to the children that you want them to plan a way of finding answers to these questions, and to find out how people carried out these activities without the use of a car.

Organise the children into groups and provide each one with a large sheet of paper, with the headings 'shopping', 'getting to work', 'getting to school', 'going out' written at the top. Ask the children to plan how they might research these areas to find out how people carried out these everyday activities. Ask them to write down what they need to find out, to identify all the places where they might find the information, and the questions they need to ask. Challenge them to think of a way to answer the question: *How did the absence of cars affect the way people lived at that time?*

During the plenary when looking at the suggested research plans, ask the children to hypothesise about the time it took to travel from one place to the next. Ask, *Why would a short journey today take, say, only 20 minutes, but in the 1950s and 1960s take two hours?* Explain to the children that buses often travelled round a number of villages so the speed of the journey was greatly reduced. Ask, *Why do you think people either worked locally, or biked or walked to work? Did anyone use motorbikes? Or trains?*

Now allow the groups to follow their research plans into the everyday activities of people who lived in the 1950s and 1960s, and how they went about them. Ask, *What impact did a lack of private transport have on the way people lived their lives, on the time taken to do everyday activities, on the places they could go, on the number of local amenities?* As a class, note the consequences of not owning a car, and then try to anticipate the consequences on the transport infrastructure, including roads and rail services.

TIRED LEGS

SUBJECT: GEOGRAPHY. QCA UNIT: 15 THE MOUNTAIN ENVIRONMENT.

LEARNING OBJECTIVE
To use mapping skills to identify how steep mountains are.

THINKING OBJECTIVE
To define the problem and plan research.

THINKING SKILLS
The children will define their enquiry and use the information to plan research on mountains around the world.

WHAT YOU NEED
A map of the local area, preferably of a hill that the children have recently climbed or walked up, on which the slope is shown in contour lines; maps showing the mountainous regions in the UK and around the world.

WHAT TO DO
Discuss with the children a time when they walked uphill recently. Ask, *How did your legs feel? Why did you get tired? Would you have gone on the walk if you had known before you went that there was a steep climb? How could you have found out?* Respond to the children's suggestions, especially if they suggest looking at a map.

Define the problem with the children: they need to know how steep a hill is before they set off on a walk, find a way to find out, and then find out. Help them to plan their research by listing all the ways they could find out the necessary information, for example, by asking someone who has already completed the walk, by looking on a map.

Look at the hill you climbed on the map, and ask the children to look at it very closely. Ask, *Can you identify what feature on the map shows you that the walk will be a steep uphill climb?* Note the contour lines, and explain that when they are closer together the hill is steeper. Identify the route you took, and the steepest part of the hill. Ask, *Does the map tell you how high or tall the hill is?*

Look at maps of the UK and locate the mountains with the children. Note their height and how steep they are.

Next, look at a map of the world and find two or three mountains and make notes in the same way. Note the coloured key at the side of the map which shows the height of the land above sea level. Ask the children how this helps us work out which is the tallest mountain. Then tell the children that you want them to find answers to the following questions:
- Where in the world are the Himalayas?
- Which is the tallest mountain?
- Which is the steepest mountain?
- How do you know?

Organise the class into four groups and ask them to

plan research that will help them find the answer to each question. Structure the plan so that for each of the questions above the children use the following or similar process:

- What do we want to find out?
- Where can we look?
- Does the source give us the answer?
- How do we know?

After ten minutes, share the research plans and then allow the groups to carry out their research. They should feed back the answers in a plenary session.

FAIRGROUND RIDES

SUBJECT: DESIGN AND TECHNOLOGY. QCA UNIT: 6C FAIRGROUND.

LEARNING OBJECTIVE
To learn how control systems are used in everyday life.

THINKING OBJECTIVE
To ask questions to inform research.

THINKING SKILLS
The children will think about their favourite fairground rides. They will describe what happens on the ride and then consider how it moves at this speed and in this direction. They will develop a series of questions to structure their thinking, and apply this when thinking of a series of questions to help them design, plan and make their own fairground models.

WHAT YOU NEED
A video showing different fairground rides; pictures of different rides, preferably with the mechanisms showing; large sheets of paper; writing materials.

WHAT TO DO
Talk to the children about their favourite fairground rides. Ask, *Why is this ride your favourite? What happens on the ride? How does it start? Which is the best bit? Does it start and finish slowly or quickly?* Prompt the children to think about what makes the ride move at this speed, in this direction and in this way. Ask, *Do you ever look at the mechanisms as you enjoy the rides? How was the car attached to the track?*

Watch the video of the first ride, for example, a

rollercoaster which goes upside down, and, with the children, think about how it works. Ask, *I wonder what is making it move? I wonder how it manages to stay on the track? I wonder why it does not fall off when it goes upside down?* Invite the children to 'wonder' about the ride and together compile a list of questions to help them find out how it works. Repeat this with different types of ride, such as a big wheel, pirate ship, waltzers, roundabouts or dodgem cars.

Start with one of the lists of general questions and add more specific questions about the mechanisms, energy source, switches, computer programs and other devices which may be used to drive the ride. Model specific language and vocabulary for the children, and encourage them to use this in the group work later.

Organise the children into groups and, giving each group a picture of a different ride, ask them to wonder how it works and why it behaves in a certain way. Move around the groups, prompting the children to ask questions which will help them analyse the components, energy source, direction of movement, how power is transferred from one part to the next, how direction can be changed and so on.

During the plenary, focus on rides that have a rotating movement. Identify a series of questions to help the children focus on the mechanisms and the way they are joined, that will be of use when designing, planning and making their own models.

LOCATION EXERCISE

SUBJECT: ICT. QCA UNIT: 6D USING THE INTERNET TO SEARCH LARGE DATABASES AND TO INTERPRET INFORMATION.

LEARNING OBJECTIVES
To use complex searches to locate information; to work with others to interpret information.

THINKING OBJECTIVE
To plan research, predict outcomes, anticipate consequences and improve ideas.

THINKING SKILLS
The children will develop a range of thinking skills in this activity, but the main focus will be on improving their ideas and finding a way to find the information they want more quickly by setting up a more refined and complex search. They will think about how they will start their search by identifying the key words. They will anticipate what they think will happen when the computer searches for this word in terms of the number of websites it is likely to find. The children will then consider what they want to gain

from the search before identifying which website is the most suitable. They will then think about how they can refine and make their search more specific to find the information they want more quickly.

WHAT YOU NEED
Internet access.

WHAT TO DO
(Check that the websites you intend to use are suitable for children. Follow the school's policy for internet access. A good search engine for young people is www.yahooligans.com Check that the children type any addresses in correctly.)

Ask the children how they could find out about the work of a charity using the internet. Ask, *How could you start to look for the information you need?* Identify with the children what they need to know first. Ask, *If you wanted to find out about a specific activity of the NSPCC, what do you think would happen if you typed these letters into a search engine?* Try it and see. Repeat the exercise with Barnardo's and UNICEF to see what happens. Note with the children that these charities have their own websites and therefore a search of this type will often take you straight to these pages, or at least tell you that they exist.

Brainstorm the names of suitable charities that the children could research. Type one or two into a search engine and see what options are offered. Note how useful the names of the charities are as 'keywords', and how they quickly find general information about the organisations, for example telephone numbers, useful contacts and addresses. Talk about how easy or difficult it is to read the site to find out specific pieces of information. Ask, *Is there a quicker way?* Refine the search by asking the children to look for a particular piece of information about the organisation, for example the latest projects or fundraising activities. Note how to set up a search using more specific keywords, for example 'Barnado's + fundraising'. Try it and see.

Extend the activity to a different context, for example, ask the children to find out if the internet holds information about Lulworth Cove. Ask, *If the key words 'Lulworth Cove' are used for a search, how many matches does the computer find? Do these matches help you to find out more information about this place?* Search for other places and identify that often the computer finds several matches.
Refine the search further by setting a specific problem for the children to research, for example, *Is the name of the local pub in Lulworth Cove called The Bell?* Ask pairs or threes to think about how they could find out. Talk about their suggestions, for

example searching websites to find the names of local pubs. Then show how, when using a search engine, you can type in more specific key words by using '+', for example 'Lulworth Cove + The Bell'.

If the search does not give the children the information they need, they should evaluate the use of the keywords and formulate another plan to find out the name of the pub. Once they have found the information it could be collected, possibly using the 'copy' and 'paste' functions, and a piece of work produced to tell the rest of the class about the information. (Remember to remind them about copyright and the importance of acknowledging sources.)

BRIGHT COLOURS

SUBJECT: ART AND DESIGN. QCA UNIT: 5A OBJECTS AND MEANING.

LEARNING OBJECTIVE
To consider how colour is used to create visual effects.

THINKING OBJECTIVE
To predict outcomes.

THINKING SKILLS
The children will look at three paintings in which contrasting colours, tints or tones are evident. They will consider how their own still life sketch would look in each of these styles. Then they will complete their sketch in each of the different styles.

WHAT YOU NEED
Copies of a painting by Cézanne or Gaudi, that uses bright contrasting colours, one by Seurat or Monet, that uses tints of the same colour, and one by Whistler that uses tones of black and white; three small black and white outlines of children's still life composition; paints; brushes.

WHAT TO DO
Look at each of the paintings in turn, and discuss how the artist has used colour to create the effect. Note how each artist uses different colour compositions to depict their still life or landscapes. Concentrate on the colours used rather that the style. Ask the children to think about their own still life composition and to predict whether it will look best if painted in bright contrasting colours, in tints of the same colour, or in tones of a central colour mixed with black or white. If necessary, recreate the still life to help the lower attaining children with their predictions.

Link with ICT by scanning in the children's pictures and filling each object with colour to create different ways of painting the picture. Others can paint their still life compositions using contrasting colours, tints and tones for each one. Ask, *Were your predictions correct? Do you like the picture that you thought would be best?*

PICTURE THIS

SUBJECT: MUSIC. QCA UNIT: 21 WHO KNOWS?

LEARNING OBJECTIVE
To use instruments and voices to compose a piece of music in response to a picture.

THINKING OBJECTIVE
To improve ideas.

THINKING SKILLS
The children will use a picture as a stimulus for musical compositions, consider how they can compose sounds to depict what the picture is showing and how they can improve on their ideas.

WHAT YOU NEED
A print which shows particular moods and effects, such as *Steamer in a Snowstorm* by Turner, *Nocturne in Blue and Gold: Old Battersea Bridge* by Whistler, or one which depicts everyday life, such as *The Gleaners* by Millet or *The Hay Wain* by Constable.

WHAT TO DO
Look at, for example, *Steamer in a Snowstorm* by Turner and talk about the mood it depicts. Ask, *What can you see? What is the weather like? Why is it called a Steamer in a Snowstorm?* Talk about what the artist is trying to depict. Ask, *What sounds can you imagine hearing when you look at this picture? How could you make these sounds? How could you use your voice as an instrument?*

Organise the children into groups and invite them to compose sounds to depict the mood and effect shown by the painting. After five minutes, ask each group to perform their compositions and to talk about the sounds they have used and why.

When each group have finished performing, talk about how their ideas could be improved using the children's previous knowledge, for example, using open and closed sounds, tense and relaxed chords, legato and staccato notes, giving the piece a definite structure.

Allow the children another five minutes to improve, adapt and change their ideas.

THE CREATION STORY

SUBJECT: RE. QCA UNIT: 6C WHY ARE SACRED TEXTS IMPORTANT?

LEARNING OBJECTIVE
To learn that all religions include a story about how the world was made, and that these stories have similarities and differences.

THINKING OBJECTIVE
To ask questions.

THINKING SKILLS
The children will ask questions about the Creation and use these to inform research on the beliefs of people from different religions. They will use the information to note similarities and differences between a range of religions.

WHAT YOU NEED
A collection of Creation stories; large sheets of paper; writing materials.

WHAT TO DO
Depending on the major religion represented in your

class, choose a version of the story of the Creation to retell the children. Invite them to recall the major events and make a list of all the important facts. For example, whether the story included a higher being, a God, whether it outlines the order of Creation and who did what, whether it identifies the part that people played in the process, how important this story is to believers of this religion. Talk about the sacred book where a version of this story may be found – this is how we know what people of this religion believe.

Look at the list of facts and ask, How could this list help you to think of questions to ask to find out about the Creation story from different religions and belief systems? Write down the questions the children suggest on a large sheet of paper or the board. Invite the children to consider whether they have listed all the questions they want and need.

Identify all the major religions of the world, then organise the children into groups: higher attainers in one, and the rest mixed ability. Allocate one religion to each group to research, giving higher attaining children a more obscure belief system such as Aborigine Dreamtime. Ask each group to start by identifying the sacred book where they might find the information, and any other sources that might help with their research. They should them set about finding answers to their questions. As they research, ask them whether the research has thrown up more questions.

ROCK AND ROLL

SUBJECT: PE. QCA UNIT: DANCE ACTIVITIES LINK UNIT

LEARNING OBJECTIVE
To recognise elements of different dance styles.

THINKING OBJECTIVE
To plan research.

THINKING SKILLS
The children will consider as a class where and how they can find out about the style and dance steps of rock and roll dancing, and use the information to select music and plan their own sequence of steps to create a dance. They will consider why female dancers wore swirly skirts and how this enhanced the way the dance looked. They will then work in groups to plan research into a dance style of their own choice.

WHAT YOU NEED
Videos, CDs, pictures and other reference materials including music from the 1950s; large sheets of paper; writing materials.

WHAT TO DO
Explain to the class that you want them to plan research into different dance crazes from the past. As a class, you will plan research to find out rock and roll steps and suitable music, and then groups can plan research in the same way into a dance of their own choice.

On a large sheet of paper, record what the children already know about rock and roll. List all the facts, including when it became a craze, the type of music it was danced to, the fashions worn at that time and any steps with which the children are already familiar. Organise the information into sections. For each fact, note how this knowledge helps with the research plan. Ask, *Do any facts help us locate suitable reference materials?* Consider all means of evidence sources, for example record sleeves, CD compilations, photographs, video, reference materials, visitors and so on, and note whether you already have these in your resource collection. List the evidence sources that the children think will help to find out the most about a particular fact.

Next, consider what is still missing from the research, what it is the children still want to find out and list these queries as questions. For example, they may want to know more about the music, the different styles in different countries, whether it can be danced in groups, individually or in pairs.

Structure the research plan with the children. Look at what you did earlier and identify the process together. Note that you should always start by listing what you already know about the subject.
◉ Write this as a question to start to structure the plan: *What do we already know?*
◉ Next pose the 'So what?' question: *So what does this tell us in terms of what we do not know?*
◉ Use this to identify questions for research: *What do we still want to learn and find out?*
◉ Next consider how this can be done: *How can we find the answer to this query?*
◉ Identify and match additional sources of evidence that can be used to give possible answers to the questions posed. *Are there any questions that do not have an evidence source identified? What else should we consider?*

Watch a video of rock and roll dancing together, and afterwards invite the children to ask further questions to inform their research plan.

Use the structure of the plan for the children to find out about a dance craze of their choice, focusing on the music, steps, fashion, time and place. Examples include the Locomotion, Twist, Shake and Mashed Potato.

EXTENDING ENQUIRY SKILLS

Subject and QCA unit, NLS or NNS objectve	Activity title	Thinking objective	Activity	Page
English NLS objectives: To identify features of recounted texts such as sports reports; to develop a journalistic style through considering balanced and ethical reporting, what is in the public's interest in events, the interest of the reader, selection and presentation of material	Newsboard	To plan research	Putting together a class newspaper or magazine to include competition pages, comic strip and sports reviews	70
Mathematics NNS objectives: To make decisions; to solve problems based on real life using one or more steps; to find simple percentages of small whole-number quantities	DIY painting and decorating	To define a problem	Solving two-step problems involving area, and requiring multiplication and addition of decimals and three-digit numbers	71
Science QCA unit: 6G Changing circuits	Bulbs, buzzers and shadows	To anticipate consequences	Anticipating what will happen to a light when circuits are changed, and to a shadow when the direction and angle of light alters	72
History QCA unit: 12 How did life change in our locality in Victorian times?	Living in Victorian times	To ask questions	Identifying questions which arise from looking at buildings and other architectural features of Victorian times	73
Geography QCA unit: 16 What's in the news?	Should the Olympics come to London in 2012?	To define a problem, anticipate consequences and predict outcomes	Defining possible problems by anticipating consequences and predicting outcomes if the Olympics were to be held in London	75
Design and technology QCA unit: 5A Musical instruments	Making musical instruments	To define a problem, anticipate consequences and predict outcomes	Considering and defining the problems the children are likely to meet when trying to make different types of sounds on home-made instruments	76
ICT QCA unit: 5F Monitoring environmental conditions and changes	Seeing plants in a different light	To define a problem	Setting up light sensors to monitor the effect of light on plant growth	77
Art and design QCA unit: 5C Talking textiles	Art to feel	To define a problem and plan research	Making a picture from textiles which people with sight impairment can 'read'	78
Music QCA unit: 21 Who knows?	Mood music	To plan research	Planning research to find the stimulus used by different composers as starting points for their music	80
RE QCA unit: 6D What is the Qu'ran and why is it important to Muslims?	The Qu'ran	To ask questions to help identify areas for research	Setting up a group research project to find out the significant learning aspects of the Qu'ran	81
PE QCA unit: 3 Outdoor and adventurous activities	Lost worlds	To define a problem	Deciding how to approach a task to find the best route between two points on a map	82

NEWSBOARD

SUBJECT: ENGLISH. NLS OBJECTIVES: TO IDENTIFY FEATURES OF RECOUNTED TEXTS SUCH AS SPORTS REPORTS; TO DEVELOP A JOURNALISTIC STYLE THROUGH CONSIDERING BALANCED AND ETHICAL REPORTING, WHAT IS IN THE PUBLIC'S INTEREST IN EVENTS, THE INTEREST OF THE READER, SELECTION AND PRESENTATION OF MATERIAL.

LEARNING OBJECTIVE

To learn how to select and present information in the form of a newspaper report.

THINKING OBJECTIVE

To plan research.

THINKING SKILLS

The children will develop the information-processing skill of analysing to plan research for creating a class newspaper or magazine. They will plan the order in which the articles will be presented, and how to set up an editorial board to make decisions as a class. Groups will then plan research into how to approach the development of their own section, and think about how they will display this for inclusion in the newspaper or magazine.

WHAT YOU NEED

Copies of various local newspapers and/or magazines; paper; writing materials.

WHAT TO DO

Tell the children that you want them to plan and organise a class newspaper or magazine for other children to read in the library. Talk about how a real newspaper or magazine is put together. List the people involved in writing the articles, taking the photographs, other contributors and editorial staff. Ask the children to suggest how to tackle the development of the newspaper or magazine. Ask, *What do you need to do first? How will you organise yourselves? How will you identify who will do what? How will you display the articles, photographs and other contributions so that you can decide what to include in the newspaper or magazine?*

Set out the order of research, for example:
◉ Analyse what types of articles and contributions are found in local magazines and newspapers.
◉ Organise a newsboard to display and organise the sections in the magazine.
◉ Allocate each section to a group.
◉ Organise the groups to carry out certain jobs.
◉ Put together the section of the newspaper or magazine.
◉ Edit the contributions (taking into account the NLS objectives).
◉ Display on the newsboard for others to decide which to include.
◉ Decide on the order of the sections.

Ask each group to put together their section, following the research plan above. Suggested sections include: news articles, competition pages, comic strip, sports reviews. Challenge each group to plan research into how to put together their own particular section in terms of what to include, how and where. Ask, *Who will decide on the titles of the articles? How will these reflect what is included in the article or other contribution?*

DIFFERENTIATION

Organise the children into mixed ability groups so that lower attaining children can work alongside others; higher attaining children can be section editors. The section editors can then form an editorial board to edit and make suggestions for inclusion into the newspaper or magazine to put to the rest of the class. Challenge them to plan how they will go about this by researching into how real editors do the job.

WHERE NEXT

Allow the children time to put together the newspaper or magazine.

ASSESSMENT

Note how well the children plan the steps in their research into how newspapers and magazines are put together before planning one of their own.

LEARNING OUTCOMES

The children will plan how to put together a class newspaper or magazine by identifying the steps for research and following these.

FURTHER ENGLISH CHALLENGES

Sell the school

Encourage the class to plan research to create an advertisement for selling the school. Develop a plan by asking questions to structure the activity: *What do you need to know before you start to write the advertisement? What information do you need to* include? What information would you like to include? What devices do advertisers use to catch the eye of the readers? What price will you charge for the school? This will lead to exciting conversations about what it is worth. Extend the activity to selling the newspaper or magazine to parents.

DIY PAINTING AND DECORATING

SUBJECT: MATHEMATICS. NNS OBJECTIVES: TO MAKE DECISIONS; TO SOLVE PROBLEMS BASED ON REAL LIFE USING ONE OR MORE STEPS; TO FIND SIMPLE PERCENTAGES OF SMALL WHOLE-NUMBER QUANTITIES.

LEARNING OBJECTIVE

To learn the process for solving two-step problems.

THINKING OBJECTIVE

To define a problem.

THINKING SKILLS

The children will think about the problem they need to solve before identifying strategic steps which will help them work in a logical way to find the answer to their problem – they will define what the problem is and what they need to do in order to solve it.

WHAT YOU NEED

Empty paint tins showing capacity and amount of coverage; labels from rolls of wallpaper showing the distance between the repeating match and consequent number of drops per roll needed for an average-sized room; room measurements for an average-sized room; calculators; large sheet of paper; writing materials.

WHAT TO DO

Tell the children that you are going to decorate your house, and that you need to go shopping for the things you will need. Tell them that you have not yet made up your mind whether to paint the walls or hang wallpaper. However, start with painting, and ask them to think about how much paint you need to buy and how much it will cost.

First of all, explain to the children what the problem is and describe this together so that the class has a clear idea of what they need to find out. Write on a large sheet of paper 'What do we need to find out? – how much paint is needed and the cost to paint the room' to demarcate the first step in defining the problem.

Invite the children to say how they would tackle this problem, noting their ideas and giving each one a number. When you have finished collecting their suggestions, review each one in turn.

The question *What do we need to know?* forms the second stage in defining the problem. Highlight any previous suggestions which address this question and add any new ideas the children might have. Make sure you have included the following: the size of the room, the amount of paint in a tin, the cost of each tin of paint.

Identify the next stage in defining the problem: *Where can we find the information?* Talk about the labels on the tins, and the size of the walls that need to be painted (provide the dimensions of an average-sized room).

Now ask, *How much paint do we need?* Draw out that the children need to know the total area of each wall, and the total area of the room that needs to be painted. They also need to know how much area each tin of paint will cover.

Next the children will need to consider *What do we need to calculate and how?*. They will need to add together the area of each wall to find the total area of the room, and divide this by the area each tin of paint will cover.

Finally ask, *How can we find the total price for painting the room?*. The children should simply multiply the number of tins by the cost per tin. Organise the children into groups and ask them to calculate the cost for different rooms in the house. Encourage them to follow the structure you have identified but let them use their own way of calculating the costs. Check the children's answers at the end of the lesson to see how accurate they are, but also whether they have understood the structure of solving the problem.

DIFFERENTIATION

Provide less able children with the dimensions of a smaller room for them to calculate the area. Use metres to keep the numbers small and simple. For example, most rooms are 8 feet tall so use 2 metres as an average height. The length of the room can be 5 metres and the width 3 metres. This keeps the calculation simple. Therefore, if the area of each longer wall is 10 square metres (and there are two which makes 20 square metres), and the area of each shorter wall is 6 square metres (and there are two which makes 12 square metres), the total area is 20

+ 12 = 32 square metres. Calculate that each tin of paint covers 4, 8 or 16 square metres to give the children a simple division sum to solve. Adapt the number for the children in your group.

Higher attaining children should be encouraged to define their own problem to solve: *How much it would cost to wallpaper the room?*. They will need to calculate the number of drops per roll and the number of drops needed for each wall. Provide them with different-priced wallpapers and rolls with different numbers of repeating patterns to investigate.

WHERE NEXT

Include the idea of checking answers in the stages of defining the problem. Use a spreadsheet format to work out the total cost of using different-priced paint and wallpaper. Define the problem first, and finish by deciding which is the most cost-effective way of decorating the house.

ASSESSMENT

Note the children who understand how to define the problem by structuring and following logical steps to find the answer to the problem. They will be ready to work independently on simple problems until you are sure they can solve more complex problems requiring two or more steps of calculation.

LEARNING OUTCOMES

Most children will understand the importance of defining a problem before attempting to solve it, and be familiar with some of the steps they need to follow. Some will be able to do this independently and apply their learning to solve new problems with one and two steps.

FURTHER MATHS CHALLENGES

Matching curtains

Tell the children that you intend to use tartan or checked fabric to make curtains. Explain that the amount of each colour in the fabric will determine the colour you will choose for the wall. Tell them that you want to use a colour that makes up less than ten per cent of the fabric you want to use. Ask the children to define and solve the problem of finding out the area of each colour in the fabric and how much this is in percentage terms. The children will need to find their own strategies for solving this problem but one way is to take a small cross section of the fabric which contains the repeating pattern, because proportionally there will be the same percentage of colour used in the smaller cross section as in the whole piece of fabric.

Kitchen and bathroom tiles

Set up a problem involving the use of different-sized tiles (larger tiles and smaller ones which are third of larger size) to redecorate a bathroom or kitchen floor. Give them an actual sized floor to cover. Again, let the children think of their own strategies to solve the problem. However, before they start, they will need to define the problem to determine what they need to find out, what they need to know, how they will find this information and what they will do with it once they have it.

BULBS, BUZZERS AND SHADOWS

SUBJECT: SCIENCE. QCA UNIT: 6G CHANGING CIRCUITS.

LEARNING OBJECTIVE

To learn that the brightness of bulbs and speed of motors in a circuit can be changed.

THINKING OBJECTIVE

To anticipate consequences.

THINKING SKILLS

The children will anticipate what will happen in different circuits when certain components are changed. They will test out their predictions by making the circuits and noting what happens to bulbs, buzzers and motors.

WHAT YOU NEED

Equipment for making a wide range of circuits including wire, switches, bulbs and batteries of different power, buzzers and motors; paper; writing materials.

WHAT TO DO

Pass the bulbs around the class and ask the children to say what they notice about each one. Draw their attention to the wattage of each bulb and ask the children to say what they think this means. Next, pass different-sized batteries around and note the voltage on these. Ask, *What do you think the voltage refers to?*

Ask the children to anticipate what will happen if a strong battery is put into a circuit with a low wattage bulb. Check out the children's predictions and ask, *What have you learned?* (That if batteries are too strong the bulbs will burn out or blow.) This is an important piece of information as resources are expensive. Relate this to everyday situations when, if sockets are overloaded, or there is too much electrical charge, the fuse inside appliances or in the main circuit board blow. Talk to the children about safety at this point and why these safety devices, fuses, have been put into electrical appliances and wiring inside buildings.

Make circuits that use bulbs, motors and buzzers. Ask the children to anticipate consequences for the changes that they make to the circuit before testing out their predictions. Help to structure their thinking by asking, *What will happen if you put a stronger battery into this circuit? What will happen to the bulb, buzzer or motor? What if you replace the wire for a shorter or longer one? What will happen if you add a switch? What if the wire is thicker or thinner? What difference does it make if the wire is covered in plastic or bare?*
Invite the children to suggest other changes for the class to anticipate what might happen.

Record the predictions and results on a table, completing the first one together as you have already tested this out and no further wastage of resources will (hopefully!) occur.

DIFFERENTIATION

With lower attaining children follow the questions above using circuits with bulbs first – to find out what happens when two bulbs are put into a circuit, when the length of the wire changes and note what happens to the light produced. Use the outcomes of this investigation to help the children anticipate what will happen to a motor when the same changes to the circuit are made. Higher attaining children should be encouraged to consider how they can make the buzzer louder so that someone with a hearing impairment can still hear the sound. Relate this to everyday uses of circuits for doorbells and anticipate the consequences of making the sound too loud.

WHERE NEXT

Provide the children with circuit diagrams and ask them to anticipate how bright the bulb(s) might be in each one. Include diagrams with buzzers and motors to familiarise the children with these

symbols. Ask them to test their predictions by following the diagrams to make the circuits.

ASSESSMENT

Assess how well the children make links between cause and effect when anticipating consequences, for example that when the energy in a circuit is shared between two bulbs the light produced by each one will be dimmer.

LEARNING OUTCOMES

The children will learn to anticipate likely consequences when making changes to a circuit. They will test out what they think by making the changes and noting what happens. They will use the information to draw conclusions about what happens when different components are changed.

FURTHER SCIENCE CHALLENGES

Wiring a house
Challenge the children to construct a circuit with several bulbs to provide light to different parts of a room in a doll's house or other working model.

LIVING IN VICTORIAN TIMES

SUBJECT: HISTORY. QCA UNIT: 12 HOW DID LIFE CHANGE IN OUR LOCALITY IN VICTORIAN TIMES?

LEARNING OBJECTIVE

To learn how places changed during Victorian times.

THINKING OBJECTIVE

To ask questions.

THINKING SKILLS

The children will use a photograph of a large industrial building to ask questions to find out how the building of this brought developments and changes to the population, and the lifestyles, environment and way of life of ordinary people.

WHAT YOU NEED

Photographs of Victorian buildings and their location.

WHAT TO DO

Look at a picture of a large industrial Victorian building, ideally located next to a river, canal or railway transport system. Ask the children questions about the building: *How do you know this building was built in Victorian times?*

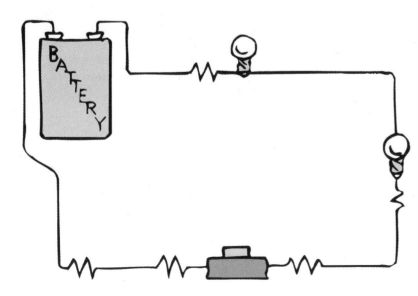

What architectural features does it have? How do you know these are Victorian in style? What design features do they have which provide a clue? What is the building used for? Does this give a clue to its age? Where is it built? Why is it built near the river/canal/railway line? What does this tell us about the transport systems in Victorian times? Why are there fewer roads? What changes would this building have made to the local area? Would there be more people living nearby to work in the (mill)? Where would they live?

Talk to the children about the history of the Industrial Revolution, and how mills and mines were built to develop these industries. Note the consequential effect of growth in population in these areas, and how many new houses were built to accommodate the workers. Note how the owners of these mills and mines became wealthy and built grand houses. These were often ornate and very flamboyant in style to show off the owners' wealth. Look at a large Victorian house and talk about what the children notice. Invite the children to consider the kind of person who might have lived in the house at the time it was built. Prompt them to think about the style, materials and design, the features that are obviously Victorian and how we know.

Note with the children the changes that these buildings brought to the area in terms of employment, environment and additional housing.

DIFFERENTIATION

Ask those who are able to consider how these old buildings have been adapted for use today, for example adapted to house a museum or art gallery, or developed into apartments. Ask the children to identify questions that would help them to find out if these developments brought an increase in the number of residents or visitors to the building, and the range of services required to meet the demand. Work with lower attaining children to identify the features and uses of the buildings. Help them to convert their sentences into a question format. Choose one question and investigate the impact of the building's development on residents and other people living locally.

WHERE NEXT

If you live in an area which was developed as a result of a new mill or mine, look at the affects this had on the locality at the time, and find out what has happened to the buildings since. Use this information as the basis on which to form questions to plan research into the changes that took place.

ASSESSMENT

Note the detail in the children's questions and how

well it directs and structures their research. Note whether the questions are linked to finding out about the way people used to live and how the construction of Victorian buildings changed the lives of local people.

LEARNING OUTCOMES

The children will consider the changes that took place in different localities by asking questions about the purpose, design and effects the development of different buildings had on the local population and people.

FURTHER HISTORY CHALLENGES
Chimney pots and rooftops

Look at photographs, pictures or actual Victorian rooftops and chimney pots, and talk about what we can learn from them. Ask, *What do they look*

like and how are they constructed? Note the design features such as height, shape and pattern on the brickwork. Ask questions about why they were designed and made in this way, and relate this to the way Victorian houses were decorated and heated. This will link back to the main activity of considering Victorian designs and how the houses, and chimneys in particular, were kept clean. This will hopefully lead the children into asking questions about domestic activities and the upstairs–downstairs lifestyles during Victorian times.

Victorian gardens

Look at pictures of Victorian gardens and talk about

the impact these had on the local population in terms of employment and new varieties of plants. Encourage the children to ask questions to structure research into the most famous garden designers of the time, and why people felt that they needed to have designers. Talk about the prestige this had for people with money.

SHOULD THE OLYMPICS COME TO LONDON IN 2012?

SUBJECT: GEOGRAPHY. QCA UNIT: 16 WHAT'S IN THE NEWS?

LEARNING OBJECTIVE
To learn about recent or proposed changes in localities.

THINKING OBJECTIVE
To define a problem, anticipate consequences and predict outcomes.

THINKING SKILLS
The children will consider the changes that hosting the Olympics brought to other venues and consider the necessary changes made to overcome potential difficulties arising from an upsurge of people to one area. They will use this discussion to identify potential difficulties and problems of holding the event in London, anticipate the consequences to the local infrastructure and predict the outcomes of certain developments, both positive and negative.

WHAT YOU NEED
A video of the opening ceremony of the Sydney (or most recent) Olympics; maps of the area where most of the events took place; maps of London and surrounding area including airports, railway stations and roads.

WHAT TO DO
Watch the opening ceremony of the most recent Olympic Games, at the time of writing this was Sydney 2000, and identify the location of the stadium on a map. Ask the children, *Why do you think the stadium was built in that location?* Note the size of the stadium, the number of people watching the event and the number taking part. Think about how all these people travelled to the event, and where they might be staying. Consider the impact that this number of people will have on the surrounding area when they all leave at the end of the ceremony. Ask the children, *How will they get to their accommodation or home?* Think about some of the building developments required to enable the city to accommodate the Games: a stadium, transport systems, accommodation for the athletes.

Identify what is likely to happen if the Olympics are held in London. Brainstorm questions about the likely difficulties and impact on the country and the city of London, the consequences and outcomes. Useful questions include: *What facilities will need to be provided? Where will these be placed? What will this mean in terms of moving people from one place to another? What impact will this have on the transport systems and roads in and around London? Where will car drivers park? Will they be allowed to park close to the event or will they park and ride? Who will pay for the improvements and developments? Where will the different events be held? How will the competitors get there? Where will the competitors stay?* And so on and so on. For each question make three lists: the difficulties that are likely to occur; the consequences of these things; and the predicted outcomes for the city of London, both positive and negative, for example improved transport systems, more and better housing and an increase in employment and business. Share all the children's ideas and decide whether it is a good or bad idea to host the games in London.

DIFFERENTIATION
Work with higher attaining children to consider the impact of hosting the Games on employment and local businesses. Invite them to anticipate the consequences of working at the venue in terms of getting to work on time and what might happen after the day's events have finished. Invite them to think of an alternative use for the accommodation when the competitors have left. Think about the transport systems with the lower attaining children, and encourage them to consider the long-term benefits of holding the event on the local population.

WHERE NEXT
Prepare a presentation to propose or oppose London holding the event. (This links to an ICT multimedia presentation.) Include the likely difficulties, the anticipated consequences of the issues which these raise, and the predicted solutions to overcome these problems.

ASSESSMENT
Assess how well the children anticipate the possible consequences of the difficulties they have raised.

Note also the children's ideas for overcoming these difficulties.

LEARNING OUTCOMES
The children will consider the impact of holding a large event on a local population and place by defining likely problems, anticipating consequences and predicting outcomes.

FURTHER GEOGRAPHY CHALLENGES
Manchester, Cardiff, Belfast or Glasgow
Invite the children to find an alternative venue in Great Britain to host the event where it will have the least impact and create the least amount of upheaval to prepare for the event. This could be your own location. Ask the children to put forward their reasons in terms of reduced consequences and negative outcomes and increased positive outcomes.
New York, Paris or Rome
Consider the other venues bidding to host the Olympics in 2012 and define the problems each area is likely to have. Anticipate the consequences to the local area, people, transport systems and local businesses.

MAKING MUSICAL INSTRUMENTS

SUBJECT: DESIGN AND TECHNOLOGY. QCA UNIT: 5A MUSICAL INSTRUMENTS.

LEARNING OBJECTIVE
To develop a clear idea of the process of making musical instruments, and to plan how to use and join materials.

THINKING OBJECTIVE
To define a problem, anticipate consequences and predict outcomes.

THINKING SKILLS
During the planning stage of this task (to design and make a musical instrument), the children will define possible problems, consider the consequences of using particular materials and attaching them in particular ways, and predict the sound quality their instrument will produce. The children will have analysed a range of musical instruments to learn how they function, and investigated a range of materials for their soundmaking qualities in an earlier lesson.

WHAT YOU NEED
CD-ROMs and reference books; the school's collection of percussion instruments; sheets of paper; writing materials; a variety of materials from which to make instruments.

WHAT TO DO
Ask the children to suggest a musical instrument that they would like to make. Note with them whether they will play these by tapping, shaking, plucking or scraping. (Encourage children who suggested woodwind instruments to choose another type of instrument to make.) Ideas include wood blocks, wind chimes, drums, guitars, shakers and rain sticks. Use CD-ROMs, reference books and the school's collection of percussion instruments to spark the children's ideas.

Model the process. Choose one of the instruments and discuss the difficulties the children are likely to encounter, the consequences of forgetting a component or using the wrong type of materials, not attaching these correctly and predicting the outcomes for these consequences. For example, for the guitar, identify the components that should be included. Define what needs to be done to make the guitar sound appropriately. Ask, *How should it be constructed? What will you need?* Identify the resources and materials and the way they will be joined and combined. Note the difficulties the children are likely to encounter in the process. Model how to record this information pictorially on one side or at the top of a sheet of paper, adding labels of the components and materials required and the way they will be joined to give added strength. Explain to the children that this form of recording will speed up the process and provide a display board from which to work. The design needs to be clear but not exact.

Next, list all the possible consequences of forgetting to include a vital part of the instrument such as the sound box (the vibrating sound will not be contained), a way of making the strings tighter (the strummed strings will not make different sounds), not using materials that are strong enough, or not joining them together firmly enough to strum and pluck (the instrument will break). Accept all the children's anticipated consequences and list these beneath or alongside your labelled drawing.

Finally, for each consequence identified, predict the outcomes, for example the quality of the sound produced will be poor, any sound made will be the same from each string and therefore boring, the instrument will fall apart and be unplayable.

DIFFERENTIATION

Make the instruments first with less able children and define the problems they are having as they work. Use these difficulties to encourage them to anticipate the consequences of not putting their difficulties right, and to predict the outcomes in terms of the sound quality the instrument will produce. Encourage higher attaining children to suggest possible problems they might have when making a pitched musical instrument, for example putting holes into a wind chime to alter the pitch but finding a way to cover them and still allow the chime to vibrate. If they cover the holes, the material will stop vibrating and therefore the sound will stop. The instrument can only be played by blowing. (This work links to the activity 'Sounding off' in this chapter.) Therefore, to alter the pitch of a wind chime, the size of the tube

will need to be changed in some way. One way of doing this would be perhaps to add a sliding mechanism.

WHERE NEXT

Allow the children time to make the instruments, encouraging them to evaluate as they work. They should refer back to their design plan to prevent the defined problems from occurring and anticipate the consequences of certain actions before getting to the stage of having to undo or rethink the making process.

ASSESSMENT

Assess how well the children put together a design plan which includes a definition of possible problems, and whether they use their plan to prevent difficulties from arising when making their instruments. Note the children who anticipate the difficulties before they start to make their instruments and so are able to predict the outcomes of choosing particular materials and making the instrument in a certain way.

LEARNING OUTCOMES

The children will learn to define the problems they are likely to encounter when making a musical instrument. They will anticipate the consequences of doing or not doing certain things in certain ways and predict the outcomes of these before they start the making process.

FURTHER DESIGN AND TECHNOLOGY CHALLENGES

Hard and soft beaters

Develop a design plan for making hard and soft beaters. Encourage the children to define the problems they are likely to have, such as which materials to use, joining and combining these to make a hard or soft end, how to attach the materials to the end of the stick etc. For each difficulty, they should anticipate the consequences of using the incorrect material, and not joining them together securely enough, and predict the outcome of these.

SEEING PLANTS IN A DIFFERENT LIGHT

SUBJECT: ICT. QCA UNIT: 5F MONITORING ENVIRONMENTAL CONDITIONS AND CHANGES.

LEARNING OBJECTIVE

To identify opportunities and design simple investigations for which the collection of data through a computer device is both feasible and advantageous.

THINKING OBJECTIVE

To define a problem.

THINKING SKILLS

The children will consider what they are trying to find out and why, how they can go about this task, what they need to use and how they will know whether they have found out what they wanted. They will use this structure to think about the problem in more detail and define the stages of their investigation.

They will then consider how ICT can help them overcome some of these problems and identify how useful it is as a tool to measure outcomes in a structured way.

WHAT YOU NEED
Light sensors attached to a suitable computer program; plants; paper; writing materials.

WHAT TO DO
Whilst growing plants, and finding out what they need for growth and what effect different light has on plants, pose the problem of not knowing just how much light the plants are exposed to. Ask the children, *How can we find out an answer to this question?* Identify the problem with the children then break it down further into steps that can be investigated through the following questions: *What are we trying to find out? Why do we need to do this? How can we go about the task? What questions need answering and how are we going to answer them?* Collect the children's ideas about how this research could be accomplished.

Ask, *What equipment will we need to use?* Show the class how the ICT monitoring equipment works at this point and how it measures the amount of light in any particular area. Ask the children to say how this will help them in their investigation. Identify possible areas to carry out the investigation and discuss potential problems, for example the need for access to power to set up the computers, the difficulty of measuring plant growth at the same time in different areas.

Ask the children, *How can we make sure the results are reliable? What problems will we have in making the test fair? Will we need to carry out the test simultaneously so that the growth is measured at the same time, in the same way but in different places? How and what are we going to measure to draw conclusions? How will we know whether we have found an answer to the problem?*

Note how these questions link closely to the process of investigation, and that by carrying out an investigation in a structured way it helps the children break down the query into smaller steps.

When you have posed all of these questions, organise the children into groups to plan the investigation. Visit each group to discuss any problems they might have both with the science and with the ICT elements.

DIFFERENTIATION
Plan the investigation with lower attaining children to link the process to the definition of the problem. Challenge higher attaining children to plan an investigation to find out whether natural or artificial light is best for plant growth. This will add an additional variable to the problem posed.

WHERE NEXT
Allow the groups to set up and carry out the investigation. It will probably be necessary to monitor the light in each growing area for at least a week before drawing conclusions about which is the best place to grow plants. Ask the children to predict the outcome of the research. Analyse the results and display the children's findings.

Use a digital microscope to video the plant and play this back at speed as another way to evaluate the rate of growth.

ASSESSMENT
Monitor the children as they work in groups and note those who question each other in an attempt to break the problem down into small steps to support the detail in their plan. This will help the children consider the fairness of their test and therefore the reliability.

LEARNING OUTCOMES
The children will consider the problem of a scientific investigation and break this down into smaller steps. They will use ICT to support the measuring part of their investigation and identify potential problems with this.

FURTHER ICT CHALLENGES
Useful or useless
Give the children a problem and invite them to say how useful sensors would be to measure the outcomes to help with analysis of the effects of temperature, sound and light on plant growth.
Thermal insulators
Whilst investigating materials as thermal insulators can the children come up with a solution for measuring the change in temperature? They will need to identify and define the problem before planning a fair test to find the best thermal insulator. They can then use the information to set up a growing area that has added protection from the frost and cold.

ART TO FEEL

SUBJECT: ART AND DESIGN. QCA UNIT: 5C TALKING TEXTILES.

LEARNING OBJECTIVE
To collect visual and other information to help them develop their ideas.

THINKING OBJECTIVE
To define a problem and plan research.

THINKING SKILLS
The children will consider how to compose a picture which tells a story mostly through touch for those people who have no or little sight. They will define the problem of why and how to compose such a picture and consider the issues raised to plan research. They will finally consider how they can enhance the picture through using the other four senses of hearing, smell and taste.

WHAT YOU NEED
A range of landscapes and portraits; a range of materials for enhancing sensory pictures; large sheets of paper.

WHAT TO DO
Look at a painting and discuss the visual elements that have been used to catch the eye of the observer. Tell the children that artists often use artistic elements to draw the eye of the observer to the main focus of the picture. Look at several landscapes and family portraits and note with the children the focal point in each one. Ask, *How do you know this is the focal point? Is it the combination of colour, a contrasting colour, use of line or perspective or some other device? Do you all agree or do some of you think differently? Why?*

Discuss how it is difficult for people who have no or little sight to appreciate this kind of visual art. Explain that you want the children to make pictures for people who have no or little sight, first defining the problem and then planning their research.

Spend a few minutes sharing the children's thoughts and opinions about the problems they are likely to encounter and what they need to find out before they can begin to create such a picture. Start them off with the first two or three points to define the problem, for example some or all of the following: Can people who can see a little see any colour? Would they be able to see the lines on the picture? Would the objects drawn be difficult or impossible to pick out?

Challenge the children to think about the consequences of this definition, asking, *How can we make the picture easier to 'see'? What can we use instead of sight? What other senses can we use instead? What techniques can we use to create a picture which uses other senses to 'see' with?* Build on this to plan research, asking, *Where and how can we find out how people with little or no sight see? What other senses do they use instead? How can we find out if colour is important still? Are there any colours that stand out more than others? Does it matter how big the finished painting is? Can the picture be composed on paper or is a different material better for the background?* Share the children's ideas, thoughts and opinions.

Consider how perspective can still be used as a device to draw the observer's attention to the focal point of the picture, by altering the size or putting it in a central position.

DIFFERENTIATION
Consider colour blindness with higher attaining children. Ask them to define the problem and plan research to find out how they can compose an interesting picture for this group of people. Challenge lower attaining children to think about defining the problem and planning research into a landscape picture using natural materials in its composition.

WHERE NEXT
Allow the children to carry out the research and plan and make a picture for people who have little or no sight. Encourage them to collect visual and other information to help develop their ideas.

ASSESSMENT
Note how many factors the children include in their research plan when defining the problem. Note how they plan to go about finding out how people with little or no sight 'see' through their other senses and how they can incorporate this into their design plan.

LEARNING OUTCOMES
The children will define a particular problem and plan research to find out the kind of art which will stimulate and interest people with little or no sight. This will give their designs real purpose.

FURTHER ART AND DESIGN CHALLENGES
Texture board
Define the problem and plan research for finding different textures to include on a texture board.

Challenge the children to think about the problem of finding man-made textures which are as realistic as possible, and to plan research to find different textures to represent everyday objects, for example plastic grass and synthetic hair.

Adding senses

Define the problems and plan research into how the children can incorporate other senses into the picture.

MOOD MUSIC

SUBJECT: MUSIC. QCA UNIT: 21 WHO KNOWS?

LEARNING OBJECTIVE

To learn how music is composed from a range of different stimuli.

THINKING OBJECTIVE

To plan research.

THINKING SKILLS

The children will consider how they can find out which stimulus different composers used as starting points for their compositions. They will then consider how the composer used different styles and musical ideas to compose music which depicts the characters, moods and feelings of the intended effect.

WHAT YOU NEED

Videos of musicals; pieces of music depicting natural sounds; film scores and/or advertisements; CD player or similar for each group to listen to their chosen piece of music; internet access.

WHAT TO DO

Listen to an extract from your chosen musical, for example, *Joseph and his Amazing Technicolor Dreamcoat* where the brothers are introduced, 'Coat of Many Colours' or 'Any Dream Will Do'. Discuss the stimulus for the musical, in this case a story from the Bible. Muse with the children about why Andrew Lloyd Webber chose this stimulus. Ask, *How can we find out? How can we plan research to find out why he chose this and other stories for his musicals? Which other stimuli did he use? How can we find out how he decided on the style for the different songs in the musicals? Where can we look and whom can we ask?*

List the research sources and the ways the children can find answers to the queries they have raised. Note the stages in the plan: *What are you trying to find out and why? What questions do you need to identify? What do you need to know about the composition before you can start to plan research?* (For example, the time in which it was set, or the reason why it was composed.) *Where can you look? Who can you ask? How will you decide whether the information is useful?*

Explain to the children that different composers use different stimulus for their compositions. Listen to some of your extracts and ask the children to say what they think the stimulus was for each composition. For example, listen to 'The Typewriter' and 'Syncopated Clock' by Leroy Anderson, 'The Flight of the Bumble Bee' by Rimskij-Korsakov and extracts from Modest Mussorgsky's 'Pictures at an Exhibition'. Look at the structure of the research plan you noted for the musicals and agree whether this is useful to plan research for the other pieces of music.

Organise the children into groups, giving them each a different musical or piece of music to plan research to find out what the stimulus was for the composition. Invite them to identify specific questions related to the particular piece of music, and how and where they can find the answers. Share the ways that the children have identified for carrying out the research such as interviewing the composer online, writing to ask the composer, looking on CD and record covers, looking in reference books or websites.

DIFFERENTIATION

Provide lower attaining children with copies of CDs of musicals on which to plan their research. Ask them to identify questions they want to ask about one of the musicals and to identify where and how they can find the answers to these. Ask them to say whether the same set of questions are useful to plan research for the other musicals. Higher attaining children should be asked to extend their research plan to find out why the composer wrote in a particular style or structure, for example why Andrew Lloyd Webber write his compositions as musicals, Tchaikovsky as ballets, Mussorgsky as orchestral pieces and so on. Plan research to find out why certain styles have been used by the different composers, for example the reason for the composition, the background and purpose.

WHERE NEXT

Allow the children to carry out the research and to list all the different stimuli, styles and backgrounds for the musical pieces in your class collection.

ASSESSMENT

Assess how well the children structure their research plan on what they want to find out and therefore what they need to know. Note the range of sources the children identify for finding out the answers to their questions.

LEARNING OUTCOMES

The children will identify a structure to their research and learn that in order to research something they first need to identify what it is they need to find out, what they already know and how they can go about finding the answers to their queries.

FURTHER MUSIC CHALLENGES

Film scores

Plan research to find out what stimulus composers of film scores used to write their music in a particular style. Use extracts from *Grease*, *Star Wars* and *Lord of the Rings*. Encourage the children to ask questions to help them research the reasons for the styles and structures of the music used. For example, they might want to look into the characters, plot and setting of the story.

Country music

Ask the children to form a research plan to find musical pieces which use nature as a stimulus. Together, identify natural features which could be used as musical stimulus (for example, the sea, fire), and consider how you could locate these on an internet search on music websites.

THE QU'RAN

SUBJECT: RE. QCA UNIT: 6D WHAT IS THE QU'RAN AND WHY IS IT IMPORTANT TO MUSLIMS?

LEARNING OBJECTIVE

To identify the significance of the Qu'ran to Muslims today.

THINKING OBJECTIVE

To ask questions to help identify areas for research.

THINKING SKILLS

The children will identify what they already know about the significance of the Qu'ran to Muslims before planning research to find out if what they know is, in fact, correct. They will then identify what further information they would like to know about the importance of the Qu'ran to Muslims. They will identify possible ways to find out and plan a way to present this information to parents and other children in the school.

WHAT YOU NEED

Reference materials about the Muslim religion; large and small sheets of paper; writing materials.

WHAT TO DO

As a class group, collect all the things that the children have learned about the Muslim religion and list these on a large sheet of paper or on the board. If there is a parent or classroom assistant who is a competent typist, ask him or her to type the children's responses into a laptop and project this onto a white screen for the children to see and refer to during the activity.

Take one of the children's responses and ask them to say how they could check whether they are right. Ask, for example, *How do you know that Muslims always wash their hands before handling the Qu'ran? Where did you find this piece of information?* Look down the list for other related pieces of information about the way the Qu'ran is treated, and how it is used to teach believers about the way they should behave and lead their lives. Ask, *Can you identify any other pieces of information you would like to know about the Qu'ran, the way it is treated and why? What questions can you ask to lead your research? Where can you find the answers?*

List the questions on another sheet of paper and identify possible sources of evidence where answers to this question may be found.

Repeat this process for one more fact about the Muslim religion. For example, talk about the five pillars of Islam or the meaning of Bismillah.

Extend the questioning and ask why these things are important and significant to Muslims rather than focusing on the what and how.

Organise the children into groups and ask them to select an item from the list (make sure it is a significant area). Ask them to identify how and where they can check their knowledge and understanding and then to raise questions to help them find out why, as well as what and how, these things are significant to Muslims.

Share what the children think at the end of the lesson.

DIFFERENTIATION

With less able children, focus on checking their understanding and help them to plan questions they wish to ask Muslim visitors to find additional information. Higher attaining children should be asked to plan research into how Muslims use the Qu'ran to ensure that their religious and cultural traditions are preserved and passed on to future generations.

WHERE NEXT

Allow the children to carry out the research plan, and to organise and plan the presentation of the information to parents and/or other children in the school. Then encourage them to carry out a similar activity to check understanding and plan research into a different religion.

ASSESSMENT

Use this activity as an assessment opportunity to find out what the children already know about Muslims and any misconceptions they may have. Note how well they ask questions to help them check this understanding for themselves and whether they use these to plan research into any gaps in knowledge and understanding.

LEARNING OUTCOMES

The children will learn how to use questions to help them check their own learning and to inform further areas for research. They will work together in groups to plan a way to present what they have found out to a range of audiences.

FURTHER RE CHALLENGES

Who and what is God?

Ask the children to work in groups to brainstorm their own ideas about God. Ask them to use this information to raise questions to ask people of different religions about their beliefs about God. Be sensitive to the religions represented in your class for this challenge.

What is prayer?

Ask the children to brainstorm what they know about prayer and worship. Ask them to work in groups to identify questions and plan research into a different religion, to check whether their understanding is correct, and to find out more about the purpose and meaning of prayers to believers and worshippers of different religions. Share the list of questions and possible sources of evidence and note similarities and differences of approach. Carry out the research plan and list all the learning, knowledge and understanding gained about the way different religions use prayer in their worship.

LOST WORLDS

SUBJECT: PE. QCA UNIT: 3 OUTDOOR AND ADVENTUROUS ACTIVITIES.

LEARNING OBJECTIVE

To see the importance of a group plan and the value of pooling ideas.

THINKING OBJECTIVE

To define a problem.

THINKING SKILLS

The children will think about what they need to do to get from one place to another. They will consider their current position and their destination before defining how they can find the route from the directions given on a map.

WHAT YOU NEED

A map of the local park or woodland with several items marked with fictional names, for example, the park gate could be 'Time barrier', one tree 'The haunt of the pterodactyls', another 'The home of the goblin king' and climbing frame 'Mystery house'; in the wood give different plants and items on trees imaginary names so that the children have to use their map reading skills to locate them. Include some tracks marked on the ground, either actual or imaginary, for the children to follow, and, if you are fortunate enough to have one, give streams names, too, which link to other things found round about such as 'Willow tree brook'.

WHAT TO DO

Visit the local park or woodland and look at the maps together. Ask the children to predict what they think they will find when they go into the park or the wood. Explain that you want them to imagine that they are entering another world and that the things they usually find are given another name.

Tell the children that you want them to locate the quickest route between two points on the map, but that they must stick to the paths.

Ask them to find the first item on the map, making sure that they cannot see this from where they are standing. Ask, *How can you find a way to this place? Which way up should the map be? How can you find out?* In this way you will be helping the children to define the problem of where they are and where they need to be in relation to the map. Encourage them to look around for a clue. Locate a tree or other item behind you that is on the map. Orientate the map so that this item is at the bottom of the map when you stand with your back to it. Ask the children, *Why should the map be this way up?* Next, find the place you are trying to find. Ask, *Where is it on the map?* Identify in which direction you need to walk by following the route on the map with your finger, pointing off the map to show the correct direction. Locate another place on the map for the children to find. Define the problem of where you are standing, which way up the map should be and therefore in which direction should you walk. Orientate the map the right way by finding a feature close by which is on the map, noting its position in relation to you and turning the map so that the feature is on the correct side, to the front or back. Identify in which direction you need to walk by following the route on the map with your finger, pointing off the map to show the correct direction.

Repeat for the other items on your map.

DIFFERENTIATION

Let higher attaining children work together in groups to find the places on the maps themselves. (The adult supervising them should let them think through the problems for themselves.) Work alongside lower attaining children, repeating the definition of the problem again if necessary until they understand what they need to do to find the place on the map.

WHERE NEXT

Ask the children to put together a map of the school grounds for younger children to use.

When on a residential visit, organise a similar activity in a safe but unfamiliar area for the children to repeat the activity.

ASSESSMENT

Note how well the children define the problems, and whether they work out the correct orientation of the map before setting off to find the place.

LEARNING OUTCOMES

The children will learn to define problems then to start to plan what to do when approaching problems for the first time. This will lead them away from solving things by trial and error and will take their learning forward.

FURTHER PE CHALLENGES

Blindfold alley
Create a track around the school grounds, placing a number of articles around it which are not too dangerous for the children to negotiate when blindfolded. For example, large and small car tyres, ropes at low levels tied between three trees in a crisscross pattern, a spider's web made from ropes tied across two trees, a plastic tunnel and high jump bar to go underneath. Organise the children into pairs, one to direct the blindfolded partner around the course. When the children have had one turn each, gather them together and define the problem. Ask, *What obstacles could cause problems? How can you get over these? What do you need to remember to do? What must you do first? What must you include in your verbal directions to enable your partner to negotiate the course? How could you help your partner feel safe?* Let the children have another turn each and ask them if, by defining the problems clearly, they could help their partner round the course quicker and more safely?

CREATIVE THINKING SKILLS

INTRODUCTION

Creative thinking is not just about creating poems, pieces of art, music, dance and gymnastic sequences, although these do provide good opportunities for children to think creatively. It is also about identifying possible solutions to problems or to get over difficulties when, for example, trying to depict a special moment in their lives. By thinking creatively children can learn to identify why an author has chosen the theme that they have or used a particular style of writing in their work. This will allow the children to consider these things when creating their own projects, thus making their learning richer and more meaningful.

Children should be given lots of opportunities to develop their own learning. Often we give them one strategy for solving a particular problem. Several activities in this book ask the children to give reasons for their ideas and strategies. The second part of this chapter focuses on the children deciding for themselves why certain things have been organised as they have, and on finding possible alternatives to solve a problem. Questions are used in the activities in this chapter to enable you to guide their thinking throughout and to get them to think imaginatively and laterally, the roots of creative thinking. A key to asking questions when trying to develop creative thinking is to give the children time to answer. For example, do not expect an answer within less than ten seconds.

The activities outlined here, while written within specific contexts, are organised so that the children can work together in groups. This allows them to collaborate and bounce ideas off each other, sparking further creativity. A key skill outlined in the National Curriculum involves the children working with others to meet a challenge. Part of the development of this key skill involves the children to learning to appreciate the experience of others, to consider different perspectives and benefit from what others think. The topic contexts of the activities in this chapter can be adapted for all subjects.

The way you organise children's learning is crucial to give the children the opportunity to think about how they will organise their own learning. Group work gives them suitable opportunities to consider and negotiate which ideas will be accepted and developed. Thought sharing or brainstorming is one way to get the children to volunteer ideas in an uninhibited way. If all ideas are accepted, everyone is encouraged to contribute. The ideas may be discarded at a later stage but the process means that good reasons have to be given for this. The creative thinking skills are:
- creating ideas
- imaginative thinking
- finding alternative innovative outcomes/lateral thinking
- hypothesising
- extending ideas.

INTRODUCING CREATIVE THINKING SKILLS

Subject and QCA unit, NLS NNS objective	Activity title	Thinking objective	Activity	Page
English NLS objectives: To use a range of dictionaries and understand their purposes; to use dictionaries efficiently to explore spellings, meanings and derivations	Crosswords	To think imaginatively	Devising a crossword puzzle to include words from recent topics	86
Maths NNS objectives: To understand area measured in square centimetres (cm^2); to use, read and write standard metric units including their abbreviations, and relationships between them	Floor tiles	To think laterally	Covering floor area with tiles of different colours and shapes	86
Science QCA unit: To learn that different variables will affect the speed with which a sweet (or other solid) dissolves	Sweet success	To hypothesise	Indentifying the variable acting on the speed with which a sweet will dissolve	87
History QCA unit: 19 What were the effects of Tudor exploration?	Feeling invaded	To think laterally	Writing an account from a different point of view	88
Geography QCA units: 13 A contrasting UK locality; 14 Investigating rivers; 15 The mountain environment	Imagine a place where ...	To think imaginatively	Thinking about a particular place by imagining they have been transported into a photograph, and considering the geographical features, the climate and time of year	89
Design and technology QCA unit: 6B Slippers	Belts and bands	To extend ideas	Designing textile belts and bands for clothing, bracelets and headdresses	90
ICT QCA unit: 5D Introduction to spreadsheets	Fairground rides	To hypothesise	Calculating how much to charge per ride and how many people need to ride each time to recuperate the cost of building a fairground ride	90
Art and design QCA unit: 5A Objects and meaning	Extending Picasso	To extend ideas	Considering a different way to portray still-life arrangements	91
Music QCA unit: 16 Cyclic patterns	Indian chants	To generate ideas	Composing chants and accompaniments for a North American dance sequence using ostinato and syncopated rhythms	91
RE QCA unit: 6C Why are sacred texts important?	What does believing mean?	To extend ideas	Defining what it means to be a believer	92
PE QCA unit: Dance activities unit 6	Australian history	To generate ideas	Creating a dance to show how Australia developed over the centuries into today's modern country	93

CROSSWORDS

SUBJECT: ENGLISH. NLS OBJECTIVES: TO USE A RANGE OF DICTIONARIES AND UNDERSTAND THEIR PURPOSES; TO USE DICTIONARIES EFFICIENTLY TO EXPLORE SPELLINGS, MEANINGS AND DERIVATIONS.

LEARNING OBJECTIVE

To learn that dictionaries are useful to check spellings and help with definitions.

THINKING OBJECTIVE

To think imaginatively.

THINKING SKILLS

The children will brainstorm words they have learned during a new topic, and think imaginatively to create a crossword puzzle to help others consolidate their understanding of this new vocabulary. They will use dictionaries to check spellings and to help them think of imaginative clues for the crosswords. The children will also use their information-processing skills to analyse the way different crosswords are structured, and their enquiry skills by identifying the order for the activity.

WHAT YOU NEED

Sheets of squared paper; completed crosswords of different structures, some enlarged or copied onto OHTs; writing materials; dictionaries.

WHAT TO DO

Explain to the children that you want them to create crosswords for each other to complete which will help them remember how to spell new topic words. Use a current topic as a context for this activity, for example the Ancient Greeks, pop groups of the 1960s or recently learned mathematical vocabulary.

Show the children a completed crossword and ask them to identify the components. Agree there are clues and a frame into which to write the answers. Note how the clues are organised; this may be into 'across' and 'down' clues or numbered in order depending on the structure. Look to see how the frame is organised. Ask the children, *How are black squares organised? Are they in a pattern or randomly spaced?* Repeat this with several crosswords.

Together with the children, brainstorm topic words to include in a class crossword. Write these on the board in alphabetical order as you go. Next, ask the children to think of imaginative clues for some of the words. Talk about how dictionaries can help with their definitions. Look at completed crosswords to give the children ideas for the different styles of clues, for example anagrams, missing word clues or

factual questions. Then encourage the children to think about the best way to construct the crossword. Ask, *What do you need to do first?* (Put the answers into the frame and number them.) *What should you leave until last?* (Put the numbered clues in the correct order for 'across' and 'down' if this is the way the crossword is structured.) If the clues are written into a word-processing package, it will be easier to cut and paste them into the correct order without having to write them all out again. The children should block out the unused squares in the frame, and then make a copy of the frame with the words left out.

Allow pairs of children to create their own crosswords to be photocopied for their friends to complete.

FLOOR TILES

SUBJECT: MATHS. NNS OBJECTIVES: TO UNDERSTAND AREA MEASURED IN SQUARE CENTIMETRES (cm^2); TO USE, READ AND WRITE STANDARD METRIC UNITS INCLUDING THEIR ABBREVIATIONS, AND RELATIONSHIPS BETWEEN THEM.

LEARNING OBJECTIVE

To learn that some shapes tessellate even when they are different sizes or have different areas.

THINKING OBJECTIVE

To think laterally.

THINKING SKILLS

The children will find a way to cover an area of floor when given certain numbers and sizes of floor tiles. They will consider how to solve the problem for themselves, whether by working out the area of each tile and then finding out how many are needed to cover the floor area, or by trial and error. The children will also be developing information-processing skills of finding pattern and relationship between the tile sizes.

WHAT YOU NEED

For each group you will need:
20 floor tiles or paper patterns of tiles in one colour measuring 30 cm^2, and 70 in another colour measuring 10 cm^2; an area of floor measuring 1.5 m^2; measuring equipment.

WHAT TO DO

Explain to the children that you want to tile your front entrance hall. Explain that you already have some tiles left over from a previous job and that you know there are enough to cover the area. You want to create an interesting pattern with the tiles you have and you want the children to think creatively about the different patterns that can be made, and to think laterally to find an innovative pattern to cover the floor.

Show them the tiles and ask them to think about how they could organise the investigation. First, identify that they need to know how many there are of each tile. Then, they need to identify the size of

the area to be covered, and work out whether there are enough of one size of tile to complete the job or whether they will need to mix the different-sized tiles to cover the area.

Organise the children into groups and give each group a set of tiles. Tell each group to measure out an area of floor (in the school hall or playground) that is the same size as your front hall. Expect them to find their own measuring equipment and find a way to do this for themselves. Next, observe them as they go about solving the problem. Note whether they do this by trial and error. This method is quite acceptable, but do question the older and higher attaining children to see if they can see another way to tackle the problem. For example, they could

predict the number of each size of tile they require by calculating the area of the floor and dividing this by the sizes of different numbers of tiles, before arranging them in different ways to make a pattern. Alternatively, the children could use centimetre squared paper and work to a scale of 1:10.

Share the different ways of making patterns as the children work, then ask them if they can create another pattern. Ask, *Do you need to have the corners of the tiles meeting? Can you use one size of tile to make a border, or to divide the area into two, three or more sections?*

Extend the activity by altering the shape or size of the tiles, or alter the size and shape of the floor area to be covered. This will require the children to work out the area of compound shapes, dividing the more complex shape into squares or rectangles.

SWEET SUCCESS

SUBJECT: SCIENCE. QCA UNIT: 6C MORE ABOUT DISSOLVING.

LEARNING OBJECTIVE
To learn that different variables will affect the speed with which a sweet (or other solid) dissolves.

THINKING OBJECTIVE
To hypothesise.

THINKING SKILLS
The children will take part in a sweet-dissolving race and discuss how they made the sweet dissolve so fast. They will consider the different variables acting upon the sweet and find a way of setting up a fair test to find out which variable affects the dissolving process the most.

WHAT YOU NEED
Fruit pastels or similar; beakers; hot and cold water; spoons; stopwatches; paper; writing materials.

WHAT TO DO
Tell the children that you want to find out the fastest way to dissolve a sweet. Explain that you want them to plan a way of dissolving a sweet faster than anyone else's. Organise the children into pairs and allow them a few minutes to think about the problem and what they will need to carry out the investigation. As each pair is ready, provide them with the equipment they request and challenge them to dissolve their sweet. They should measure how long the sweet takes to dissolve using a stopwatch. When all the pairs have dissolved their sweet, find out whose sweet dissolved the fastest. On the board,

list anything the pairs did to speed up the process, for example using hot water, stirring the sweet, filling the beaker to the top, breaking the sweet into smaller pieces and so on. Tell the children that these are all variables and they need to be considered when setting up a fair test. Explain that to make the test as fair as possible only one of these variables should be changed at any one time.

Look again at the list showing what the pairs did to speed up the dissolving process. Ask, *How do you know whether all or some of these affected the rate at which the sweet dissolved? How can you be sure?*

Together, think of a way to test each variable to find out whether it affects the rate with which the sweet dissolves. Agree that to make the test absolutely fair only one variable will change each time.

Join pairs to make small groups to investigate the effect of *one* variable on the rate of dissolving. Encourage them to plan the test first and discuss this as a class to make sure the children are absolutely clear about what they are testing, how and why. For example, one group could investigate the stirring rate. They should keep the amount and temperature of the water the same, the sweets whole and the beakers the same size and material. Make sure that, apart from the variable being tested, all other aspects are kept as constant as possible. The colour of the sweets may be more difficult.

During the plenary, ask each group to share the outcomes of their test. They should note which variables they kept constant, the one variable they changed, what they measured and what conclusion they have drawn. Agree which variables affect the rate of dissolving and run the race again. Was it a draw this time?

Use the information to draw conclusions and suggest ideas about whether two variables combined will speed up the dissolving process even more. Reverse the idea by asking the children to use the information to suggest how they could make their sweet last for longer to prolong the taste.

FEELING INVADED

SUBJECT: HISTORY. QCA UNIT: 19 WHAT WERE THE EFFECTS OF TUDOR EXPLORATION?

LEARNING OBJECTIVE
To compare and contrast very different perspectives of the same event.

THINKING OBJECTIVE
To think laterally.

THINKING SKILLS
Before tackling this activity, the children should have researched Sir Francis Drake's voyage and have a good understanding of the many voyages to the Americas. They will need to have a good understanding of the difficulties that faced settlers, and have considered the reasons these people left their homeland and how they viewed the indigenous people who already lived there. They will then think laterally to imagine what it might have been like to be a native North American at that time, and write a diary of events describing some of the activities that occurred.

WHAT YOU NEED
Information about the way native North Americans lived their lives, the activities and tasks they engaged in, and the ways in which they lived; large sheets of paper; writing materials.

WHAT TO DO
List what the children already know about settlers and native North Americans at the time of Tudor exploration, and think about how we know this. Ask the children to consider how the children of the settlers' might have felt and what they might have thought when they saw the natives. They can also consider the feelings of the native North American children. Ask, *How did the settlers view the natives? How do you think the natives might have felt to be viewed in such a way?*

Organise the children into groups and ask each group to consider a different sequence of events: the settlers arriving, taking over the land, building homes and other events which would have seemed alien to the native North Americans. As a class, draw out and discuss the difficulties faced by the settlers, and compare this with the way the native North Americans had adapted to the climate and terrain. Challenge the children to think laterally about how the settlers were viewed by the native North Americans as they continued to fail in building a successful colony. Ask them to write a diary, detailing the thoughts of a native North American child and recounting the events that occurred. Ask the children to work in their groups, to discuss and collect their ideas and to plan their diary entries on a large sheet of paper. Pairs should then each write one diary entry which, when collected with the other entries, describe the sequence of events as the settlers attempted to carve out new lives observed by the native North Americans.

Again as a class, compare and contrast the possible feelings of other indigenous people when settlers arrived in their lands, such as Aborigine,

Maori and native South Americans. Use the ideas to write a group description or poem.

IMAGINE A PLACE WHERE ...

SUBJECT: GEOGRAPHY. QCA UNITS: 13 A CONTRASTING UK LOCALITY – LLANDUDNO; 14 INVESTIGATING RIVERS; 15 THE MOUNTAIN ENVIRONMENT.

LEARNING OBJECTIVE
To use the features of an environment when considering its qualities.

THINKING OBJECTIVE
To think imaginatively.

THINKING SKILLS
The children will look at photographs and postcards of different environments and note the geographical, physical and human features. For each feature they will consider how this makes them feel in terms of the beauty of the place, and what they can see, hear, touch and smell. They will consider the climate, the people who live or visit this place, and finally whether they would like to go there and why. They will then work together to write a group imaginative description or poem stimulated by this place, based on the features and feelings identified. (There are links with literacy through the use of imagery, metaphors and similes.)

WHAT YOU NEED
Photographs and postcards of different mountain environments and seaside places in different parts of the world, and other places with distinct features

and weather patterns; large sheets of paper; writing materials.

WHAT TO DO
Look at an enlarged photograph or postcard of one of your chosen places. On a large sheet of paper, list all the physical and human features the children can see. Together, think of several sentences to describe what this place is like physically.

Tell the children that for this activity, you want them to imagine what it would be like to be in this place.

Ask them to imagine they have been transported into the photograph. They have already described what they can see, now ask them to imagine what they can hear, smell and feel. Write the children's suggestions next to the feature on your list, for example, 'the sweet-smelling perfume of the heathers', or 'the cold, icy touch of the snow'. Finally, talk about the weather shown, asking, *What is the temperature likely to be? How do you know? What time of the year is it? Would you feel a breeze, wind or gale? At what time of the year are you likely to experience these weather conditions? How will this inform the clothes you would be wearing? How can you find out?* List these questions on the board as prompts for the children to use later.

Organise the children into small groups, allow them each to choose one postcard or photograph, and ask them to follow the same process as above to imagine what it would be like to be transported into that place. Check they have listed all the physical and human features before imagining what they can see, hear, touch and smell. Ask them to write their thoughts next to the geographical feature which promoted the idea. Finally, ask the groups to think about the climate and to imagine what it would be like to live in that place at certain times of the year. Ask each group to describe their ideas to the rest of the class. They should use appropriate geographical vocabulary to refer to the features and the patterns and processes of this place.

BELTS AND BANDS

SUBJECT: DESIGN AND TECHNOLOGY. QCA UNIT: 6B
SLIPPERS.

LEARNING OBJECTIVE

To design a pattern for slippers, belts or bands.

THINKING OBJECTIVE

To extend ideas.

THINKING SKILLS

The children will analyse native North American
designs and the materials used to make slippers,
belts or bands before designing and making their
own. They will extend their initial ideas by designing
and labelling fully a detailed drawing of the materials
and techniques they will use. They will try out their
designs to make sure they work properly before
making a final version.

WHAT YOU NEED

Paper patterns for belts, headdresses and slippers;
a selection of fabrics, embroidery threads, sequins,
beads and needles; writing materials; drawing
materials.

WHAT TO DO

Look at pictures of native North American Indians
and analyse the patterns, colours and designs
on their braids, headdresses, belts, slippers and
moccasins. List the materials that have been used
and the techniques for producing the designs and
patterns.

Ask the children to choose an item, either a belt,
headdress or slipper, and provide them with blank
paper patterns, cut to the same size as the chosen
item. Using the patterns, ask them to brainstorm
a range of appropriate patterns and designs.
They should also label in detail the materials and
techniques they would use to make the item.
Then the children should choose one favourite
pattern, and practise making the patterns and
designs on offcuts of fabric, choosing the one best
suited to each particular item. Get the children to try
and improve any stitching and appliqué techniques
and skills.

Allow the children to make the final designs by
embroidering with threads, wool and silks and adding
simple appliqué, beads or sequins.

FAIRGROUND RIDES

SUBJECT: ICT. QCA UNIT: 5D INTRODUCTION TO
SPREADSHEETS.

LEARNING OBJECTIVE

To change data in a spreadsheet to answer 'What
if... ?' questions and check predictions.

THINKING OBJECTIVE

To hypothesise.

THINKING SKILLS

The children will think about the cost of building
and operating a fairground ride. They will use a
spreadsheet format to work out how many rides they
need to sell to recuperate the costs before making a
profit. Questions such as 'What will happen
if... ?' will help them to hypothesise whether they
will make more or less profit with different numbers
of people going on the rides. The children should
have knowledge of how to enter formulae on a
spreadsheet and use the 'SUM' function.

WHAT YOU NEED

A suitable spreadsheet program, which
allows the children to create a formula
using multiplication and division
operations.

WHAT TO DO

During the topic on
fairgrounds challenge
the children to
establish the
cost of making a
particular piece of
equipment. Using
this information,
ask them to
hypothesise how
much the owners
would need to
charge each person
for a ride to cover
the cost of running
the ride, pay off
the loan for building
the ride, and make a
small profit to pay for
day-to-day living expenses.
Encourage them to think about
the following questions and to add
questions of their own: *What would
happen if the ride was only half full each
time? What would happen if the ride was full each
time? What would happen if most of the people riding
were children and paying half fare?*

The children could then decide on the fare for a
ride for adults and children, and create a formula to

work out how many people they need to ride to cover the running costs. Then they could create a formula to calculate how many times one person would need go on the ride before they had made enough money to pay for the equipment. The formula should be such that it will calculate the total cost of the equipment divided by the fare, divided again by the number of people in one full ride. For example, if the equipment cost £100 000 and the fare was £5 per adult, then it would take £100 000 ÷ £5 = 20 000 adults to cover the cost of the equipment. If 20 adults could ride at once then this would take 20 000 ÷ 20 = 1000 full rides. In this way, the children can calculate how long it would take to pay for the ride for each of the scenarios in their 'What if … ?' questions.

Differentiate the activity by working in whole pence and pounds. Change the number of people that can ride to give a different number of times the ride will need to operate to recoup the cost.

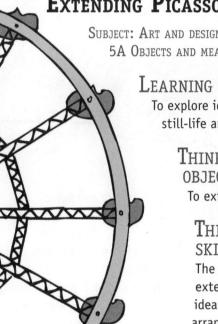

EXTENDING PICASSO

SUBJECT: ART AND DESIGN. QCA UNIT: 5A OBJECTS AND MEANINGS.

LEARNING OBJECTIVE
To explore ideas for a still-life arrangement.

THINKING OBJECTIVE
To extend ideas.

THINKING SKILLS
The children will extend their ideas of still-life arrangements by combining line, shape and colour in the style of Picasso. They will portray the objects in their own still-life arrangements in a different style.

WHAT YOU NEED
A print of Picasso's *Violin and Grapes*; two pictures of objects chosen by the children; paper; scissors; glue.

WHAT TO DO
Look at the painting *Violin and Grapes* by Picasso and talk about what the children can see. Ask, *Why do you think the painting is called* Violin and Grapes*? How does this relate to what the picture contains?* Talk about the colours and way the painting is divided into sections. Ask, *How has Picasso used line to make these sections different each time? Has he used straight or curved lines? How do the curved lines follow part of the outline of the violin?* Locate the different parts of the violin. Ask, *Where are the grapes? What other symbols has Picasso used to show that this is a picture of a violin? Why has he used browns for the background?*

Invite the children to think about how they might create a picture of their own, in the style of *Violin and Grapes*, but also extending the idea. They should cut up the two pictures they have (or draw and colour two objects), using straight lines, to form a number of irregular straight-sided shapes. They should then spend time arranging and rearranging the pieces until they have created a composition they are happy with. Now they should consider a background that will best reflect the objects to be placed on top. Suggest they divide the background into sections, using straight lines and lines which follow part of the outline of the cut-out shapes. Then prompt the children to use sympathetic tones and tints to colour in the background.

When the background is dry, the children should glue the cut-out pictures to the background to produce a picture in the same style as Picasso, but having extended his ideas.

INDIAN CHANTS

SUBJECT: MUSIC. QCA UNIT: 16 CYCLIC PATTERNS.

LEARNING OBJECTIVE
To learn that different rhythmic patterns can fit together so long as they contain the same number of beats.

THINKING OBJECTIVE
To generate ideas.

THINKING SKILLS
The children will compose, adapt, improvise and develop rhythms to create an interesting accompaniment for a North American dance. They will build these into a structure of ostinato or syncopated rhythms to repeat and develop the beat and rhythmic moves of a dance.

WHAT YOU NEED
A piece of music from the native North American culture; drums, tambours and claves; large sheets of paper; writing materials.

WHAT TO DO

As a class, listen to a piece of music from native North American culture and identify the beat. Count the number of beats in each bar carefully. Work out with the children where the strong beat is and how the other beats are weaker. Listen to a four-beat pulse and decide if one of the remaining three beats (the third one), is stronger than the other two but less strong than the first one.

Listen next for the rhythms that fit into the beat. Ask, *Are any repeated? How are they repeated? How many bars does each rhythmic pattern cover?* Note that these are called 'phrases'.

Invite the children to compose a one-bar, four-beat rhythmic phrase with a partner, which fits the pulse. Invite them to test out their ideas with one child clapping the pulse or beat and the other clapping the rhythm over again to make ostinato rhythms. Ask them to perform their pattern and record this on paper: use numbers to show the pulse or beat and vertical lines to indicate the rhythm. Using vertical lines is close to the formal notation the children will use later and they will be able to see how closely this matches real musical score.

Start the children clapping the pulse, indicating the strong and weaker notes, for example they could clap the first stronger beat and tap the other three beats on their knees. As they clap, model how to develop the four-beat rhythm by changing the notes, adding rests, clapping on the offbeat to make a syncopated rhythm and so on. Show the children how the pattern can be continued for a fairly long time. Organise the children into pairs and let them take turns to practice this. Regroup in a circle and, with the rest of the class clapping, ask each child in turn in the circle to clap out a four-beat one-bar rhythm. Play the piece of music again, this time asking the children to repeat their rhythms in turn around the circle, repeating until the music has finished. Note with the children the range of ideas they have created to fit the pulse and how they have varied the rhythm.

In groups, create ideas for a drumming accompaniment to a simple Indian chant, such as 'Indian Warrior' or 'Land of the Silver Birch' by adding ostinato or syncopated rhythms.

WHAT DOES BELIEVING MEAN?

SUBJECT: RE. QCA UNIT: 6C WHY ARE SACRED TEXTS IMPORTANT?

LEARNING OBJECTIVE

To understand that sacred texts give messages about the way believers should live their lives.

THINKING OBJECTIVE

To extend ideas.

THINKING SKILLS

The children will think about what they have learned during this unit of work and why sacred texts are important to believers regardless of their faith. They will draw out the commonalities between the different groups of believers before extending their ideas to define what believing means. They will consider values such as faith, trust, commitment, consideration and honesty.

WHAT YOU NEED

Suitable sacred texts from different religions.

WHAT TO DO

Before the lesson, look through the sacred texts and locate some references to values.

As a class, consider together what it means to be a believer. Ask, *How do believers know there is a God? Is it because they just know he exists because they have faith?* Discuss what the word 'faith' means and whether faith is the same for all believers regardless of their religion. Agree that believers all believe in one supreme being even though he is referred to in different ways. Discuss the names that different religions use to refer to this supreme being.

Challenge the children to think of all the values and beliefs that believers from different religions have in common. For each value consider how the children know this. Ask, *What references in the relevant sacred texts teach the believers about the way they should lead their lives?* If necessary, tell the children about these references and where they can be found. Accept all the children's ideas so long as they have suitable reasons and can justify their opinions.

Organise the children into groups and ask them to discuss the values together, and to extend these ideas to write a statement which describes what it means to be a believer. Agree on a class statement of what it means to be a believer which is relevant for any religion or faith.

AUSTRALIAN HISTORY

SUBJECT: PE. QCA UNIT: DANCE ACTIVITIES UNIT 6.

LEARNING OBJECTIVE
To create and structure motifs, phrases and sequences into a whole dance.

THINKING OBJECTIVE
To generate ideas.

THINKING SKILLS
The children will work together in groups to create a dance to depict the birth and development of Australia as a country. They will consider how they can structure the whole dance by combining pictures of the different stages of Australia's development. They will then work in groups to develop motifs, phrases and sequences to depict each stage before finally joining together to build the dance sections into a whole. This idea will take at least six weeks or a half term to develop.

WHAT YOU NEED
Various pieces of evocative music: slow music to depict the landscape, music to portray different Australian animals (perhaps composed by the children), music for an Aborigine dance, for the coming of the convicts, and for building modern Australia (perhaps an extract from Track 3 from Disney's *Millennium Celebration*).

WHAT TO DO
Talk to the children how modern Australia grew and the different social groups which make up its modern society. Discuss and make a note of the beginning with the earth, sun and creatures, the Aborigine culture, the arrival of the convicts and the way all of these groups now live together with other people who have emigrated to make up modern Australia.

Organise the class into five groups and allocate each group one of the following areas from the history of Australia:
- the landscape: sun, rocks, Great Barrier Reef coral, fish and sea creatures
- the animals: kangaroo, cassowary, lizard, snake, spider
- the Aborigines
- the arrival of Captain Cook
- the arrival of convicts.

Give the groups time to talk about how their alloted aspect could be depicted through music and movement. Ask, *What kind of music would best describe the scene? What kinds of movements would be appropriate?* For example, the Aborigines could be hunting and dancing in a rhythmic way; the convicts could be dragging their chains and looking bedraggled after a long journey. Then encourage the children to try out their motifs and build them into phrases and sequences to depict this part of the dance without the accompanying music. Each group should aim to produce a repeating phrase that can be joined to the other groups' dance sections to make the complete dance.

Over a number of weeks, set the ideas to music, working on one section together as a class group, and focusing on extending and developing the skills and techniques of the particular group who will be performing this bit of the dance.

Encourage the children to help each other evaluate, develop, refine and improve each phrase and sequence. Build the ending of the dance together. Include in the ending the building of famous Australian landmarks and modern Australians taking part in the full range of leisure activities and sports of today.

Put the dance together with each group performing their section before joining together at the end to perform the big finale.

EXTENDING CREATIVE THINKING SKILLS

Subject and QCA unit, NLS and NNS objective	Activity title	Thinking objective	Activity	Page
English NLS objectives: To understand the differences between literal and figurative language e.g through discussing the effects of imagery in poetry and prose; to understand aspects of narrative structure e.g. how the passing of time is conveyed to the reader	This old house	To hypothesise	Hypothesising from the setting description in *Tom's Midnight Garden* what might be happening at midnight	95
Maths NNS objectives: To know that a diagonal is a straight line drawn from a vertex of a polygon to a non-adjacent vertex; to know that two lines that cross each other are called intersecting lines and the points at which they cross is an intersection; to recognise positions and directions, and use co-ordinates	Taking a line for a walk	To think laterally	Drawing shapes without taking the pencil off the paper. Creating shapes which cannot be drawn without taking the pencil off the paper and thinking of a reason why this is the case	96
Science QCA unit: 6F How we see things	An eye-catching number	To generate ideas	Making a chart or poster to show the difference between a shadow and a reflection	97
History QCA unit: 14 Who were the Ancient Greeks?	Imagine a time when ...	To think imaginatively	Imagining life as a person who lived at the time of the Ancient Greeks	98
Geography QCA unit: 18 Connecting ourselves to the world	Communication	To hypothesise	Hypothesising how much people in different countries know about other parts of the world	99
Design and technology QCA unit: 6A Shelters	Newspaper technology	To generate ideas and to think laterally	Making structures from newspaper	100
ICT QCA unit: 5E Controlling devices	Clever clown	To think imaginatively and laterally	Making a model with features that move, light up and sound a buzzer, and which are controlled by a simple computer program	101
Art and design QCA unit: 5B Containers	Salt and pepper	To think imaginatively	Designing and making salt and pepper pots	102
Music QCA unit: 18 Journey into space	Space music	To generate ideas	Creating a film score for a journey into space or under the sea	103
RE QCA unit: 6C Why are sacred texts important?	Sermon of the day	To generate ideas	Writing a sermon or talking about part of the Bible or Qu'ran	104
PE QCA unit: Striking and fielding games unit 2	Quick cricket	To extend ideas	Developing a scoring system for a game of quick rounders and a team sports' day	105

THIS OLD HOUSE

SUBJECT: ENGLISH. NLS OBJECTIVES: TO UNDERSTAND THE DIFFERENCES BETWEEN LITERAL AND FIGURATIVE LANGUAGE E.G THROUGH DISCUSSING THE EFFECTS OF IMAGERY IN POETRY AND PROSE; TO UNDERSTAND ASPECTS OF NARRATIVE STRUCTURE E.G. HOW THE PASSING OF TIME IS CONVEYED TO THE READER.

LEARNING OBJECTIVE

To understand how one author conveys the passing of time to the reader.

THINKING OBJECTIVE

To hypothesise.

THINKING SKILLS

The children will consider the beginning of a story and, by comparing the descriptions of the setting, they will begin to hypothesise what the author is trying to convey regarding the passing of time. They will think about the imagery of the clock and how this is used as a practical clue to this concept.

WHAT YOU NEED

A copy of *Tom's Midnight Garden* by Philippa Pearce (Puffin); several large sheets of paper divided into four rectangles; writing materials; a photocopy of Chapter 3 for each group.

WHAT TO DO

In a previous lesson, read the first chapter of the book, and as a class discuss the characters and Tom's feelings about staying with his aunt and uncle during the holidays rather than at home. Note how much Tom likes gardens and that his aunt and uncle do not have one. Think about how Tom feels when he sees his new home. Review the description of the hallway, the cold flagstones, the dusty smell and the things that can be seen, such as the posters, milk bottles and laundry box. Pay particular attention to the description of the old grandfather clock and its owner, and the fact that it never strikes the right number of times. Ask, *Why do you think the author has included a grandfather clock in the hall? What is the purpose of this?* Draw out that it could be because the author wants to draw the reader's attention to the passing of time, to give them a clue as to what may be happening in the story.

Organise the children into groups and ask them to write down the salient points of the description in the top left-hand section of their large sheet of paper.

At the beginning of the next lesson, review these points and also summarise the first part of Chapter 2. Start reading to the class from the part when Tom is in bed and the clock begins to strike. Listen to how Tom reasons that there could be thirteen hours in the day and ask the children to infer what this could mean for Tom. Ask, *What is he thinking? Does he think that he can go out for one hour and not be missed because there will still be enough time to fit in ten hours sleep?*

Organise the children into groups and give each group a photocopy of Chapter 3. Ask them to read through Chapter 3 together, noting in the top right-hand box on their sheet of paper the description of the hall and the grandfather clock. They should also note any new characters.

In the bottom left-hand corner box, ask the children to refer closely to the text to note the description of the garden. In particular, they should note down any inferential comments such as the smell of the hyacinths and the texture of the tree trunks. Ask, *How is this garden making Tom feel about his home?*

When you have shared the descriptions as a class, ask the children, *Who could the maid be? Why did the clock strike thirteen? What could happen on the thirteenth hour? What happens in the house? What happens to the garden?* Encourage the children to refer closely to the text when sharing their ideas.

Ask the children to hypothesise the kind of things that could be happening to Tom in the house: he could be dreaming, the house could be haunted, the house could live in a different time warp. Note down the children's ideas for later comparison.

DIFFERENTIATION

Provide higher attaining children with the extract at the end of Chapter 13 which starts after Hatty sings the chorus of 'Sweet Molly Malone': *Suddenly Tom said – he blurted it out before he could help himself.* This is when he asks Hatty what it is like being a ghost. Discuss the conversation Tom and Hatty have and ask the children to hypothesise who is right.

Talk with lower attaining children about why the title of the book is *Tom's Midnight Garden* to give them clues and ideas for their hypotheses.

WHERE NEXT

Continue to read the story as a class, checking back to the children's hypotheses.

Dip into later chapters and identify with groups of children how the author is setting the time. Ask them to hypothesise what is happening in the story and how they know that Tom is moving from one time to another.

ASSESSMENT

Assess how well the children interpret the text to look for clues to help them hypothesise what is happening in the story, and if they notice how the author uses language to paint the picture of time passing, in this case with two threads running concurrently.

LEARNING OUTCOMES

The children will learn to locate how the text helps readers to hypothesise how time is passing in the story.

FURTHER ENGLISH CHALLENGES

Time after time

Look at familiar stories, poems and openings of novels and note how the author sets the time. Ask the children to hypothesise whether the story is set in the past, present or future and to say how they know for each of the texts they look at.

Time traveller

Watch the opening extract from *Back to the Future* and talk about how we can hypothesise that Marty will go back in time. Ask, *What time clues are in the dialogue? What device has the film-maker used?*

TAKING A LINE FOR A WALK

SUBJECT: MATHS. NNS OBJECTIVES: TO KNOW THAT A DIAGONAL IS A STRAIGHT LINE DRAWN FROM A VERTEX OF A POLYGON TO A NON-ADJACENT VERTEX; TO KNOW THAT TWO LINES THAT CROSS EACH OTHER ARE CALLED INTERSECTING LINES AND THE POINTS AT WHICH THEY CROSS IS AN INTERSECTION; TO RECOGNISE POSITIONS AND DIRECTIONS, AND USE CO-ORDINATES.

LEARNING OBJECTIVE

To describe diagonal lines using mathematical terms and know that two lines that cross each other are intersecting lines.

THINKING OBJECTIVE

To think laterally.

THINKING SKILLS

The children will look for a pattern when drawing shapes without taking their pencil off the paper. They will look at each shape and note the features that are the same and those that are different. They will then create shapes which cannot be drawn without taking the pencil off the paper and think of a reason why this is the case.

WHAT YOU NEED

Several large sheets of paper; writing materials.

WHAT TO DO

Draw a variety of shapes on the board, some of which can be drawn without taking the pencil off the paper, and some which cannot. Include a pentagon which looks like a house with the square base corner diagonals linked, and one with all points joined with a line.

Look at each shape one at a time and ask the class to predict whether the shape can be drawn without taking the pen off the paper. Tick them if they think they can and cross them if they think they can't. Test these all out on the board.

Challenge pairs to find a way of drawing the pentagon 'house' shape without taking their pencil off the paper. Ask, *Can you find more than one way? How will you show the order in which you drew the lines? If you start in a certain place, does this prevent the shape being drawn without taking the pen off the paper? Where should you start, for example, where more than two lines meet?*

Encourage the children to write a rule for drawing this shape without taking the pen off the paper. At the end of the lesson, identify how many ways the children found of drawing this shape. Ask, *How many different starting points were there? What did these points have in common? Were there any starting points which prevented the shape being drawn?* Share the rules that the children have written to guide their investigations and solving of the problem. Note the different ways that different children approached the task.

DIFFERENTIATION

Sit with the lower attaining children to ensure they understand the purpose of the task. Start with a simple shape, such as a triangle, which can be drawn without taking the pen from the paper. Move onto shapes which are made from a series of triangles in a pyramid pattern and organised in a line.

Ask higher attaining children to investigate a square and hexagon with intersecting lines as well as the pentagon shape. Ask, *What do you notice about* these shapes? Why can't they be drawn? Can you think of a rule? What is different between these shapes and the pentagon in terms of the member of sides and corners but also the number of times the lines meet in the corners?

WHERE NEXT
Investigate other shapes following the rules.

ASSESSMENT
Note which children think of a possible rule to explain how they solved the problem and which will help them solve similar problems. Note those children who solve the problem by trial and error but who are beginning to realise that they need to start from a point that has more than two meeting lines.

LEARNING OUTCOMES
Most children will be able to solve the problem by thinking laterally and by starting from different points to solve the problem.

FURTHER MATHS CHALLENGES
Continuous patterns
Challenge the children to create other patterns for their friends to draw without taking the pen off the paper. Ask the children who are accepting the challenge to predict whether these can be done and why before they start.

Pylons
As a class, count the number of triangles and trapezium in an electric pylon. Ask the children, *What do you notice about the shapes?* Challenge them to reproduce the shapes in the pylon on paper but without taking their pencil off the paper. Ask, *Can you think of a rule to predict whether or not this may be possible?*

Circular pattern
Ask the children to create a pattern for their friend to try to draw without taking their pencil off. Patterns made by drawing compasses or Spiro graphs are good starting points for this.

AN EYE-CATCHING NUMBER

SUBJECT: SCIENCE. QCA UNIT: 6F HOW WE SEE THINGS.

LEARNING OBJECTIVE
To understand the difference between a shadow and a reflection.

THINKING OBJECTIVE
To generate ideas.

THINKING SKILLS
This assessment task will demonstrate the children's thinking in terms of their understanding of the difference between a shadow and a reflection. They will create their own symbols or pictures to show how each is formed.

WHAT YOU NEED
A3 sheets of paper; crayons.

WHAT TO DO
Talk to they children about what they know about the way shadows are formed, and together write a statement to explain this. For example, 'Shadows are formed when a light beam is blocked by an object or material.' Talk about whether a shadow is the same shape as the object blocking the beam of light. Ask, *Are the edges of the shadow always clear?*

Next, ask the children to say how shadows are different from reflections. Discuss how reflections are made and agree that this is because a beam of light changed direction when it hit the surface of an object or material.

Explain to the children that you want them to create a poster or chart to show their understanding of the way shadows are formed and how reflections occur. Tell them they can use any ideas they wish but that you want the posters or charts to be informative to people who do not understand the difference between the two. Allow the children ten minutes to brainstorm and try out different ideas before asking them to select one idea to show how a shadow is formed and another to show how a reflection occurs. Encourage them to show what is happening to the beam of light in each case.

Share the children's ideas at the end of the lesson and agree which posters convey the message quickly and clearly. Why do the children think these posters do this the best?

DIFFERENTIATION
Encourage higher attaining children to think about the position and size of the light source and the consequent impact on the shape of the shadow and relative position. Encourage them to label the reflection using scientific vocabulary to show their thinking.

Sit with lower attaining children as they work, probing their understanding and encouraging them to use this to produce interesting and creative posters.

WHERE NEXT
Encourage the children to make concept maps to show their thinking, perhaps in pictures and diagrams rather than words.

ASSESSMENT

This is an assessment activity to show the children's understanding, but note also how they portray their understanding in a creative way to make the difference between shadows and reflections clear.

LEARNING OUTCOMES

The children will create their own ideas for portraying their understanding of the difference between shadows and reflections.

FURTHER SCIENCE CHALLENGES

In the shadows

Challenge the children to create ideas for showing where the shadows are in different pictures. Ask higher attaining children to create a picture of an outside scene and to place the sun in its position before drawing the shadows of the objects in their pictures. Ask the children to include water in their pictures and to show the reflections of the objects in this.

Be seen at night

Look at reflective materials and ask the children to create a slogan and/or posters to convey the message 'Be seen at night'. They should include that fact that reflective materials on clothing reflect the light from car headlights and such, enabling drivers to see pedestrians.

IMAGINE A TIME WHEN ...

SUBJECT: HISTORY. QCA UNIT: 14 WHO WERE THE ANCIENT GREEKS? (THIS ACTIVITY CAN BE SET WITHIN ANY OF THE UNITS.)

LEARNING OBJECTIVE

To summarise what life was like for the Ancient Greeks.

THINKING OBJECTIVE

To think imaginatively.

THINKING SKILLS

This activity can be used as an assessment activity to find out what the children have learned about life during the time of the Ancient Greeks. They will base their imaginative writing on research information and facts they have investigated.

WHAT YOU NEED

The children's previous research into the different aspects of life at the time of the Ancient Greeks: the events that took place, the groups of people that lived at that time and the activities they took part in; paper; writing materials.

WHAT TO DO

Choose one of the people the children have learned about during the unit of work, for example a soldier, ordinary citizen, slave, athlete or actor. Discuss with the children all the activities these people would have been involved in. Imagine what life might have been like for them. Encourage the children to think about the day-to-day routines, but also about that person's beliefs and feelings. As a class, use the children's ideas to write an entry for one day in the life of this person, noting the things that they did and why.

Ask the children to work independently, in pairs and groups, and to choose one person and imagine what their life was like. Remind the children to think about the things their chosen person would do in a typical day, but also to imagine how they might have felt, what they might have been thinking and what they believed. Encourage them to brainstorm lots of possibilities and to plan the detail of the content before writing an entry for a diary, in the first person, based on the point of view of their chosen person.

DIFFERENTIATION

This activity is based on the children choosing which person they would like to be. Ask higher attaining children to consider being a non-competitor in the Olympic Games, either as a woman or a slave, and ask them to imagine what these people might have been thinking and feeling as they watched the competition. Monitor lower attaining children closely to make sure that they are using the facts and information as prompts for their imaginative ideas.

WHERE NEXT

Choose one of the battles of the time and prompt the children to imagine what this event might have been like for the soldiers on both sides. Write and act out the diary entries together as a simple cameo role-play activity for the plenary session of the lesson.

ASSESSMENT
Talk to the children as they work, prompting them with questions to probe their understanding of life at that time. Note how well they use this information to imagine life as their chosen person.

LEARNING OUTCOMES
The children will use the information from research to imagine what life was like for different people living at the time of the Ancient Greeks.

FURTHER HISTORY CHALLENGES
Acting lessons
Take one of the diary entries and ask the children to work in small groups to act it out for the rest of the class. Challenge them to find a way of showing, through the action and dialogue, what life might have been like for this person during the times of the Ancient Greeks.

COMMUNICATION

SUBJECT: GEOGRAPHY. QCA UNIT: 18 CONNECTING OURSELVES TO THE WORLD.

LEARNING OBJECTIVE
To learn that people around the world communicate in different ways, but that many ways are the same.

THINKING OBJECTIVE
To hypothesise.

THINKING SKILLS
The children will consider the many different ways that they communicate with friends and family who live nearby and those who live further afield. They will consider the different types of communication available in different countries which are used by people living in different geographical regions. (There are links with evaluation skills when considering the best way to communicate in different situations.)

WHAT YOU NEED
Maps; newspapers; magazines; TV and radio magazines; access to a fax machine; internet and email access; mobile phone.

WHAT TO DO
Brainstorm the different ways in which the children communicate with close family and friends – visiting,

talking on the telephone, sending emails, cards and possibly sending faxes. Ask the children to hypothesise if families in other countries use these means of communication. Ask, *In which countries do you think people communicate in the same way? Why do you think this?* Next, ask the children to hypothesise if there are countries in which people do not communicate in this way. Correct any misconceptions at this point and explain that people living in all countries in the world have access to the same communication systems that we do but that they often live in remote areas so do have immediate access. Relate this to people who live in the more remote parts of the British Isles who cannot always use their mobile phones.

Talk about other ways that we keep in touch with what is happening around the world. Consider how the media gives us information, for example newspapers, magazines, TV and radio. In the same way, hypothesise in which countries these ways are used and whether there are any countries where they are not. Agree the wide range of communication systems in use around the world and our increasing reliance on satellite systems. Discuss cable TV and the range of facilities available to those who subscribe.

Organise the children into groups and ask them to consider other children around the world. Give each group a different country and ask them to hypothesise how the children keep in touch with each other, whether they go to school and, if not, do they learn in some other way. They should note down the wide range of ways that people all around the world keep in touch.

Still in groups, prompt the children to think laterally and to list all the reasons why people keep in touch. For each reason, identify the different ways that this can be done. For example, when someone celebrates a birthday, we can send a card by post or over the internet, send a text message with a photograph attached, telephone by land or mobile phone; or when exchanging weather statistics with another school we can send this by email, fax or telephone. Note the strengths and weaknesses of each method, then decide on the best way to communicate for each particular reason, allowing the children to disagree if they wish, so long as they can give reasons for their opinions.

As a class, share the children's hypotheses.

DIFFERENTIATION
Organise the children into mixed ability groups, except for the higher attaining children. With this group, introduce additional ways that people keep in touch by discussing the use of radios in outback

Australia. Hypothesise with the children why the people living in the outback use radios rather than mobile phones to keep in touch with the world. Think about the increasing use of computers by this group of people. Next, consider how children go to school. Ask, *Do they travel hundreds of miles each day or do they keep in touch with their teacher in some other way?* Talk about the School of the Air in Alice Springs and the work that it does. You might like to visit the website at www.assoa.nt.edu.au List all the ways children who live in the outback keep in touch with their classmates in Australia, for example post, radio, email, faxes and telephone. Again do not reinforce misconceptions. Explain to the children that most children go to schools in Australia the same way that they do.

WHERE NEXT

Prompt the children to research different countries and regions within countries and note the different ways that people keep in touch.

Ask the children to consider the equipment needs for the different ways of communication and hypothesise how this affects the means of communication in different types of physical geographical places.

ASSESSMENT

Note the children's hypotheses about the ways that people around the world can communicate with each other and why. Note those who hypothesise correctly that different people find some methods of communication more useful than others, depending on the geography of the region in which they live rather than the country. For example, those who live in rural areas are more likely to communicate by land phone than mobile phone because of the limitations of satellite systems.

LEARNING OUTCOMES

The children will learn to hypothesise which communication systems are available to different people around the world, and that the chosen method depends on the kind of place they live, whether they live in remote areas or more populated areas. They will learn that different people find some methods of communication more useful than others, depending on the geography of the region in which they live rather than the country.

FURTHER GEOGRAPHY CHALLENGES

When is the best time to communicate?
Consider the best way and time for communicating with different parts of the world. Hypothesise why we should not telephone Australia mid afternoon, for

example. Ask, *Why is it better to send an email at this time? If we sent an email at 2.30pm English time, when would an Australian receive it (Australian time)? When could we expect to see a reply if they replied straight away? What if we sent the email in the morning?* Make a list of countries around the world and identify the best time to send an email. Do the same for telephone conversations or faxes.

Stuck up a mountain, or up a creek without a paddle
Prompt the children to consider a trip up a mountain or down a river, and to list the equipment that they would take with them so they could keep in touch wherever they were. Hypothesise with the children the different places they could visit, for example, the River Amazon, the Nile or the Indus. Ask, *Would you take different ways of communicating depending on which river you were visiting? Why or why not?*

NEWSPAPER TECHNOLOGY

SUBJECT: DESIGN AND TECHNOLOGY: QCA UNIT: 6A SHELTERS.

LEARNING OBJECTIVE

To learn that structures can be strengthened by reinforcing them with materials that have been folded and rolled.

THINKING OBJECTIVE

To generate ideas and to think laterally.

THINKING SKILLS

The children will consider how to make newspaper stronger before using it to build a shelter. They will consider how they can reinforce their model by inserting pieces of plastic or wooden dowelling. They will generate their own ideas for changing the shape of the newspaper, and think of alternative ways to join these to make a structure strong enough to hold a cotton sheet. It will be useful if the children have analysed how tent frames are put together and how pylons are strengthened by triangulation before tackling this unit.

WHAT YOU NEED

Sheets of newspaper; sticky tape; a cotton sheet.

WHAT TO DO

As a class, talk about how structures are strengthened by triangulation, for example in a simple tent. Look at the sheets of newspaper and ask, *How could you change the shape of the sheet to make it strong enough to stand up? How could you test out how strong the newspaper is before and after you change its shape?* (For example, how easy or difficult it is to tear the newspaper in half.)

Challenge the children to say how they could join the newspaper tubes to make a tower structure that could be covered with a sheet to make a simple shelter. Encourage the children to generate their own ideas for this and accept any imaginative alternatives they might suggest.

Organise the children into groups and challenge them to make a structure which is tall enough to stand up inside and strong enough to support a sheet to make a shelter. Provide them with shorter plastic tubes or wooden dowelling to reinforce their structure if necessary.

Evaluate the structures together and look at the different ways the children have rolled and folded their newspaper poles and joined these to build their structures. Which do the children think are the most effective?

DIFFERENTIATION
Build a tent frame with lower attaining children and work alongside them as you continue to oversee and monitor the work of other groups. Ask this group to make a structure, inside which a person can sit or lie down, and which will support a sheet of paper or lightweight sheet. Challenge higher attaining children to create a telescopic structure that can be folded away into a small portable box, or to make a curved structure like an igloo shape with their tubes of newspaper.

WHERE NEXT
Use the children's ideas to make the shelters with other materials such as aluminium poles, plastic tubing (like that used to bury cables under ground) and wood. Set this within a survival theme if you wish.

ASSESSMENT
Note the creative ideas the children come up with for making and joining the newspaper structures.

Note those children who find alternative solutions for joining the different components of their shelters and the different shapes into which they build these.

LEARNING OUTCOMES
The children will learn to generate ideas for strengthening and reinforcing structures using a range of materials. They will think of alternative ways to join these shapes to make a structure strong enough to hold a sheet and tall enough to stand inside.

FURTHER DESIGN AND TECHNOLOGY CHALLENGES
Snookered
Challenge the children to make a snooker cue, table and balls from newspaper. Talk to them about how they can make the material stronger by folding and rolling it into different shapes and densities. Play a game of snooker in numeracy lessons as a mental arithmetic activity.

Home from home
Go outside and use willow to make a structure strong enough to stand on its own and tall enough to stand inside. Let the children generate their own designs before thinking of ways to join them all together to make an interesting structure for younger children in the school to explore during playtimes and to use for imaginative play. Encourage the children to use their ideas from the newspaper activity to design the structure first, and to plan how each group will contribute to its production before organising the activity themselves.

CLEVER CLOWN

SUBJECT: ICT. QCA UNIT: 5E CONTROLLING DEVICES.

LEARNING OBJECTIVE
To generate a sequence of instructions which can control a number of output devices.

THINKING OBJECTIVE
To think imaginatively and laterally.

THINKING SKILLS
The children will think imaginatively to create a model which moves in a circle, lights up and makes a noise after a certain number of seconds. They will think about how they can have more than two devices working at once. They will then think laterally about how they can put together a computer program to control how their model works in a particular sequence.

The children will need to have completed most of the activities in Unit 5E. There are links with Unit 6C Fairgrounds and an idea recently published by QCA of supplementary activities.

WHAT YOU NEED
Equipment to make circuits, including batteries, wire, buzzers, motors and bulbs; a buffer box or similar to link the devices to input and output connections; software to write a simple program to control the movement and sensors of a model.

WHAT TO DO
Ask the children to think imaginatively to design a model which moves, lights up and makes a sound at the same time. Explain that you want them to design a toy which will engage the interest of a younger child. This could be a clown's face with a nose that lights up, eyes or a bow tie which rotate and which makes a buzzer noise at the same time that the nose lights up. They should think about the order in which each device will start and stop, the length of time that each one will work for and the gap between and include this in their design plan.

Link the wires from the devices – the eyes, tie and nose – to the output and input sockets on the control box, showing the children how these start and stop the device. Then match the number of devices to the sequence of actions the children have planned. For example, input 1 makes the nose light up while output 1 makes it stop. Write on the plan the amount of time between each device working and, as a class, turn the plan into a set of instructions to put into the computer software. The children should think about how they can start the buzzer at the same time that the nose lights up. Children will need to consider where wires, lights and buzzers can go so they don't hamper the movement of the model.

DIFFERENTIATION
Some children may manage to use one device successfully, others may be able to incorporate more.

WHERE NEXT
Around the school and at home, encourage the children to look for objects which are controlled by computer programs such as microwaves, CD players, video recorders, drink dispensing machines and so on. Create ideas for programming these in different ways.

ASSESSMENT
Note how the children work out how to write the correct sequence to control the devices in their models. Share their innovative ideas to help others to think laterally.

LEARNING OUTCOMES
The children will work out for themselves how they can write a simple program to control the devices in their models.

FURTHER ICT CHALLENGES
Crystal rainforest
Set up this commercially produced program and ask the children to find the sequence for filling the drinks with juice.
Burglars beware
Write a program to control a sensor mat so that a buzzer sounds each time the pad is stepped on. Ask the children to think about when this would be useful. Reverse the program so that the buzzer sounds each time weight is removed. Again, encourage the children to think about possible applications for this device.

SALT AND PEPPER

SUBJECT: ART AND DESIGN.
QCA UNIT: 5B CONTAINERS.

LEARNING OBJECTIVE
To create interesting 3-D forms.

THINKING OBJECTIVE
To think imaginatively.

THINKING SKILLS

The children will design and make salt and pepper shakers from clay. They will think imaginatively to create innovative designs.

WHAT YOU NEED

A collection of different salt and pepper shakers of different materials, shapes, colours, sizes and designs; sketchbooks; card; scissors; sticky tape; clay.

WHAT TO DO

As a class look at the range of salt and pepper shakers in your collection and note that they are all containers. Discuss why they are containers and what they contain. Note the range of materials from which they are made and discuss why these have been chosen. Ask the children to consider the different styles and designs and talk about why these particular designs have been used. Look specifically at those which have been made from clay. Ask, *How have they been formed? Have they been made from coils of clay or built by forming a shape and scooping out the middle? Have they been made from a sheet of clay formed into a container shape?*

Explain to the children that you want them to think of an imaginative design for salt and pepper shakers. They should consider the stimulus they want to use, perhaps by looking on the internet or in books for ideas. Prompt their thinking by considering the latest film or book, a tree, animal, fruit or plant. Give them free reign to try out a number of ideas and to sketch these in their sketchbooks. Encourage them to think about where they will put the holes for the salt and pepper to flow. Ask, *Where will you put the hole and stopper to enable the salt and pepper to be refilled when empty?*

When the children have finished their design, ask them to label the resources they will need and to make notes on the making process. Ask, *How will you form the clay into a shape which will contain salt or pepper? How will you add any extra features like ears, petals, leaves or stalks?* Explain how they can do this with slip (watery clay).

DIFFERENTIATION

Encourage less able artists to use actual objects with definite shapes as a base for their designs, for example apples, plums and pears, balls and eggs. Challenge higher attaining children to consider imaginative places to put the holes for pouring the salt and pepper, such as ears and noses.

WHERE NEXT

Prompt the children to make the shakers from clay, either by coiling, forming or on a wheel (with expert help!).

This activity could just as easily focus on teapots and mugs if you find these easier to make.

Challenge the children to make containers with papier mâché.

ASSESSMENT

Use the children's designs to note the imaginative way they approach the task. Note how they plan and go about creating their imaginative salt and pepper shakers.

LEARNING OUTCOMES

The children will learn that containers come in many materials, shapes and sizes and that this depends on the imagination of the designer.

FURTHER ART AND DESIGN CHALLENGES

Totem poles
Challenge the children to work in groups to use boxes and paper folding techniques to make totem poles. They should base their ideas on North American Indian cultures but use their imagination to design their own faces and other images.

Easter Island statues
Encourage the children to use clay to form statues like those found on Easter Island and surrounding South Sea Islands. They should add interest by creating surface textures, and/or adding smaller cut-out shapes of clay to make features.

SPACE MUSIC

SUBJECT: MUSIC. QCA UNIT: 18 JOURNEY INTO SPACE.

LEARNING OBJECTIVE

To use sounds to create an intended effect.

THINKING OBJECTIVE

To generate ideas.

THINKING SKILLS

The children will consider how they can compose a film score for a film set in space.

WHAT YOU NEED

The *Star Wars* theme tune; extracts from the film *Star Wars*; pitched and non-pitched instruments; tape recorders which can reverse the tape and sound; theme tunes from different TV programmes and films.

WHAT TO DO

Play a game with the children identifying different theme tunes to TV programmes and films with which they are familiar. Ask the children to say why they remember these tunes.

Listen to the *Star Wars* theme and talk about the tune and what it is trying to depict. Ask, *Why does it sound triumphal? What is the music trying to portray?* Watch the opening of the first *Star Wars* movie and talk about what is happening. Ask, *How does the film score support the action on screen?* Talk about the air of mystery that has been created and how this has been achieved.

Use a different extract from the same film, for example when Luke Skywalker, Chewbacca, Princess Lea and Han Solo are trapped in the waste disposal unit. Turn the sound off and ask the children to imagine the sounds that could be added to this as they watch. Organise them into groups and challenge them to create different sounds for this extract. They should make a storyboard showing the different frames and then decide on different sounds to accompany each frame. Play the extract through several times for the children to practise their compositions. Ask the groups to perform the compositions and use those that the children like best as a basis for a class-composed film score.

DIFFERENTIATION

Ask more able musicians to incorporate tunes and chords into their film score, to add tension or more relaxed feelings. Ask them to explain what tunes and chords they have used and why, and to think of a way to record their score using graphical or traditional notation. Less able musicians should be encouraged to consider the noises that are likely to be heard as the water splashes around and the walls move inwards. Ask them to create ideas for sound effects rather than a film score.

WHERE NEXT

Extend the children's ideas by thinking about sound textures – they could add pitched tunes and reverse some sounds on a tape recorder. Encourage them to consider the effects of these ideas and whether or not to include them in different parts of the film score.

Challenge the children to generate ideas for the score for a film entitled *Journey Under the Sea*.

ASSESSMENT

Assess the range of ideas the children generate to support the visual effects on screen, from sound effects to pitched tunes and chords. Note which children use pitched tunes and chords to create certain effects, such as tension or more relaxed feelings, and who can explain how and why they did this in musical terms.

LEARNING OUTCOMES

The children will generate ideas for a film score to accompany a piece of film.

FURTHER MUSIC CHALLENGES

Computerised music

Ask the children to use keyboards with headphones or other computer-based programmes to create sound effects and film scores for another extract from *Star Wars*. Set up the equipment in the corner of the classroom, with the TV screen facing away from the rest of the class, and encourage groups to create and record their ideas, change the voices and style to convey their intended effect.

SERMON OF THE DAY

SUBJECT: RE. QCA UNIT: 6C WHY ARE SACRED TEXTS IMPORTANT?

LEARNING OBJECTIVE

To understand how a sacred text is used in worship.

THINKING OBJECTIVE

To generate ideas.

THINKING SKILLS

The children will consider an extract from the Bible and identify what we can learn from this. They will use this learning point as a basis for a sermon or talk to teach worshippers how they should conduct their lives. They will consider how they can set this into a suitable context for younger worshippers.

WHAT YOU NEED

A selection of parables.

WHAT TO DO

Read the parable of the Sower (Matthew 13) and talk about what it means. Ask, *What are the important learning points? What is the real story of this parable? What is its message? What values and beliefs are expected from us as readers? What can we learn from this story?* Talk about how the Bible is a message to Christians from God and gives guidance on the way people should behave. Explain that Christians learn from the stories it tells.

Explain to the children that in a Christian church, the vicar, priest or leader gives a sermon about a particular part of the Bible each week. This is a way of teaching people what the Bible tells us about the way we should behave. It teaches us about Christian values and beliefs and how we should behave towards one another. Gather the children's ideas about how they could deliver a sermon on the parable of the Sower. Ask, *How could you put across the main message about the values and beliefs that the parable teaches us?* Tell the children that they need to refer to the text to do this. Ask, *How could you explain that some people will not always behave properly, but that God will bring them back into the fold? How could you explain that some people will not live or may have difficulties to face in life?* Consider drama, role-play and short sketches to reflect the values and beliefs, and discuss the possible use of pictureboards and artefacts.

Organise the children into groups, ask them to list the values and beliefs conveyed by the extract and to generate ideas for passing this message on to younger children.

DIFFERENTIATION

Different groups could consider different extracts depending on their ability, for example the lower attaining children could consider the Ten Commandments as these explain the morals clearly. Higher attaining children could consider the more difficult concepts covered in the Prodigal Son or the Lost Sheep, and how they could convey the morals in a meaningful way to younger children.

WHERE NEXT

With the children, look at extracts from the Qu'ran and Torah in the same way.

Look at fables and other similar stories and identify the message each one conveys. Ask the children to develop short dramas to act out the message in a way that younger children will understand.

ASSESSMENT

Assess how well the children generate ideas to present the values and beliefs of the stories to younger children.

LEARNING OUTCOMES

The children will learn that the Bible and other sacred texts teach believers of the faith morals, values and beliefs and how to behave. The children will generate ideas of how they can get these messages across to younger children.

FURTHER RE CHALLENGES

Holy messengers

Talk about the people who are messengers from God, such as angels, prophets including Mohammed and Jesus, and religious people the children know. Ask the children to consider what message they would send if they were a messenger from God. Ask, *What would you like to teach people about the way they should live their lives?* Ask them to create their own ideas about this and to think of a way of sending their message so that it would be well received.

What do you make of this?

Give the children a moral dilemma and ask them to say how they would behave. This could be finding a £20 note in the street, deciding not to share something with a friend or not keeping an appointment because they would rather do something else. Ask, *How do you think Jesus or Mohammed would react? How is this different to how you would behave? What does this tell us about the values and beliefs we have learned from the Bible and Qu'ran?* Ask them to think of other moral dilemmas to discuss with the rest of the class.

QUICK CRICKET

SUBJECT: PE. QCA UNIT: STRIKING AND FIELDING GAMES UNIT 2

LEARNING OBJECTIVE

To practise batting and fielding skills in a large group team game.

THINKING OBJECTIVE

To extend ideas.

THINKING SKILLS

The children will practise their batting and fielding skills. They will extend their knowledge of scoring systems of familiar games to create a new game. They will consider how they can prevent a batter from scoring by placing themselves around the field, and how, as batters, they can score more rounders by hitting the ball into a space.

WHAT YOU NEED

Rules for playing quick cricket; a large sheet of paper; equipment for rounders; writing materials.

WHAT TO DO

Before going outside for the games lesson, talk about the rules of quick cricket with the class. Identify why it is called quick and revisit the skills involved in batting, running and fielding. Note the tactics used by both teams and how the runs are scored.

Tell the children that you are going to develop a game of quick rounders by extending the scoring system from quick cricket to create a new game.

Ask the children why they think the game is called 'rounders'. (Because the batters score rounders by running round a pitch.) Identify with the children how the rounders pitch is marked. Note where the batter stands and where the posts are located, in a circle or round.

Organise the children into groups and challenge them to think of a new game. They should consider how to make the game continuous by the batter running around the rounder's pitch until a rounder is scored, whether to have a bowler, what happens if the batter misses the ball, whether they will be out and so on.

Share the group's ideas and agree one way of playing the new game. The following is a suggested model.

Quick rounders: rules

◉ There should be four posts and a hoop to mark the batting position.
◉ The batter hits one, two or three balls in quick succession by throwing the ball up in the air and then batting. (You should decide on the number of balls – see 'Differentiation' below.)
◉ The batter starts to run around the posts.
◉ The fielders must field the balls and send them back by throwing to the person at the hoop.
◉ No one must run with the ball.
◉ The ball(s) should all be inside the hoop before the runner gets to the fourth post.
◉ If the balls are back in the hoop before the runner gets around the pitch no rounder is scored.
◉ The runner can run around as many times as they like until all the balls are back in the hoop. They can therefore score two or three rounders, depending on how far they hit the ball(s) or how long it takes the fielding team to get the ball(s) back.
◉ Each batter has two or three turns.
◉ When the batters have all had two or three turns the teams swap over.

Ask the children why the game is called 'quick' rounders. Explain that like quick cricket the game

is continuous and that when the batter has hit the ball(s) he must try to run a rounder before the ball(s) are back in the hoop.

Agree the scoring system: batters gain a rounder each time they run round the pitch. If they fail to run round the pitch, they do not score. Agree how many times a batter will bat – two or three are usually enough, depending on the number in each team. By not having the batter given out, all children get the opportunity to practise their batting skills.

Talk about the tactics and where the fielders should stand to prevent the batter from hitting the ball too far or into too big a space. Ask, *How many players do you need at the starting point to collect the balls when they are returned by the fielders? How close to the batter should they stand? Why should they not stand too close? How many players should there be in each team?* Develop the children's batting skills by talking about where the batters should send the ball and how they can make sure that the ball will go in this direction.

Go outside and play the game!

DIFFERENTIATION

Let children with poorer batting skills hit three balls, all of which must be returned to the starting point, while good batters should only have one or two.

WHERE NEXT

Develop the game by introducing a bowler.
Use some or all of the children's ideas to extend the game.

ASSESSMENT

Note how well the children extend the ideas from the quick cricket game to develop a game of their own.

LEARNING OUTCOMES

The children will extend the ideas of the traditional quick cricket game to create another game.

FURTHER PE CHALLENGES

Pass the ball

Challenge the children to extend the game by using one ball which must be passed from post to post to reach the final post before the running batter. This will extend the game into the full traditional game of rounders.

Team sports' skills

Plan a sports competition which includes a range of team games covering a variety of skills: throwing, target, running, jumping and ball skills. Teams should take part in each activity. Find ways of scoring the games so that you get a winning team at the end.

EVALUATION SKILLS

INTRODUCTION

The ability to evaluate gives the children a useful insight into their own learning and helps them to identify what they need to do next to improve still further. This is a key skill within the National Curriculum and one that is often developed well when the children have performed or made something, but not practised extensively in other aspects of learning. Many teachers already encourage children to say what went well, or what was good about something they have done. However, although the children can say what went well, often they are not given the opportunity to say what it was that made it good. Encouraging this kind of evaluation can help develop the children's ability to make suggestions for improvement.

The activities in this chapter focus on the children considering carefully what they are doing and what they have done and identifying for themselves where they need to improve. There are examples of how these skills can be developed and can be adapted to suit other contexts equally well. For example, the activity in which the children evaluate the usefulness of historical sources is equally valid for other research projects and leads to children questioning what they are reading, seeing and hearing. The skill of evaluating the usefulness of information for its purpose is the starting point for identifying which information to collect and which to reject in any research project. This type of activity will help the children to think independently about why the information they are analysing is important to the task. The importance of the activity 'Symmetrical movements in the gym' is in the children's planning of apparatus to perform their sequences, deciding for themselves which pieces will be useful for the task and which will not. This will help children develop

the necessary skills of organising and supporting their own learning needs independently and help them develop initiative. The skills are:
- evaluating information – judging value, usefulness and quality
- suggesting improvements
- developing criteria for judging.

INTRODUCING EVALUATION SKILLS

Subject and QCA unit, NLS or NNS objective	Activity title	Thinking objective	Activity	Page
English NLS objective: To evaluate a range of instructional texts in terms of their purposes, organisation and layout, clarity and usefulness	Getting it together	To evaluate information (judging usefulness and quality)	Reading instructions to put together a shelving unit	109
Maths NNS objective: To solve problems about real life	Finding the answer	To evaluate information and to judge the value of information	Judging whether information given will allow them to find the solution to a word problem	109
Science QCA unit: 5D Changing state	Presenting scientists	To evaluate information and to judge the value of presentation	Evaluating the way an investigation is presented to enable them to interpret information quickly	110
History QCA unit: 16 How can we find out about the Indus Valley civilisation?	A useful source	To evaluate information (judging usefulness)	Judging the value of different historical sources in terms of answering research questions	111
Geography QCA unit: 12 should the high street be closed to traffic?	Traffic calming	To evaluate information and to judge the value of information	Judging the value of information gained from a traffic survey	111
Design and technology QCA unit: 5A Musical instruments	Shake, rattle and roll	To develop criteria for judging quality and to suggest improvements	Considering and making improvements to the quality of sound produced on home-made instruments	112
ICT QCA unit: 5C Evaluating information, checking accuracy and questioning plausibility	What's up?	To judge the usefulness of information and to suggest improvements	Finding errors in a database	113
Art and design QCA unit: 6A People in action	Dancing figures	To evaluate information (judging quality)	Evaluating how artists create the impression of movement in their work	113
Music QCA unit: 19 Songwriter	Fur trade	To evaluate information (judging quality)	Judging how well the lyrics of a song build to depict a moral discussion and debate	114
RE QCA unit: 5B How do Muslims express their beliefs through practices?	The five pillars of Islam	To judge the usefulness of different sources of evidence	Looking at a range of reference materials and evaluating their usefulness in terms of clarity of information and presentation, and how well each one explains the purpose and meaning of the five pillars to Muslims	115
PE QCA unit: Athletic activities unit 3	Relay race	To develop criteria for judging the quality of baton-passing techniques and suggest improvements	Suggesting how a partner can improve their running, jumping or throwing techniques	116

GETTING IT TOGETHER

SUBJECT: ENGLISH. NLS OBJECTIVE: TO EVALUATE A RANGE OF INSTRUCTIONAL TEXTS IN TERMS OF THEIR PURPOSES, ORGANISATION AND LAYOUT, CLARITY AND USEFULNESS.

LEARNING OBJECTIVE
To learn to read and follow a sequence of instructions accurately, note its structure and any weaknesses in its clarity, organisation and layout.

THINKING OBJECTIVE
To evaluate information (judging usefulness and quality).

THINKING SKILLS
The children will look at the components in a shelving unit and follow the diagrams and texts to put it together. They will note the content of the instructions and evaluate the usefulness of the diagrams and written instructions. They will evaluate the layout and organisation of the information and decide whether they could make these clearer to help another group put the unit together more efficiently.

WHAT YOU NEED
A shelving unit with the tools to put it together; the accompanying instructional leaflet which includes diagrams and written text (enough photocopies for the children to have one each).

WHAT TO DO
In small groups in turn, possibly as a focused activity in the literacy lesson, look at the components of the shelving unit and the picture of the finished product. Ask the children, *How will you put these shelves together?* Produce the instructional leaflet and talk about its features and the way the information is organised. Ask, *Can you see straightaway what you need to do first? How do you know? Is the first instruction numbered? What about the next instruction? Are other devices such as bullet points or organisational language used? What other helpful information is included on the leaflet? What about the diagrams? Do they help or would written instructions be better? Why is this?*

Help the group to put the shelving unit together, encouraging them to note any difficulties they may have due to lack of clarity in the instructions. Prompt the children to talk about about any improvements they could make to the instructions as they work. When they have finished, ask them to decide whether they have put the unit together correctly. Ask, *Have*

all the pieces been used? Are there any screws left over?

When everyone has had a turn to make the shelves, ask the children to work individually or in pairs to edit the leaflet to make it more useful. They may decide to change the layout or to make the steps clearer depending on their evaluation. Give the original leaflet a mark out of ten to evaluate its overall usefulness and compare this with the usefulness of the children's revised version.

You may wish to use different instructional texts for different groups to evaluate. They can then share their opinions with the rest of the class during an end-of-the-week plenary. The children can evaluate each other's improved leaflets and say why they are better than the original.

FINDING THE ANSWER

SUBJECT: MATHS. NNS OBJECTIVE: TO SOLVE PROBLEMS ABOUT REAL LIFE.

LEARNING OBJECTIVE
To learn the steps needed to solve real-life problems involving measures, money and all four operations.

THINKING OBJECTIVE
To evaluate information and to judge the value of information.

THINKING SKILLS
The children will consider the information given in a number of word problems and judge whether there is enough detail to allow them to solve the problem.

WHAT YOU NEED
A set of word problems for the children to evaluate (make the problems easy or difficult to match the differing abilities of the children. The examples below include a problem for each level of problem solving and involve everyday situations, money, time and numeracy. The units have been kept simple so that you can concentrate on the evaluation rather than the computation); writing materials.

WHAT TO DO
Explain to the children that you want them to judge the value of information given in word problems and whether this is enough for them to solve the problem. Do the following example together first:
⊙ A family of two parents and two children decide go to a theme park. The tickets cost £10 each for adults. How much will the entrance fee cost altogether?

Remind the children of the process. Ask,

What do we already know? The number of people going, the price of the adult ticket.
What do we need to find out? The total cost.
How are we going to do this? Will we add, subtract, multiply and/or divide?

Remind the children that the clue is in the vocabulary and in this example the 'altogether' is the key. Discuss with the class how they could add the price of each ticket together, or multiply and then add. Now, either try to solve the problem and find the answer together, thus finding out that some crucial information is missing about the price of the children's ticket. Or you could ask the children to evaluate the information, checking to see if there is anything missing. Ask, *Which piece of information is missing?*

Tell the children that the child's entrance is half the adult's ticket price. Ask, *Can you solve the problem now?* Work out the steps for solving the problem and find the answer together. Some children may be able to do the sum quickly in their heads.

Repeat this process for the next problem:
⊙ A train gets into London at 4.10pm. The journey takes 180 minutes. At what time does it leave? What does the journey cost for one adult and two children? And this one:
⊙ A swimming pool has a maximum capacity of 70 people. How many more people can swim before the pool is full?

Organise the children into groups and provide each group with a sheet of problems. Match these to the ability groups by giving the lower attaining pupils one-step problems, and the higher attaining pupils three-step problems to solve. Adapt some that you use in problem-solving lessons by removing some of the necessary information. Challenge the children to evaluate the problems and to say whether all the information is available to enable them to solve the problem. Challenge them to say which bit is missing, and provide them with the original versions to check. Sit with the higher attaining pupils to discuss their strategies and, while you check the remaining groups' work during the plenary, challenge them to write problems for each other to evaluate.

PRESENTING SCIENTISTS

SUBJECT: SCIENCE. QCA UNIT: 5D CHANGING STATE.

LEARNING OBJECTIVE
To interpret information from graphs, tables and charts and use this to make improvements to an investigation.

THINKING OBJECTIVE
To evaluate information and to judge the value of presentation.

THINKING SKILLS
The children will judge the value of recording temperature differences as line graphs instead of bar charts.

WHAT YOU NEED
IT temperature sensors; boiling water in a suitable container (keep the boiling water well away from the children at all times).

WHAT TO DO
Explain to the children that you want to find out how quickly water cools after it has been boiled, and whether it cools faster or slower once it has reached a particular temperature. Ask, *How could you investigate this question?*

Agree, if the children suggest this, that one way is to boil water and to take the temperature at regular intervals to note how much it has cooled each time. By finding the difference between how much the temperature drops each time, we can find out whether the water has cooled by the same, less or greater amount.

Carry out the investigation with the children, recording the temperature after every four minutes. Put the information into a computer graphing program after each reading.

After about an hour, display the information as a bar chart. Note how well the information allows you to find the interval of cooling after each reading. With the class, note whether there is a pattern to the rate of cooling which allows them to predict what the next reading will be. Ask, *Can you make a fairly accurate prediction? Can you suggest a range within which the next reading is likely to fall? Can you tell from the way this information is displayed what the temperature would have been after two minutes, one minute or three minutes?*

Show the children how they can display the information as a line graph, which shows the gradual fall rather than the precise readings every four minutes. By noting the halfway point between the two readings the children can predict the likely temperature of the water after two minutes rather than four. Ask, *Is this way of displaying the information more useful than the bar graph?* Repeat the process with pie charts and agree that this is not a suitable way at all of displaying this type of information as it makes interpretation impossible. Agree that the bar chart is useful for working out the interval of cooling between each reading, and that the line graph is valuable for showing the likely temperature at intervals between the readings and is a good way of displaying constantly changing readings or measurements.

A USEFUL SOURCE

SUBJECT: HISTORY. QCA UNIT: 16 HOW CAN WE FIND OUT ABOUT THE INDUS VALLEY CIVILISATION?

LEARNING OBJECTIVE
To learn factual information about the Indus Valley civilisation.

THINKING OBJECTIVE
To evaluate information (judging usefulness).

THINKING SKILLS
The children will evaluate sources of evidence and judge which is most useful with regard to their list of research questions. They will use the evaluation to produce a quick reference guide to help others locate the information when carrying out similar research.

WHAT YOU NEED
A range of historical sources which will provide answers to the children's questions; large sheets of paper; writing materials.

WHAT TO DO
Carry out this activity at the end of the unit of work when the children have some factual knowledge of the Indus Valley civilisation.

Tell the children that you want them to provide a list of useful sources of evidence which the next class can use to help them find out about different aspects of the Indus Valley civilisation.

Start by asking the children what they found most interesting about the topic. Ask, *What do you think the next class will find interesting? Will it be the same as you or could it be different?* Brainstorm a list of questions that the next class may want to ask about the Indus Valley civilisation. Keep these simple and general to begin with before focusing more closely on the way the people lived, what they ate and wore, and the jobs they did. Suggestions include: *Where was the Indus Valley civilisation? How, when and by whom was it discovered? When did it exist? What evidence of the past is available today? What did the people look like? What did they wear? What did they eat? How did they cook? What did they use? How did they write? What language did they speak?* Organise the children into groups to identify as many enquiry questions as they can.

Then, share the questions as a class, and note how many the children have thought of in total. Then ask them to identify and note by the side of each question the most useful source of evidence to provide an answer to the question. Evaluate the range of sources of evidence together. Ask, *Can some questions be answered by more than one source? Is one source more useful than another because it answers lots of questions?*

Ask, *How could you organise the information so that it would be readily available and easy to use?* Encourage them to think about creating a quick reference guide to enable the next class to locate what they are looking for quickly. They could do this by listing the questions or aspect headings and identifying all the sources of evidence to help find the answer, or by listing the sources of evidence and listing by the side all the aspects and questions it provides information on. Let the children decide which way they want to present this guide.

TRAFFIC CALMING

SUBJECT: GEOGRAPHY. QCA UNIT: 12 SHOULD THE HIGH STREET BE CLOSED TO TRAFFIC?

LEARNING OBJECTIVE
To undertake fieldwork.

THINKING OBJECTIVE
To evaluate information and to judge the value of information.

THINKING SKILLS

The children will carry out a traffic survey at a certain time if the day and evaluate whether the information is valuable enough to inform a decision about whether traffic-calming measures should be carried out in the area. They will then improve on their collection of evidence by carrying out surveys at different times of the day to inform a decision about which is the best traffic-calming method. The children will also develop their enquiry skills of defining a problem and planning research, and reasoning skills of making judgements and decisions.

WHAT YOU NEED

Clipboards; sheets of paper; writing materials.

WHAT TO DO

Ask the children to describe how difficult it is for them to cross the road at a local spot, which is well known for being difficult to cross. This could be outside the school, a local supermarket or in the local high street.

Ask, *What measures could be taken to slow down or eliminate the traffic?* Collect their ideas. Ask, *How could you convince the local councillors to consider your ideas? What do you need to do first? Do you need evidence to back up your argument?*

Discuss the idea of carrying out a survey of the amount of traffic which passes the spot. Talk to the children about how they would conduct the survey and the range of information they wish to collect, bearing in mind it needs to be a comprehensive but uncomplicated survey. Show them how to organise a tally chart into three sections, one for cars, one for delivery vehicles and one for lorries. If the children suggest at this point that they should investigate different times of the day because the results may be different, follow their lead. Organise supervised groups to visit the chosen spot and, over about twenty minutes, to collect the number and range of vehicles that go past. The children should also record the start and finish time of their survey.

Back in the classroom, evaluate the value of the information. Ask the children, *What does your survey tell you about the traffic?* Encourage the children to answer this question in precise terms such as, 'There are more delivery vans than cars between 11am and 11.20am.' Go on to discuss what the information does not tell you, such as, *Do lorries use this particular stretch of road at certain times of the day?* List these queries and next to each one write down the children's suggestions for how they could find out the answer (linking enquiry skills of defining the problem and planning research).

Help the children to use the information given by the surveys to decide on the best method of traffic calming, the one they could suggest to the local council. Discuss how they could present their persuasive argument in a literacy session, and how they could present the information in an ICT session.

SHAKE, RATTLE AND ROLL

SUBJECT: DESIGN AND TECHNOLOGY. QCA UNIT: 5A
MUSICAL INSTRUMENTS.

LEARNING OBJECTIVE

To note how the quality of sound of a musical instrument can be improved by adapting the design features or changing the materials used.

THINKING OBJECTIVE

To develop criteria for judging quality and to suggest improvements.

THINKING SKILLS

The children will play their musical instruments to a partner, discuss the level of quality of the sound produced and why the level of sound quality is as it is, and suggest improvements to the design feature or changes to the amount and types of materials that have been combined or used.

WHAT YOU NEED

The children's home-made musical instruments completed in earlier DT lessons; an instrument you have made; a large sheet of paper; writing materials.

WHAT TO DO

Look at the instrument that you have made earlier. Describe its design features and ask the children to say how the sound can be produced. Play the instrument in the way they suggest. Ask the children, *What do you think of the sound? Can you describe its quality? Does it have a strong tone? Does it sound tinny? Is the sound full or empty, open or closed? Why does it sound like this? Is it because of the way it has been made? Is the sound box large enough? Are the materials suitable? What materials would produce a better sound quality?* Once the children have identified the reasons for the quality of the sound production, list these and by the side of each one note their suggestions about how these features could be changed or adapted to improve the sound quality.

Organise the children into pairs. Explain that you want them to evaluate the quality of each other's instruments in terms of the quality of sound produced. Challenge them to identify what makes the instrument sound the way it does. Once they have done this, they will be able to suggest improvements to these components, material choices or combinations to improve the quality of the sound. In a later lesson, try out the suggestions to see if they work.

What's up?

SUBJECT: ICT. QCA UNIT: 5C EVALUATING INFORMATION, CHECKING ACCURACY AND QUESTIONING PLAUSIBILITY.

LEARNING OBJECTIVE
To identify and correct implausible and inaccurate data.

THINKING OBJECTIVE
To judge the usefulness of information and to suggest improvements.

THINKING SKILLS
The children will look at a database and note the information it contains. They will identify a series of questions to interrogate the database in order to find answers. They will identify why some of these questions are not answered correctly. They will judge the overall usefulness of the database, before identifying that there are too many errors for it to be reliable. They will then suggest ways to improve the reliability.

WHAT YOU NEED
Database software with a database containing information about a range of breads, linked to Design and technology unit: 5B Bread. Use fields including name, country of origin, preparation time and cost.

WHAT TO DO
Set up a database containing information on breads from around the world using the fields above. Decide in which field you will make obvious mistakes so that when the children search for particular information it will be clear that some information is incorrect. For example, include a spelling mistake to make the database unreliable or the information implausible. You could enter an incorrect cost for foccacia bread so that when you display the information as a graph, the cost of foccacia is hugely more expensive than the other breads and the mistake is obvious to the children!

Gather the children around the computer screen or use an interactive whiteboard and enter some more breads into the database together to remind them how it works. Note the fields and ask the children to suggest what information the database will display, for example a graph of the time it takes to prepare different recipes, the breads which cost less than a certain amount of money and so on.

Brainstorm a list of possible searches with the children. Show them how to interrogate the database by asking it to display graphs showing different information, or a more complex search to find a specific type of bread. Tell the children that there are some mistakes in the database and that, through their searches, you want them to find as many of these as they can.

After 20 minutes or so, ask the children to share the mistakes they have found. Ask, *What kind of mistakes are they? Can some of them be put right, for example the spelling mistakes and amounts? Are there some mistakes which are so wildly wrong that it is easier to re-enter the information?*

Decide whether the database is reliable or not, and if not why not. Note how useful the database format is for finding certain pieces of information but only if the information is entered into the database correctly.

Evaluate the databases that are used in everyday life and hypothesise what could go wrong if the wrong information was entered.

Dancing figures

SUBJECT: ART AND DESIGN. QCA UNIT: 6A PEOPLE IN ACTION.

LEARNING OBJECTIVE
To identify how artists create movement in photographs, paintings, statues and figurines.

THINKING OBJECTIVE
To evaluate information (judging quality).

THINKING SKILLS
The children will look at a range of different paintings in different genres and evaluate the quality

of each in terms of how successfully the artist has depicted movement. They will consider the range of art elements and techniques used, and evaluate how the artist achieves the finished effect.

WHAT YOU NEED

Pictures of classical figures (preferably those in mid-movement), paintings showing people moving, such as Fernard Léger's *Les Constructeurs*, Georges Seurat's *Le Chahut*, Pablo Picasso's *The Three Dancers*, suitable examples of the work of Umberto Boccioni, and any LS Lowry crowd scene; photographs of people moving from magazines and newspaper; the children's work in PE and games lessons; paper; pencils.

WHAT TO DO

As a class, look at the pictures and photographs and discuss what the people depicted are doing. Look at the position of the bodies and limbs and agree how these depict movement clearly. They look as though they are moving because the pictures mirror the actions we do when we are running, walking and moving in other ways. Relate this to the work of classical artists and how they made their figures look as realistic as possible by drawing or sculpting precisely the positions of the limbs and body.

Look at *The Three Dancers* by Picasso and encourage the children to identify the artistic elements and techniques that have been used to create the idea of movement. Prompt them to evaluate how well Picasso has created the idea of movement despite the angular features in the painting. Help them to evaluate the overall quality of the painting in these terms. Ask the children to think of all the adjectives which describe the movement of the dancers. Next, look at paintings by other artists in your collection, noting how Bocciano blurs the edges of his figures to depict the movement, Seurat uses flowing lines and colour, and how Lowry creates the effect by using one main colour and lots of people looking purposeful in his paintings.

Provide the children, in pairs or threes, with a photograph or painting and ask them to think of all the adjectives which describe the quality of the painting in terms of how well it creates the idea of movement. Ask them to sketch a similar scene in the style of one of the other artists, using the range of techniques discussed to create the idea of movement. Prompt the children to collect further pictures, photographs and figures which show different ways of depicting movement.

FUR TRADE

SUBJECT: MUSIC. QCA UNIT: 19 SONGWRITER.

LEARNING OBJECTIVE

To consider how words and music create moods and feelings and portray moral themes.

THINKING OBJECTIVE

To evaluate information (judging quality).

THINKING SKILLS

The children will learn a song describing how animals are bred in captivity for their fur. They will think about how the composer conveys this message by evaluating the way words and music have been used to create certain effects, moods and feelings.

WHAT YOU NEED

A copy of 'Do You Know the Fox?' by Sandra Kerr (from *Birds and Beasts*, A&C Black); a copy of the lyrics and the music to display.

WHAT TO DO

As a class, learn the first verse of the song, making sure the children sing the last tied note at the correct pitch.

Discuss the words and consider what the song may be about. Ask the children, *How is the fox feeling? How does the composer make this obvious in the words?* Display the words for the children to see and highlight those that depict the way the fox is feeling.

Display the tune for the children to see. Discuss how it rises and falls with certain words, for example how the tune falls *With her tail drooping down and a price on her head*. Think about how the last note keeps the singer and listener hanging on. Talk about how the children wanted to sing this last note. Ask, *Why did you want to go down one more note? Which note would this be?* Show the children how, if they had continued down one more note, they would have ended on the same note as the first one thus 'finishing off' the song. Ask, *Why did the composer not wish to create this finishing-off effect? What kind of mood does the song create by ending on a hanging note?*

Help the class to learn the second and subsequent verses. Discuss how the words change in the last verse and the mood these depict. Highlight the words which reveal how the fox is feeling in this verse. Talk about how the coda gives the song a finishing-off effect and therefore depicts the mood of freedom. If the children are sufficiently mature, discuss the farming of animals for the fur trade and consider the morals associated with this type of farming. Fox hunting may or may not be a suitable topic to debate with the class.

Link the lesson to the consideration of other fur trade animals, asking the children to write new words to depict this, to fit the same tune. Evaluate how well the words depict the feelings of the animals in the verse.

THE FIVE PILLARS OF ISLAM

SUBJECT: RE. QCA UNIT: 5B HOW DO MUSLIMS EXPRESS THEIR BELIEFS THROUGH PRACTICES?

LEARNING OBJECTIVE
To learn facts about the five pillars of Islam.

THINKING OBJECTIVE
To judge the usefulness of different sources of evidence.

THINKING SKILLS
The children will work as a class to evaluate which sources of evidence are most useful for finding out about the first pillar of Islam, Shahadah, before working in groups to evaluate the sources for finding out about the other four pillars. They will look at a range of sources of evidence and decide which is

the most useful to them, both in terms of the facts given, and the way the information is presented to enable speedy recovery of facts. They will also consider how well the source provides information about the meaning and purpose of each of the five pillars. By the end of the lesson, they will have identified which sources are most useful overall, and which are more useful for some pillars and not for others, and why.

WHAT YOU NEED
A range of evidence sources including a written first-hand account from a Muslim visitor, reference books, the internet and CD-ROMs.

WHAT TO DO
Tell the children about the five pillars of Islam, what they are and why Muslims follow them. Explain to the children that you want them to work in groups to find out as much as they can about each of the pillars.

Choose Shahadah, the first pillar, and evaluate the resources available together as a class. Ask the children, *How easy is it to find out whether the resource contains information on Shahadah?* Prompt them to look at an enlarged version of the account from your Muslim visitor and to scan it for the word Shahadah. When they have located it, ask them to quickly identify how useful the account is. Ask, *Is Shahadah explained clearly? Does it explain the importance to Muslims and why they declare their faith so openly?* Look for similar references to Shahadah in other sources. Ask the children, *Is Shahadah located in the index so that you can locate it quickly? If not, could it be included under another title, such as 'The Five Pillars of Islam'?* Demonstrate how to look for these references in the contents and index pages.

Using the computer, show the class how to search for Shahadah on the internet and on any CD-ROMs you have. (Make sure you have identified suitable websites first.) When you have located references to Shahadah decide, with the children, which is the most useful source of evidence and why. Agree that this is probably the practicing Moslem's account. Ask, *Why this was the most useful piece of evidence? How it could be made even more useful?* Agree that it would probably be better to invite a Muslim into school so that the questions can be asked directly.

Organise the children into four groups to evaluate the sources for the other four pillars of Islam, Salah, Zakah, Saum and Hajj. They should decide first of all how to organise their group – who within the group will focus on which pieces of evidence. They should evaluate the different sources of evidence, considering the questions: *How quickly can we locate* material about our particular pillar? How clearly is the information presented? How useful it the source in giving facts? How well does it present information about the purpose and meaning of each pillar? When they have finished, share the information found as a class, and discuss which is the most useful piece of evidence for each pillar. Ask, *Is there one source which is more useful than the others? Is there one source which is useful for finding out about one pillar but not another?* List the five pillars of Islam and note next to each one the most useful sources of evidence for researching the facts.

When the children have a list of useful evidence sources, they can then begin their research, finding the materials they have identified as the most useful.

RELAY RACE

SUBJECT: PE. QCA UNIT: ATHLETIC ACTIVITIES UNIT 3.

LEARNING OBJECTIVE
To describe and evaluate the effectiveness of performances in running relay races.

THINKING OBJECTIVE
To develop criteria for judging the quality of baton-passing techniques and suggest improvements.

THINKING SKILLS
The children will work in groups of four to evaluate each other's running and baton passing techniques, and use the information to suggest how these can be improved. They will consider the position of the body at the start, the follow-through and the finishing position in their observations and evaluation. They will start by describing what they see before considering how the way the action is performed impacts upon the quality of outcome in terms of the speed in which the distance is covered.

WHAT YOU NEED
A baton and a stopwatch for each group of four; writing materials; a TV extract of a relay race. Carry out a risk assessment for this activity and ensure the children follow rules of where to observe from, when and where to start.

WHAT TO DO
Show the children a video of a relay race where the baton has been passed successfully from person to person. Explain that many relay teams are disqualified because they drop the baton or do not pass it over in the designated area. Watch the video again, this time showing the pass-over in slow motion. Stop it at the right time and describe what is happening. Ask the children, *In what position is the receiver? When does he/she start to run? How quickly?* Move the film forward frame by frame, encouraging the children to watch and describe what the two people are doing. Ask, *What has the receiver done with the baton? In which hand is it? How is he/she holding it? In what position does the giver finish? How quickly, and when, do they start to stop?*

Explain to the children that they are going to practise the same skills and techniques in pairs outside. One pair in each group of four will observe the other pair, describing what they do and noting how they can improve their techniques. They will measure the improvement by timing whether they have improved the speed of covering the relay distance.

Go outside and, after a suitable warm-up, run a relay race with the children in groups of four. Allow time for the groups of four to work as two pairs, each observing the other and suggesting improvements to the running and passing techniques and skills.

The purpose of this activity is not to find a winning team but to note the time for each team's first run so that a comparison can be made with the second run. The winning team will be the one who improves on their first time the most. This way, slower runners have an equal chance of 'winning' and you can organise them into friendship, ability or mixed ability groups as you wish.

Run the relay race a second time and compare the times of the two teams. Ask, *Who has improved the most?*

EXTENDING EVALUATION SKILLS

Subject and QCA unit, NLS or NNS objective	Activity title	Thinking objective	Activity	Page
English NLS objectives: To compare and evaluate a novel or play in print and the film/tv version; to investigate different versions of the same story in print or on film, identifying similarities and differences, recognise how stories change over time and differences of culture and place that are expressed in stories; to evaluate a range of texts, in print and other media, for persuasiveness, clarity and quality of information	Harry on the big screen	To evaluate information (judging quality)	Comparing film and written versions of the same story	118
Maths NNS objective: To solve a problem by representing, extracting and interpreting data in tables, graphs and charts	Tables and graphs	To evaluate information (judging usefulness)	Judging the clarity of how information is presented by how easy it is to extract information	119
Science QCA unit: 6C More about dissolving	How much sugar will it hold?	To evaluate whether a test plan is fair and reliable for finding out solubility of some solids, and if not what needs changing to make it fair and reliable	Evaluating whether a test plan is fair and reliable, and if not what needs to be done to make it fair and reliable	120
History QCA unit: 20 What can we learn about recent history from studying the life of a famous person?	Beatlemania	To evaluate information and to judge the value of information	Judging the reliability of a range of sources of evidence and the value of the information each one contains	122
Geography QCA unit: 14 Investigating rivers	River uses	To evaluate information (judging usefulness)	Evaluating the importance of rivers to humans	123
Design and technology QCA unit: 5D Biscuits	Charity biscuits	To evaluate information (judging quality) and to suggest improvements	Judging the quality of a biscuit recipe for taste and suggesting ways to improve the texture and taste	124
ICT QCA unit: 6A Multimedia presentation	What's happening?	To evaluate information (judging quality) and to suggest improvements	Writing a newsletter or report, making sure that the important information is immediately conveyed to the reader	126
Art and design QCA unit: 6B What a performance	Dressing it right	To evaluate information (judging quality) and to suggest improvements	Evaluating costumes and suggest improvements for suitable costumes for an end-of-year show	127
Music QCA unit: 20 Stars, hide your fires	Singing to an audience	To evaluate information (judging value) and to suggest improvements	Evaluating how structure improves the quality of performance	128
RE QCA unit: 6F How do people express their faith through the arts?	Every picture tells a story	To evaluate information and to judge the value of information	Evaluating interpretations of the same event, and noting that different interpretations convey the same feelings and moods to the observer	129
PE QCA unit: Gymnastics activities unit 5	Symmetrical movements	To evaluate information and to judge the value of information	Judging the value of different pieces and ways of organising apparatus to support symmetrical sequences	130

HARRY ON THE BIG SCREEN

SUBJECT: ENGLISH. NLS OBJECTIVES: TO COMPARE AND
EVALUATE A NOVEL OR PLAY IN PRINT AND THE FILM/TV
VERSION; TO INVESTIGATE DIFFERENT VERSIONS OF THE SAME
STORY IN PRINT OR ON FILM, IDENTIFYING SIMILARITIES
AND DIFFERENCES, RECOGNISE HOW STORIES CHANGE OVER
TIME AND DIFFERENCES OF CULTURE AND PLACE THAT ARE
EXPRESSED IN STORIES; TO EVALUATE A RANGE OF TEXTS, IN
PRINT AND OTHER MEDIA, FOR PERSUASIVENESS, CLARITY
AND QUALITY OF INFORMATION.

LEARNING OBJECTIVE

To learn that the chara cters, culture and places in
stories often change when film or TV versions are
made.

THINKING OBJECTIVE

To evaluate information (judging
quality).

THINKING SKILLS

The children will listen to a
story read over a number of
weeks and think about the
characters, setting and
plot. They will watch the
same story as portrayed
through a film or TV
series and evaluate the
quality in terms of
how well the film- or
programme-makers reflect
the author's intended
mood, feelings, suspense
and excitement. They will
evaluate whether the written
text is a better representation
of these factors or whether the
film version is more successful and
why.

WHAT YOU NEED

A film/TV version of a children's story (for example:
The Borrowers, any *Harry Potter* film, *The Sheep Pig*,
Charlotte's Web or *The Jungle Book*); A3 sheets of
paper; writing materials.

WHAT TO DO

Read your chosen story over a number of days or
weeks to make sure the children are familiar with
the characters and events. As they listen, ask them
to imagine what they think the characters look like.
If possible, allow time for the class to draw or paint
pictures of these. Talk about how the events make

them feel. Ask, *How does the author convey the moods
and feelings, the suspense and excitement?* Working
in groups, ask the children to list the characters,
settings and events that appear in the written text
on one side of an A3 sheet of paper divided into
three rows.

Over a few days, watch the film together and, as
they watch, ask the groups to tick the features that
are the same in both the book and the film and to
note in the relevant box on the right-hand side of the
paper the differences between the film version and
the written text.

Share the children's observations after you have
seen the film. Note together all the things that are
the same, all the things that are portrayed differently
and all the things that have been omitted.

Together, evaluate how well the film or TV
version represents the author's
intention. Ask, *Did the film/TV
version paint the same
picture as the one you
imagined when you
first listened to the
story? Did the
characters look
as you imagined
them to be?
How were they
different? Did
the events take
place in the
same way as
you imagined
them when you
listened to the
story? How well
did the film- or
programme-makers
convey the suspense
and excitement? Was the
story more exciting and the
suspense greater in the book or
film/TV version? Why? What about the
feelings and mood? Who expressed these best?
Why? Ask the children to express a preference for
the written or film/TV version. Ask, Why do you have
this view?* Ask the children to say whether they
prefer to read a book before watching the film or TV
programme or vice versa.

DIFFERENTIATION

Higher attaining children should be challenged
to note the accuracy of the finer details, such as
the dialogue, rules of any competitions, character
descriptions, colour and design of places, props and

costumes and to evaluate how well the film version reflects this.

WHERE NEXT
Repeat the activity in reverse and watch a film version of another story before reading the book to the class. Ask the children, *Have you changed your opinion about whether you would watch the film first or read the book? Why or why not?*

ASSESSMENT
Note those children who can evaluate the quality of the film and written versions by spotting the similarities and differences of character, setting and plot, and how well the author's intention has been reflected, whether it has been improved and if so how.

LEARNING OUTCOME
The children will learn to evaluate the quality of a film production of a story they know by comparing the characters, settings and plot. They will decide which one they like best and why, based on how well the film-makers reflect the author's intended mood, feelings, suspense and excitement.

FURTHER ENGLISH CHALLENGES
Film drama
Read a short story extract or poem and challenge the children to write a film script for this. Invite them to act it out and to make a video recording for the rest of the class to watch. Compare the different ways that the different groups have interpreted the story and evaluate together how well this has been done. Discuss how well the mood and feelings have been captured with regard to the author's intention, and whether the characters have been reflected as intended or exaggerated. Evaluate the quality of the drama in terms of whether it accurately reflects the written text. A suitable example to use for this challenge is the Witches' scene from *Macbeth*.
Sports magic
Prompt the children to read different newspaper accounts of the same football fixture and to note the facts and opinions that the reporter includes. Then watch a TV recording of the same match and ask the children to note the similarities and differences. Encourage them to evaluate the quality of the written accounts in terms of how accurately they reflected the suspense and excitement of the match. Ask, *Which of the two versions conveyed this the best? What about the factual information? Which medium most successfully conveyed the range of facts about the match? Why do you think the two versions were successful in part?*

TABLES AND GRAPHS
SUBJECT: MATHS. NNS OBJECTIVE: TO SOLVE A PROBLEM BY REPRESENTING, EXTRACTING AND INTERPRETING DATA IN TABLES, GRAPHS AND CHARTS.

LEARNING OBJECTIVE
To interpret information on different types of graphs.

THINKING OBJECTIVE
To evaluate information (judging usefulness).

THINKING SKILLS
The children will look at bar charts, tables, line graphs and pie charts and decide which is the most useful way to present different types of information to enable them to find the answers to their questions quickly.

WHAT YOU NEED
One month's weather statistics recorded by the class in a graphing package. The data should include the daily rainfall, the temperature taken at different times of the day, the number of sunny days in the month and wind direction.

WHAT TO DO
Ask the children to recall the range of weather statistics that have been entered into the graphing package. Ask, *What was the purpose of this exercise? What information do we want to gain from it? How useful is the information to people putting together a holiday brochure, for instance, when trying to attract visitors to the area?*

With the children, brainstorm a set of questions to ask the program, for example, *What percentage of sunny days was there? What was the average temperature at 2.00pm? 12 noon? 3.00pm? What was the average daily rainfall?*
Look at the first question together and display the information first as a frequency chart, noting the answer to the first question. Display the information as a line graph, pie chart and table. Ask, *How easy was it to find the answer when displayed as a frequency chart? What about the other ways of presentation? In which way was it impossible to find the answer?*

Repeat the process for the other questions above, identifying the most useful presentation for finding the answer to the questions. Ask pairs to decide which is the most useful presentation format for finding the answer quickly to each of the other questions. Remind them that the purpose of the exercise is not to find the answer, although it will be an added bonus, but to find the most useful way to find the answer quickly.

THINKING SKILLS: AGES 9–11

During the plenary, make some generalisations from the activity, for example line graphs are the most useful presentation when measuring constant changes, such as temperature and distance; frequency graphs are most useful for presenting data about the number of times something occurs; tables are useful for pinpointing specific data on particular days or times; pie charts are useful for finding proportion or percentages.

DIFFERENTIATION

Ask higher attaining children to predict which they think is the most useful way of presenting data to answer each of the questions and to give reasons for their hypotheses, before checking out if they were right. Ask less able children direct questions such as, *Does the graph show a percentage, a number or a measurement?* Begin to draw their attention to the generalisations: if they want a measurement they need a line graph, if they want to know how many times something happens they need a frequency chart and so on.

WHERE NEXT

Provide opportunities for the children to practise these evaluation skills when handling information in other lessons and activities.

As a homework activity, ask the children to look for and collect examples of when these presentation formats are used in everyday life, for example information about performance or spending of the local council services.

ASSESSMENT

Monitor the children as they work and make a note of those who clearly recognise which is the most useful format to answer specific questions. Make a particular note of those who start to make generalisations and are able to predict which is the best format, based on the type of question being asked.

LEARNING OUTCOMES

The children will learn to recognise for themselves which is the most useful format for presenting certain types of information to give answers to questions in a clear and speedy way. Some will do this by displaying the information in different formats and then finding out how easily and quickly they can answer their questions, while others will make generalisations to make their judgements.

FURTHER MATHS CHALLENGES

Tennis tables

Provide the children with a copy of the competition table showing the order of play at Wimbledon. Note some of the tennis players with whom the children are familiar. Prompt them to track the possible progress of Tim Henman's route to the final. Ask, *Who could he meet on the way?* Judge how useful this format is for tracking potential competitors in the competition. Ask, for example, *Could Agassi play Hewitt?* Discuss other sporting fixtures which use the same format, such as snooker championships and the final stages of the World Cup. Evaluate how well the information helps sports people to prepare for the competition and ask the children to consider why this format is not used in the FA cup. Challenge the children to set up a football competition in the same way so that the two favourites are likely to meet up in the final.

Apple pie

In groups, prompt the children to look at a range of commercial food packaging and note the amounts of the main ingredients. Provide them with the opportunity to enter the data into a database and use it to ask and answer questions, for example, *Which product contains the most water? Which product contains apple and sugar?* For each question, ask the children to say which is the most useful way for finding the answer.

HOW MUCH SUGAR WILL IT HOLD?

SUBJECT: SCIENCE. QCA UNIT: 6C MORE ABOUT DISSOLVING.

LEARNING OBJECTIVE

To set up a fair test to investigate the rate of solubility.

THINKING OBJECTIVE

To evaluate whether a test plan is fair and reliable for finding out solubility of some solids, and if not what needs changing to make it fair and reliable.

THINKING SKILLS

The children will evaluate a recent investigation and decide why it was fair and reliable. They will consider how the way the investigation was conducted helped them to find out about the speed with which a sweet dissolved and how they speeded up the process. They will be able to give reasons for their conclusions because of the fairness of the test and they will use this knowledge and understanding of measurement and changing one variable at a time to evaluate the quality of other scientific investigations. This will help them to practise general principles every time they set up an investigation.

WHAT YOU NEED
Outcomes of the investigation in 'Sweet success' in Chapter 4 of this book; large sheets of paper; writing materials.

WHAT TO DO
Recap and discuss how the children found out how to make the sweet dissolve the fastest. Talk about the variables that affected the speed and how they measured each one to find out which had the biggest effect. Agree that it was important to alter only one variable each time and that the other variables remained the same. Agree what the variables were. Talk about how the children can use this information to set up a similar investigation into how fast sugar will dissolve in a cup of tea, and to assess how they transfer and apply their learning to a similar situation.

Tell the children that you now want to find out how much sugar can be dissolved in a set amount of water. Ask, *Will there become a point where the solution will not dissolve any more sugar because the liquid becomes dry – the solution becomes saturated?*

Discuss first of all possible ways to find out how much sugar a set amount of water will dissolve. Prompt the children to consider the variables that are involved, such as the amount and temperature of the water, whether to stir, the size of the containers holding the water. Encourage them to consider how and what they will measure. Ask, *How will you know when the solution is saturated – that it will not dissolve any more sugar?* Agree this point together and discuss why, if they all decide on a different point, the test will not be fair. Finally, ask the children to consider how they can record the information to help them draw a conclusion from the test.

Let the children work in groups to plan how they can approach the task. Encourage them to identify the equipment they will need before planning how they will carry out the test. Ask, *How many times will you need to carry out the test? One time for each variable being tested and changed, or more? How many times do real scientists check their results, once or more than once? Is twice enough, or should it be carried out more than this?* Agree that twice may suffice for this test while in other situations you may need to repeat it more.

Share the plans as a class, and ask the the children to evaluate whether each plan allows the results to be reliable or not. They should give reasons for their judgements.

DIFFERENTIATION
Organise the children into mixed ability groups, keeping an eye on the less able children to make sure they are not being left out of the discussions, and the higher attaining children to make sure they are not dominating the discussions.

WHERE NEXT
Evaluate whether sugar dissolves in other liquids and whether the saturation point is the same.

Evaluate whether you can find out about the dissolving properties of other solids in the same way.

ASSESSMENT
Note the children who understand that certain tests are not reliable and fair because too many variables are changed at once, or that measurements are not precise or accurate.

LEARNING OUTCOMES
The children will learn how to make a test fair and reliable by evaluating the quality of measurement and noting the changes in variables each time.

FURTHER SCIENCE CHALLENGES
Is it fair?
Provide the children with an outline plan to find out whether the same masses of different solids need different amounts of water to dissolve in, or whether they will dissolve in the same amount of water. Make obvious generalisations on the plan, such as 'Get a beaker and fill it with water. Put a spoonful of sherbet into the first beaker, a spoonful of salt in the next and so on.' Ask the children to evaluate the quality of the plan and to edit it to make it more fair and reliable. Share the outcomes and use the information to set up a fair and reliable test into finding out whether different solids become saturated in different amounts of water or whether they

become saturated in the same amount.

Testing conclusions

Provide the children with a series of conclusions and ask them to plan a way of testing these out. Encourage them to swap plans and to edit each other's to evaluate whether they are fair and reliable.

BEATLEMANIA

SUBJECT: HISTORY. QCA UNIT: 20 WHAT CAN WE LEARN ABOUT RECENT HISTORY FROM STUDYING THE LIFE OF A FAMOUS PERSON?

LEARNING OBJECTIVE

To consider a range of historical sources and note whether they provide facts, fiction or opinion.

THINKING OBJECTIVE

To evaluate information and to judge the value of information.

THINKING SKILLS

The children will judge the value of a range of historical sources and decide whether certain snippets of information provide fact, fiction or opinion. They will use this analysis to judge the reliability of the evidence in terms of what we can learn about the recent past from studying the lives of famous people (in this unit John Lennon and the Beatles).

WHAT YOU NEED

A range of historical sources of evidence which report on the different stages, achievements, beliefs and values of the Beatles: record sleeves, information from CDs, websites (there are many – research the most suitable in advance), pictures, photographs, CD-ROM encyclopedia, TV and newspaper archive footage; Beatles' records and record player; a large sheet of paper for each group divided into four columns; writing materials.

WHAT TO DO

Tell the children about the Beatles, how they were brought up immediately after the war and had been part of the teenage revolution that took place at that time. Talk to them about the kind of attitudes many teenagers had and how many wanted to become pop stars like Elvis Presley and other famous American singers. Revise what life was like in the late 1950s and early 1960s and consider the impact the Beatles had on teenagers nationwide at that time. Look at a large photograph of the Beatles in their early days and compare their appearance to photographs of people just after World War II. Note the differences in hair length and style of clothes. Listen to a song from the 1950s such as 'I'm a Blue Toothbrush' or similar by Max Bygraves, or 'How Much is that Doggy in the Window?' or similar by the Beverley Sisters, and ask the children what they think of these songs. Listen to an early Beatles song – the first was 'Love Me Do' which was a minor hit, followed by 'Please, Please Me', which went straight to number 1, and then 'From Me to You'. Note how this music is different from the other 1950s songs. Ask the children, *What do you think people thought of the Beatles' music at the time? How do we know it was very popular with teenagers?* (It went to number 1 in the pop charts.) Next, prompt the children to look at the clothes and hairstyles of the early Beatles. Ask, *Do you think this style was popular with teenagers? What do you think older people thought of the Beatles? How do we know?*

On a large sheet of paper draw four equal-sized columns. In the left-hand column write the sentence 'The Beatles were popular with teenagers' and head the other three columns 'fact', 'fiction' and 'opinion'. Ask the class to judge whether this statement is fact, fiction or opinion. Agree that it is a fact, tick the correct column and write the reasons for this in the same column. Ask, *How valuable is the pop chart as a source of evidence? What other sources of evidence would prove reliably that this sentence is a fact?*

Underneath the first statement write 'The Beatles were not popular with older people'. Discuss the children's opinions, agree to tick the opinion column, and write down the reason. Ask, *Is there a source of evidence which categorically shows that this statement is a fact?* Prompt the children to list all the possible sources of evidence, including newspaper accounts and vox pop of the time. Discuss how these sources indicate that the statement *could* be a fact but are in reality not 100 per cent reliable as they do not put forward *everyone's* opinion or point of view. Ask the children, *Why is this statement* not *fiction?* Again, identify that there is *some* evidence which indicates that it could be partly based on fact – newspapers and TV shows are evidence that several people at that time held this view.

As a class, compose a set of statements about the Beatles, some of which are facts ('They were born in Liverpool'), some which are opinion ('The Beatles made good pop songs'), and some which may be fiction ('The Beatles did not like fish and chips'). Record these on your master sheet. Then ask the children to work in groups of four to research and agree which statements are fact, which are fiction and which are opinion or point of view. They should also identify the most valuable sources of evidence, the ones which helped them make their judgements. After about 15 minutes, share the children's ideas and record their agreed response on a class sheet. Together, judge which sources of evidence are the most valuable for providing facts and which for providing points of view or opinion.

DIFFERENTIATION

Work with lower attaining children to identify all the statements that tell a fact plus the related source of evidence, before moving on to statements which are fiction and noting any evidence or lack of it. Finally, discuss those statements which are opinion or point of view, noting with the children the evidence which helps them to make this judgement. Higher attaining children should be challenged to work in pairs to consider different sources of evidence, for example a newspaper and TV report of the same event (perhaps John Lennon's and Yoko Ono's bed-in), analysing how much of the text is factual information and how much is opinion or point of view. They should then share their findings with other groups and agree on a judgement about how valuable these sources are in terms of providing an accurate and reliable account of this event.

WHERE NEXT

Provide the children with the opportunity to compare the range of evidence available today which helps us to find out facts about a favourite band.

ASSESSMENT

Note whether the children understand that some sources of evidence are more valuable than others for providing factual information about the past. Note those who understand that some, while not 100 per cent reliable in terms of providing facts, nevertheless provide valuable evidence about people's points of view or opinions at that time.

LEARNING OUTCOMES

The children will learn to judge the value of each source of evidence before reaching conclusions about what they have learned about the past. They will start to question the reliability of evidence and think about how valuable it is to their research into the facts of events.

FURTHER HISTORY CHALLENGES

Biographical details

Prompt groups of six to select sources of evidence which detail a particular event in the life of the Beatles, and to use this factually correct information to write a short dramatic piece. They should also include items that are opinion and others that are fiction. When they perform their piece to the rest of the class the audience should evaluate which parts of the drama is fact, which is fiction and which is opinion. Discuss how, from a range of sources of evidence, the group picked out the one source which was most valuable in terms of providing the factual information about the event.

Oasis versus the Beatles

Challenge the children to judge which sources of evidence will help them to find out which is/was the most popular band of its day: Oasis (or some other current group) or the Beatles. Ask them to judge how reliable each piece of evidence is in helping them reach this point of view, and to identify the most valuable source.

RIVER USES

SUBJECT: GEOGRAPHY. QCA
UNIT: 14 INVESTIGATING RIVERS.

LEARNING OBJECTIVE

To learn that rivers are valuable to humans as a source of water and food.

THINKING OBJECTIVE

To evaluate information (judging usefulness).

THINKING SKILLS

The children will consider the uses that people make of rivers and evaluate how important a particular river is to the settlements it passes en route to the sea. They will analyse the value of the river for each purpose, and agree how valuable the river is to humans from all points of view. This activity will extend the children's learning about geographical patterns and processes, as well as increase their knowledge about the environment and geographical facts. This activity could be linked to fieldwork research of a local river, or carried out as part of an enquiry project into rivers around the world.

WHAT YOU NEED

A map of the children's chosen river; secondary

sources of evidence about the chosen river; previous research and knowledge of geographical facts; a large sheet of paper; writing materials.

What to do

Choose a local river that the children have studied recently and recall some of the facts they found out: its journey, factual information such as the river's measurements, and the human uses such as irrigation for crops, water supply to industry, leisure activities, food and water for animals. Using an enlarged copy of the map, OHP transparency or computer projection, ask the children to track the journey of the river, noting its many uses along the way. Mark each use and make a list of these. Agree how valuable the river is to humans from all points of view.

Tell the children you want them to do the same for the river they have chosen to investigate. Tell them that, using the factual information they have about the river, you want them to evaluate its usefulness and value to humans. Plan with them how they will do this: by noting the settlements it passes through, and looking in secondary sources for any activities linked to the river, such as industry, farming, leisure pursuits, and food source. This may take more than one lesson depending on the children's ability to locate factual information. Organise the children into pairs or groups of three and encourage them to discuss their ideas.

At the end of the activity, consider the value of each river investigated as a class. Prompt the children to make judgements based on the amount and range of activities each river provides for. Ask, *How important is this river to the people who live and work alongside it?* Note the importance of keeping the river clean and free from pollution, so that plant life and fish can survive.

Differentiation

Ask higher attaining children to evaluate the impact on a river of human leisure activities such as fishing, canoeing, boating and diving. Ask them to judge the usefulness of the river in terms of these activities, and the value of these activities in terms of human need. Ask them to think laterally and to judge whether human activity is at all useful or valuable to the river. This will challenge them to think about the way humans sustain rivers. Organise lower attaining children into mixed ability groups so that they can learn from their partners.

Where next

Prompt the children to think about how rivers have changed over the years in terms of size, purpose and water quality, and why these changes have occurred.

Note whether this is due to human activity or natural elements, such as drought and flooding.

Assessment

Listen to the children's conversations and look at their lists to assess how well they evaluate the river's usefulness and value to human activity. Note those who start to consider the environmental issues of caring for the river to maintain its usefulness and value.

Learning outcomes

The children will learn that rivers are useful and valuable to a range of human activity, and if we wish to sustain this we have a responsibility to maintain them.

Further geography challenges

Desert rivers
Evaluate the use of water in desert regions where there is no or only one river source. Consider the value of desalination plants and how these supplement human use of water.

Polluted areas
Evaluate how responsibly humans use rivers and judge whether they are being looked after properly. Investigate issues such as industrial deposits, chemicals from farming land and the deposition of sewage. Evaluate which rivers are cleaner than others and whether this because there are fewer settlements and industrial use. Make a judgement about whether the river will be as useful and valuable in ten years time if humans continue to treat it in the way they are.

Charity biscuits

SUBJECT: DESIGN AND TECHNOLOGY. QCA
UNIT: 5D BISCUITS.

Learning objective

To learn that products are designed for different users and that this is an important consideration.

Thinking objective

To evaluate information (judging quality) and to suggest improvements.

THINKING SKILLS

The children will consider the range of sweet biscuits available to buy today before choosing a type that will suit the taste buds of most of the children in the class. They will consider why certain ingredients should not be used, such as peanuts and other nut products, and make sure these are not included in small amounts in any of the ingredients. They will then make up batches of their favourite recipe, making variations of the same theme, and carry out a tasting activity to either identify an absolute favourite of the class, groups and individuals, or to suggest how the recipe could be improved to suit these tastes. They will evaluate the quality of the finished biscuits to inform further attempts. You may wish to organise this activity over two lessons (planning one day, baking the next).

WHAT YOU NEED

Recipes for basic sweet biscuits and the ingredients.

WHAT TO DO

With the class, brainstorm the range of sweet biscuits available to buy and decide which one each child likes and why. List the ingredients which inform their choice.

Look at a basic recipe for sweet biscuits, and discuss the purpose of each ingredient. Ask the children, *What is the purpose of each ingredient? Does it add to the taste, the colour or texture?*

Ask pairs to consider the basic recipe, and to add some of the ingredients from the class list of favourites. They should then make a shopping list and, if at all possible, go to the supermarket with an adult to buy what they need. Alternatively, you should have the ingredients available, or give parents and carers time to organise this.

Working in groups, prompt the children to make batches of biscuits, varying the basic recipe. Organise a tasting event to select the variation that the children like best. Ask them to explain why one particular variation is their favourite. They should base their judgement on the quality of the flavour and texture of the biscuit – whether it is too dry or soggy, sticks to the roof of the mouth

and so on. They should also suggest how the non-favourites could be improved. Based on the children's evaluation, make batches of the favourite biscuits.

DIFFERENTIATION

Organise the children into friendship and mixed ability groups during the baking task so that they can make their favourite recipe. Challenge higher attaining children to work out how many batches they would need to bake to make one biscuit for every child in the school.

WHERE NEXT

Ask the children to write an evaluation of why they chose the recipe they did. Ask them to write an evaluation of the flavour and the texture and to list any improvements that could be made.

Groups could make batches of biscuits, leaving out one of the ingredients to find out what happens. Ask, *Why it has this ingredient been included? How does its omission change the taste and texture of the biscuit?*

ASSESSMENT

Note the children's comments as they taste the biscuits and whether they make relevant comments about the texture as well as the flavour. Note those who are then able to use this evaluation to suggest how the biscuits could be improved.

LEARNING OUTCOMES

The children will learn to evaluate the recipes of biscuits and consider why certain ingredients are important to the quality of taste and texture. They will evaluate the purpose of the ingredients when deciding which they like best and why.

FURTHER DESIGN AND TECHNOLOGY CHALLENGES

Red nose biscuits

Prompt the children to design and make biscuits to celebrate Comic Relief's Red Nose Day. Agree as a class that the biscuits need to be red or have a red feature, and discuss what these could be. Then consider, for example, how red to make any mixture, how to make the correct colour noses to complement the flavour (perhaps by using tomatoes for savoury biscuits, strawberries or raspberries for fruit ones and smarties for chocolate flavoured ones). Encourage the children to evaluate the quality of the biscuits against set criteria of taste, presentation and style, and to make improvements to the mixture and decoration.

Savoury challenge

Challenge the children to evaluate the quality of a

range of commercially produced savoury biscuits and to note the ingredients in each one. They should list what they like about the taste and texture and note any improvements they would want to make, for example, adding more cheese to the cheesy biscuits. Make batches of savoury biscuits to suit the taste buds of individuals and groups of children.

WHAT'S HAPPENING?

SUBJECT: ICT. QCA UNIT: 6A MULTIMEDIA PRESENTATION.

LEARNING OBJECTIVE
To design and create a page to include text, graphics and sound.

THINKING OBJECTIVE
To evaluate information (judging quality) and to suggest improvements.

THINKING SKILLS
The children will work in pairs to produce an item for the class or school newsletter. They will then work as a class to put this together in draft form, and use this in an evaluation and editing exercise. They will identify the most important pieces of information and think of ways to catch the reader's eye. They will evaluate each other's ideas and choose the presentation which they think is the clearest.

WHAT YOU NEED
Desktop publishing software; computer access; printers; paper; writing materials.

WHAT TO DO
Plan the next newsletter as a class and discuss what the children wish to include. Make sure that this includes relevant dates and times of planned events, news items and other important prices of information about the school. Allocate pairs of children to produce one item to published quality which includes pictures and text. (This activity assumes the production of a simple, folded four-page newsletter, but you might wish to stick to one page only.) Pin all the items on a board for the class to see. Select items for the front page, and, moving the pieces around physically, agree where the children want to place them on the page to make the newsletter look attractive and interesting. They

should consider the balance between text and graphics, and leave space for the title graphic. When the class have agreed on the presentation format, model how to do this on the computer.

Explain to the children that you want them to work in pairs, to think about how to make the important pieces of information stand out. First they should note down what the most important pieces of information are (any dates, times, prices, headings and subheadings and so on), then suggest how these particular pieces of information can be highlighted (through italics, bold, the use of different colours, size and style of font, underlining and use of bullet points and arrow symbols).

As a class, use the pairs' suggestions to design and lay out each page of the newsletter, selecting which articles to put on each page as you go. (You might like to challenge a small group of higher attainers to design one or two pages by themselves.)

Print out the completed newsletters, enough for one copy for each pair, and ask the children to evaluate the class design, and to suggest changes and improvements to make the information more interesting and eye-catching. As a class, share the suggested improvements, agree on the best ideas and make the changes to produce a final version.

DIFFERENTIATION
Challenge higher attaining children to include a moving picture and sound in their newsletter so that if it is sent electronically, it will immediately catch the eye of the receiver. Less able children should

work in mixed ability pairs so that their literacy skills can be supported.

WHERE NEXT
Challenge the children to practise these skills independently by putting together the next newsletter in a similar way.

ASSESSMENT
Listen to the children's conversations as they discuss the changes they are making to the style of presentation. Note whether they are evaluating the quality of presentation each time rather than the content, and whether their suggested improvements are in response to this evaluation rather than what they have written.

LEARNING OUTCOMES
The children will evaluate the quality of the presentation of important information in terms of how well it catches the eye of the reader, and suggest further improvements to the design.

FURTHER ICT CHALLENGES
Noisy bookmarks
Prompt the children to use an author-packaging software to produce a 'bookmark' with an eye-catching slogan and moving picture, inviting the viewer to find or read a certain book that is on display on a computer, in the library or another class. Encourage them to insert a sound to add interest. Evaluate how eye-catching the bookmark is in terms of catching the attention of potential readers. Help the children to create a 'Press here' label which, when pressed, will run the programme inviting viewers to find the chosen book. Change the bookmark every day to help develop the reference skills of younger children.

Reference posters
Ask the children to make posters for the school library to encourage different groups of children to read. They should include pictures and text, and evaluate the use of these features, making sure they add to the clarity and interest of the poster. If possible, allow them to create this on a whiteboard so that a sound can be introduced.

DRESSING IT RIGHT

SUBJECT: ART AND DESIGN. QCA UNIT: 6B WHAT A PERFORMANCE.

LEARNING OBJECTIVE
To learn how costume and make-up add effects to a performance.

THINKING OBJECTIVE
To evaluate information (judging quality) and to suggest improvements.

THINKING SKILLS
The children will consider how professional designers design costumes for a professional show. They will evaluate how the designers have managed to reflect the personalities of the different characters, and suggest ways that these could be improved. They will then use this information to design a costume for the school show, or similar event.

WHAT YOU NEED
A video of a West End show such as *Joseph and his Amazing Technicolour Dreamcoat, Cats, Chicago, The Lion King* or *Bombay Dreams* (posters will do).

WHAT TO DO
As a class, look at the costumes used in the production of *The Lion King* (or other show you have chosen) and note which characters are which. Talk about why certain colours have been chosen and how these reflect the personality of the character. Note the range of textures and fabrics that have been used, the style and patterns, and talk about the way these have been produced. Note how the designer has produced the headwear, the techniques that have been used and how these fit onto the heads of the performers. Talk about why they need to be secure.

Organise the children into groups and, providing each group with a poster from a different show, ask them to evaluate the quality of the costumes in relation to how they reflect the story, characters, setting, time and place. They should evaluate the costumes in terms of colour, style, texture, choice of fabrics and pattern.

Share the children's evaluations during the plenary and agree whether the costumes reflect the show's setting, time and place. Challenge them to say which costume is the most effective and why, and whether they would change any elements of the costume design.

DIFFERENTIATION
Provide groups of lower attaining children with a picture of one of the characters from *The Lion King* and outline the story and role that this character plays. As you relate the action, ask them to note how the costume reflects this. Prompt them to make an overall evaluation on the costume in terms of how well it reflects the personality of the character. Ask higher attaining children to note the way the designer uses hats and make-up to create effects. (This will provide a useful starting point to the

designing and making hats task in the QCA unit of work.)

WHERE NEXT
List the techniques, style and elements that have added to the effectiveness of the costumes, ready for the children to consider when designing and making their own costumes.

ASSESSMENT
Note whether the children are evaluating the costumes in terms of how well they reflect the personality of the character portrayed. Note how they link this evaluation to the use of certain artistic elements and techniques. Make a particular note of those children who use this evaluation to suggest improvements to the overall quality of the design and are able to give reasons for this in terms of portraying the character more effectively.

LEARNING OUTCOMES
The children will learn to evaluate how well designers reflect personality, time and place through the techniques and use of colour, patterns, fabric choices, texture and style.

FURTHER ART AND DESIGN CHALLENGES
Top hat and tails
Look at a collection of hats and agree how these can be used to create certain effects. Give the children the title of a traditional tale and ask them to suggest designs for hats to depict the characters, both human and animal, in the story.

Face paints
Look at a poster of the musical *Cats* and evaluate how effectively the make-up artist has used face paints to create and reflect the different personalities of the characters. Evaluate the use of colour and pattern and how these add to the overall effect. Invite the children to say whether they would make any changes and why, and whether they can suggest any improvements. Evaluate, select and design suitable decorations for face paints at the next school fête.

SINGING TO AN AUDIENCE

SUBJECT: MUSIC. QCA UNIT: 20 STARS, HIDE YOUR FIRES.

LEARNING OBJECTIVE
To perform a song from memory giving thought to expression.

THINKING OBJECTIVE
To evaluate information (judging value) and to suggest improvements.

THINKING SKILLS
The children will learn a new song and consider how well knowledge and understanding of the musical elements involved help them to add expression to their performance.

WHAT YOU NEED
Copies of the song 'Stars, Hide Your Eyes', enough for one between two or three; an OHP copy; OHP; highlighter pens in a range of colours. Learn the song as a class in advance so the children are familiar with the context, tune and words.

WHAT TO DO
Explain to the children that today they will identify how musical elements help us judge how to add expression to our performance of the song. Tell them that they will look at the words and music and identify how the composer adds variety to the performance through musical direction, which is easy to see, and through musical elements, which are not. Sing the song through once to remind the children of the words and music.

Look at the score of the song together on an OHP and identify the musical directions regarding dynamics. Identify what these mean. (Mp – *mezzo piano* or fairly quiet, f – *forte* or loud, mf – *mezzo forte* or fairly loud, p – *piano* or quiet.) Highlight these on the OHP, inviting the children to locate the same on their copy and to highlight the same directions. Sing the song through, responding to the musical direction, for example starting fairly quietly, but singing *webs of treason* loudly. Ask, *Do you think the performance was better this time? How? Why? Why has the composer directed you to sing this section more loudly? Is it because they want to add expression, mood, emotion and effect? How does this change in dynamics alter the meaning and intention of the words? How does it add dramatic effect?* Repeat this for other musical directions of dynamics.

Look at tempo next and decide what 'rit. last verse' means. Ask, *Why does the composer want you to sing the last part of the last verse gradually getting slower? How does this add dramatic effect?* Ask the children to work in pairs or threes to highlight the parts they think should be sung legato and those parts that should be sung staccato in two different colours. After five minutes, share the children's ideas, singing the different alternative ways. Choose the version the class think best adds the most expression and achieves the best dramatic effect.

Evaluate how this analysis helps them to add dramatic effect to their performance and give it more expression. Ask the children, *How have these changes improved the quality of performance?*

DIFFERENTIATION

Work with more able musicians to note additional directions such as dimuendo in the last two bars, the pause at the very end and crescendos and diminuendos in the introduction. Discuss how this adds dramatic effect and helps to set the mood of the song. Concentrate on the dynamics with lower attaining children, reinforcing the musical direction on copies of the words only.

WHERE NEXT

Complete a similar activity with the accompaniment, prompting the children to consider how its analysis helps them decide how it should be played. As a class, learn the second part and add it to the performance.

ASSESSMENT

Listen to the children's performance and note how well they use the musical directions and elements to add expression.

LEARNING OUTCOMES

The children will learn to judge the value of musical direction and elements in helping to add expression and dramatic effect to improve their performance of a song.

FURTHER MUSIC CHALLENGES

Tuneful elements

With the children, look at how changes in pitch

create suspense or resolution. Discuss how the interval of the octave is used to cause suspense in bar 12, and how it is resolved in the penultimate and final bar of the singing part. Ask the children, *How does this help the performance?*

Rhythmic accompaniment

Together, look at how the accompaniment follows the rhythm of some of the words. Ask, the children, *How does this help to tie the song together? How does this help with the performance?*

EVERY PICTURE TELLS A STORY

SUBJECT: RE. QCA UNIT: 6F HOW DO PEOPLE EXPRESS THEIR FAITH THROUGH THE ARTS?

LEARNING OBJECTIVE

To identify how artists express beliefs through painting.

THINKING OBJECTIVE

To evaluate information and to judge the value of information.

THINKING SKILLS

The children will look at a range of different paintings and note how they reflect the beliefs of Christians. They will look at the subject matter of the paintings first and then consider how the artist has used colour and line to show mood and emotion, and how facial expressions portray feelings to the observer. They will reach a final judgement about the beliefs the painter has portrayed by noting how different artists approach the same subject matter and yet the overall feelings, moods and effects are similar.

WHAT YOU NEED

Prints of paintings from the Italian renaissance, making sure that the subject matter is suitable for this age, for example Botticelli, Giotto, Michelangelo and da Vinci.

WHAT TO DO

Compare two paintings that portray the birth of Jesus, for example Botticelli's *The Mystic Nativity* and Leonardo da Vinci's *The Virgin and Child with St Anne and St John the Baptist* (both available via the National Gallery website www.nationalgallery.org.uk). Look at the first painting and ask the children to say what the subject is. Ask them, *How do you know? How does the painting makes you feel? Do you think this was the artist's intention? How do you know that the artist was pleased about the birth of Jesus? What colours are used? In what style have the* characters been painted? Do they look pleased? Are any sad? Look closely at Mary's face. What expression is she wearing? How does this make you feel? How do you think Mary felt? Does the artist portray the story exactly or is it an interpretation? How do you know? Does the painting portray the artist's beliefs? Contrast this with the second painting and prompt the children to note the differences in the use of colour and line. Ask them to look closely at Mary's face again and note her expression. Ask, Does ths painting make you feel the same as the first? Why? How does the artist portray his beliefs?

Repeat this by contrasting two paintings which depict the death of Christ for example, Giotto's *Lamentation* and da Vinci's *The Last Supper*. Note with the children the value of paintings for depicting feelings and mood and how they portray beliefs.

DIFFERENTIATION

Work with lower attaining pupils to help them understand that art is a means of expressing beliefs where the artist doesn't have to be overly concerned with how. Higher attaining children should be encouraged to consider the value of paintings for expressing key beliefs – Jesus was sent by God to tell us about life after death – and this is reflected in both *The Mystic Nativity* by Botticelli and *The Last Supper* by da Vinci.

WHERE NEXT

Look with the children at art from religions other than Christianity and judge its value in portraying the beliefs of the people of that religion.
Look at statues and religious buildings and prompt the children to note the way the sculptors and architects have reflected the beliefs of the worshippers in their designs.

ASSESSMENT

Assess how well the children evaluate the feelings conveyed by the different paintings and begin to link these to the beliefs of Christians.

LEARNING OUTCOMES

The children will learn to judge the value of religious paintings in portraying beliefs through the evaluation of how expression, colour and line are used to evoke feelings, emotion and mood.

FURTHER RE CHALLENGES

Hallelujah

Listen together to the 'Hallelujah Chorus' by Handel and talk about the mood that this creates. Ask the children, How does the composer convey this mood to the listener? What is the tune like? What about the harmonies? Is it joyful piece of music? Note all the emotion the children feel as they listen to this chorus. Compare this to the *Dies Ire* from Beethoven's 'Mass in C Minor'. Note how the composer conveys emotion to the listener through the soulful tune and use of a minor key. Ask the children, What religious event are the two pieces of music portraying? Why do you think this? Prompt the children to judge the value of the music in terms of how each piece portrays the beliefs and feelings of the two composers about the birth and death of Jesus.

Prayer

As a class, look at Muslim designs and talk about why these designs are used. Ask, What do they reflect? Do they show the beliefs of the people who worship Islam? Explain how Islamic patterns always contain a mistake and are never perfect because only Allah is perfect. Discuss and judge the value and importance of the designs in prayer.

SYMMETRICAL MOVEMENTS

SUBJECT: PE. QCA UNIT: GYMNASTICS ACTIVITIES UNIT 5.

LEARNING OBJECTIVE

To select and refine sequences of symmetrical movements.

THINKING OBJECTIVE

To evaluate information and to judge the value of information.

THINKING SKILLS

The children will put together a floor sequence with a partner over a number of weeks before this activity. They will then evaluate a range of PE apparatus before deciding on the best pieces and organisation to support a symmetrical performance of their sequence. They will evaluate their performance in terms of the variety of journeys, and levels and dynamics it allows them to build in, before suggesting a way of ensuring they keep their movements together.

WHAT YOU NEED
A gymnastic sequence for each pair of children; photographs of a range of gymnastic apparatus available for use, including tables, benches, planks, ladders, mats and wall bars.

WHAT TO DO
Organise the children into pairs with the photographs of the available gymnastics apparatus. Explain that you want them to evaluate each piece of the apparatus for its value in supporting a performance of their sequence. They should then use the evaluation to create a simple, combined piece of apparatus on which they can perform. As they work, ask them, *Why have you chosen or discarded these pieces of apparatus? Have you chosen pieces which will allow you to move in the different ways already developed? How do you know that your sequence will still be symmetrical? Will you move alongside each other, perhaps one on the floor and another on the apparatus, or move towards each other to meet in the central table before crossing over to complete the sequence moving away from each other?*

After about 20 minutes, share the children's ideas as a class. Ask the class, *Do you like any particular idea you have just heard? Can you incorporate this idea into your own sequence? How will the piece of apparatus help you to add variety to the movements, such as varying the levels, dynamics or direction of travel?* Allow the children another five or ten minutes to reconsider their choices, to re-evaluate and make improvements.

DIFFERENTIATION
Expect higher attaining children to work in groups of four to work out how they can perform their sequences on the same pieces of apparatus in canon. Lower attaining children should be encouraged to evaluate and use two identical sets of apparatus, which run alongside each other. This way the children can reflect each other's movements directly.

WHERE NEXT
Organise the apparatus and allow the children time to practise and refine their sequences.

ASSESSMENT
Talk to the children as they work to find out whether they are considering the value of each piece of apparatus in relation to how well it supports the performance of their sequences, especially in terms of moving symmetrically with their partner.

LEARNING OUTCOMES
The children will evaluate the value of different pieces and organisation of PE apparatus to particular gymnastic sequences, and will use this information in selecting those most suitable to their own ideas.

FURTHER PE CHALLENGES
Class act
As a class, use the evaluations to select the most suitable pieces of apparatus so that all pairs can perform their sequences as a class performance. This may mean some pairs refining their sequences to fit the chosen pieces. Organise the agreed apparatus on a large plan and, with pairs working in groups of six with a copy of the plan, allow the children time to decide where they will start and finish each performance and in what order they will perform. Some pairs may be able to perform their sequence simultaneously while others may perform in canon. In the hall, invite each group to perform in front of the rest of the class who should evaluate the value of the apparatus chosen for each of the groups. They will use this information before choosing the most valuable pieces and organisation to support the performance of every group and pair. Perform the sequences as a class, with some pairs working at the same time and others working on their own.
Musical movement
Prompt the children to evaluate the value of different pieces of music in helping them synchronise their movements. You might like to evaluate 'Bolero' by Ravel, many songs by Kylie Minogue, the film score from *Titanic* and Track 3 from Disney's *Millennium Celebration*). Include pieces that are not suitable; those with an irregular tempo or beat.

CROSS-CURRICULAR PROJECTS

INTRODUCTION

The two cross-curricular topics in this chapter show how activities can be approached differently to develop different thinking skills. You may decide to re-organise the focus to develop a different thinking skill by arranging the learning differently or by asking different questions.

The first topic combines several QCA units of work and shows how these can be organised differently to support learning across the curriculum. Some are extension activities which link well to the context of the subject units, for example, Galileo is a summative activity linking the knowledge and understanding of the Sun, Earth and Moon.

The second topic develops the children's evaluative and enquiry thinking overall. In many of the activities they will be making enquiries about and evaluating the information from a range of venues and using some of the ideas to plan their own school trip.

ITALY

This series of activities is set within the theme of Italy. The activities are examples of the types of task the children can take part in to raise their awareness of another country. As they work through the tasks they will be developing a range of thinking skills due to the nature of the activities and the way they are organised. The activities could easily be set within another country and used as a means to extend the children's cultural development. Greece is an obvious alternative as links can be made with the history units 14 and 15, through which the children study how the country has evolved and its legacies to the world community such as the Olympic Games, Greek words, food, architecture and theatre. The thinking skills are already identified in these units of work,

and so the context of Italy has been chosen for this chapter to show how the activities can be organised to develop thinking and understanding, rather than knowledge and facts.

PLANNING A SCHOOL TRIP

This project encourages the children to think about the usefulness of a school trip for educational reasons as well as social reasons and for having fun. They will evaluate leaflets and make informed choices, giving reasons for these, collect relevant information about particular types of places to visit and work out the relative costs of visiting each one before making decisions about the best place to go and the cheapest option for travelling to the venue.

ITALY

Subject and QCA unit, NLS or NNS objective	Activity title	Thinking objective	Activity	Page
English NLS objectives: To collect and investigate the meanings and spellings of words using the following prefixes: *auto, bi, trans, tele, circum*; to use word roots, prefixes and suffixes as a support for spelling	Rooting words	To look for pattern and relationship; to sort and classify	Looking for pattern and relationships in words and classifying them by root derivative	134
Maths NNS objectives: To make decisions; to solve problems about real life using one or more steps; to begin to find simple percentages of small whole number quantities	Holiday destination	To use skills of deduction and to make decisions	Planning and deciding on a suitable holiday to Italy	135
Science QCA unit: 5E Earth, Sun and Moon	Who was Galileo?	To think creatively; to extend ideas	Organising a quiz to recall and consolidate knowledge and learn new facts	136
History QCA unit: 13 How has life in Britain changed since 1948?	Eating habits	To collect and sort information; to plan research; to ask questions	Researching how people's holiday habits have changed and the impact of travel on people's eating habits	137
Geography QCA unit: 24 Passport to the world	Beach location	To locate, collect and classify information; to ask questions	Locating different beach holiday areas in Italy	139
Design and Technology QCA unit: 5B Bread	Italian bread	To collect and analyse information	Analysing different Italian breads and producing a new product	140
ICT QCA unit: 6A Multimedia presentation	Pepperoni pizza	To generate ideas	Creating a presentation to sell a product	142
Music QCA unit: 18 Journey into space	Operatic genius	To think imaginatively	Listening to Italian opera, to imagine what feelings are being conveyed and the story being told by the musical styles and elements used	143
RE QCA unit: 6A What can we learn from Christian religious buildings?	Roman Catholics	To use the skills of inference and to give reasons	Completing a concept mapping activity to link different prayers to their purpose or service, giving reasons for the link	144
PE QCA unit: Dance unit 6	Italian calendar	To generate ideas and to suggest improvements	Developing motifs, phrases and sequences and extending the ideas by using different structures	146

Rooting words

SUBJECT: ENGLISH. NLS OBJECTIVES: TO COLLECT AND INVESTIGATE THE MEANINGS AND SPELLINGS OF WORDS USING THE FOLLOWING PREFIXES: *AUTO, BI, TRANS, TELE, CIRCUM*; TO USE WORD ROOTS, PREFIXES AND SUFFIXES AS A SUPPORT FOR SPELLING.

LEARNING OBJECTIVE
To understand that words often have prefixes, suffixes and root words which derive from another language.

THINKING OBJECTIVES
To look for pattern and relationships; to sort and classify.

THINKING SKILLS
The children will look at the way suffixes derived from Latin determine meaning of many words in the English dictionary. They will consider the link between English and Italian and other languages, such as French and Spanish. They will look for the pattern and relationships within the words to help them think what the word might mean before looking it up in the appropriate dictionary.

WHAT YOU NEED
Dictionaries (English and Italian – check that the words you will be focusing on can be found in the dictionaries available); thesaurus; a list of common Italian or Latin words; paper; writing materials.

WHAT TO DO
Explain to the children how our language developed over a number of years and now has several links to other languages around the world. Show them the word for 'water' in French (*eau*), Spanish (*agua*) and Italian (*aqua*). Ask, *What do these words have in common?* Explain that they are all derived from the Latin word *aqua* meaning 'water'. Tell them that Latin is one of the oldest known languages in the world and that it originated in Italy.

Prompt the children to think for a few moments about words in the English language which use *aqua* as a root. Brainstorm these and list them on a sheet of paper. Look up their definitions in a dictionary and record these alongside. Note that all the definitions relate to water. Agree that *aqua* means 'water'. Provide groups of children with different roots to identify pattern and relationship. When they have collected several words with the same prefix or root word, challenge them to say what they think their root word means. Words to use include those outlined in the NLS objective plus *domin* and *cent*. Encourage the children to look them up in an appropriate

dictionary to check whether they were right.

As a class, sort the children's collection of words into sets according to their meaning. Set up a classification system to find the country of origin of different words, suffixes and prefixes, for example *geo*, *tech* and *photo*.

DIFFERENTIATION
Provide higher attaining children with more word derivatives to sort and classify. Less able children should be encouraged to collect complete words to begin with so that they learn to identify the pattern and relationships between prefixes and suffixes and to understand the meaning of these terms.

WHERE NEXT
Investigate the pattern and relationship and collect, sort and classify other prefixes and suffixes as outlined in NLS Years 5 and 6: *auto, bi, tele, trans, circum, omni, aero, audi, cede, clude, con, cred, duo, logo, logy, graph, hydro, hydra, in, micro, oct, phobe, photo, port, prim, scribe, scope, sub, super, tele, tri, ex.* Prompt the children to look some of these words up in Italian dictionaries to find out which have Italian origins.

ASSESSMENT
Assess the children's understanding of suffixes and prefixes through their ability to note the pattern and relationships between the groups of words they have collected. Note those who are able to set up a sorting and classification system for identifying the language of origin.

LEARNING OUTCOMES
Most children will note the similarities and differences between the root, suffix and prefixes by noting the pattern and relationships of these. Some will begin to note the country of origin from familiar words in that language.

FURTHER ENGLISH CHALLENGES
Spaghetti junction
Prompt the children to look for words which come from other countries that are now used in everyday language. Collect these and sort them according to their country of origin. Places to look include holiday brochures, food cartons and the local high street. Words to include: *restaurant, café, gateau, cul-de-sac, bungalow, boutique, rendezvous, pasta, pizza* and *spaghetti*.

Word definitions

Ask the children to combine a prefix with a suffix to make a known word, and to work out the literal meaning of these words using the information gained from earlier classification and analysis, for example *photograph*, *omnibus*, *conclude* and *circumscribe*. Encourage the children to use the pattern and relationships of prefixes and suffixes to invent new words, for example *aquapool* – 'a pool of water', *centitable* – 'a hundred tables'.

HOLIDAY DESTINATION

SUBJECT: MATHS. NNS OBJECTIVES: TO MAKE DECISIONS; TO SOLVE PROBLEMS ABOUT REAL LIFE USING ONE OR MORE STEPS; TO BEGIN TO FIND SIMPLE PERCENTAGES OF SMALL WHOLE NUMBER QUANTITIES.

LEARNING OBJECTIVE

To solve real-life problems involving money, using more than one step and using the information to make decisions.

THINKING OBJECTIVE

To use skills of deduction and to make decisions.

THINKING SKILLS

The children will consider the travel options to different places in Italy. They will calculate how much it will cost for a family of four to go on holiday to the same place with different travel companies. They will compare the costs to decide which company offers the best holiday deal for this family. They will consider the costs of supplements in their calculations and work out savings of ten and fifteen per cent offered by different travel agents when reaching their decisions.

WHAT YOU NEED

Holiday brochures to Italy which offer discounts on certain hotels, plus travel and accommodation supplements; calculator; large piece of paper or whiteboard; paper; writing materials.

WHAT TO DO

As a class, look at the information presented in travel brochures from different companies, and discuss the steps required to find out the total cost of a holiday for a family of four. List the steps on a large piece of paper or whiteboard for the class to refer to later. Tell the children that you want them to work in groups to find the best holiday option for a family of four to the same destination with different travel companies. Provide each group with the same holiday destination in Italy for which a number of holiday companies offer deals. Challenge them to look in their brochures to deduce the total cost of the holiday for a family of four from the information provided. Ask, *Which is the cheapest hotel? Is this the cheapest hotel in all the brochures? Which airport offers the best deal so that the family do not need to pay supplements? Which company offers the best discount?* Challenge them to use the information to decide which is the best hotel and travel company to go with to this particular holiday resort.

Gather the children together at the end of the activity and share what they have found out. Share the total costs of each holiday and make a class decision about the best holiday option for this family. Extend the learning by considering what happens to the overall costs when one child goes free. Note how the supplements may change because this child will not be included in the number of people travelling for calculation purposes. Decide how valuable this free child place is to the family.

DIFFERENTIATION

Invite higher attaining children to calculate the costs of travel from different airports and to find the difference or savings when travelling from the one with the lowest supplements. Challenge them to find the cheapest travel company when one offers ten per cent (the cheapest so far) and the other fifteen per cent (the most expensive so far) discount. Provide lower attaining children with two brochures only and ask them to calculate the cost of the holiday using the same hotel in both brochures. They can then make a direct comparison to identify which is the cheapest option. If necessary, work with this group to help them with the calculation. Extend to include the ten per cent discount depending on the ability of the children.

WHERE NEXT

Organise a group to use a spreadsheet format to calculate the cost of holidays within a certain amount. Decide which is the best offer.

Evaluate which high-street travel agent offers the best last-minute deal by deducing the total cost for a family of four and comparing this to the full-price cost of the holiday. Some may offer particular deals on travel insurance, which higher attaining children could take into account

ASSESSMENT

Assess how well the children use all the available information to deduce which is the best holiday offer. Note the children who use the information to inform their decisions about the best holiday deal.

LEARNING OUTCOMES

Most children will learn to plan and decide which is the best holiday offer between two companies by calculating the total cost of the holiday from the information in the brochures. Some will go beyond this and deduce which is the best airport from which to travel.

FURTHER MATHS CHALLENGES

Cruising

Prompt the children to calculate the cost of different cruises at different times of the year, and for different cabins and numbers of people. They should decide which is the best cruise to take and when, and with which company. Encourage the children to build the destinations into their decision-making, for example they could decide whether, although one cruise is slightly more expensive because it visits more Italian cities, it is a better option to choose.

When to go

Ask the children to look at different types of holidays available to Italy at different times of the year and to deduce the best time to take a skiing, beach or city break. They will need to read the information about snow, weather and particular events that may be happening to help them make decisions.

WHO WAS GALILEO?

SUBJECT: SCIENCE. QCA UNIT: 5E EARTH, SUN AND MOON.

LEARNING OBJECTIVE

To learn facts about the Sun, Earth, Moon and beyond.

THINKING OBJECTIVES

To think creatively; to extend ideas.

THINKING SKILLS

The children will complete this activity at the end of the unit of work to review what they have learned about the Sun, Moon and Earth. They will think creatively to extend the ideas of familiar formats to devise a quiz of their own choice. For the purpose of this activity the children will follow the quiz format for *A Question of Sport*, but *The Weakest Link*

and *Blockbuster* formats are also suitable. They will evaluate how the way this activity is organised helps them to recall, consolidate or learn new facts about the Earth, Sun, Moon and the Universe and the way that it works.

WHAT YOU NEED

A picture board (see below); pictures of planets and famous astronomers, including Galileo, and other people famous for their work on space research; video extracts from the quiz *A Question of Sport* to identify the rounds; access to work completed during the unit of work; paper; writing materials.

WHAT TO DO

Tell the children that you want them to devise a quiz to help them learn, consolidate and revise the facts they have learned about the Sun, Earth and Moon during the recent unit of work. Explain that, in addition to this, the quiz must be interesting to motivate children to take part.

Watch the video extract from *A Question of Sport* and identify the round titles. List these for the children to refer to as they put together their own quiz. Include the 'Picture board', 'True or false?', 'Odd one out', 'One-minute round', 'Mystery guest' and 'What happens next?'.

Collect the children's ideas about the kind of things they could include on the picture board and record these for reference. Talk about how the 'What happens next?' round can be related to the topic, for example, 'The Moon moves around the Earth every

28 days and spins on its axis. This means that ...'. Collect one or two suggestions from the children. Discuss the format of the 'Odd one out' round, for example, you could show pictures of the Earth, Sun and the Moon, where the Sun is the odd one out because planets orbit around it while the Earth and Moon themselves orbit the Sun or Earth. Encourage the children to include questions which will develop their reasoning and concepts about shadows.

Organise the children into groups and give them time to plan out possible answers and facts to include in the quiz for the rest of the class to learn, consolidate or revise. When they have a list of facts and answers, challenge them to think creatively to organise the answers as questions to match the rounds as identified earlier.

Share the ideas and agree a class quiz format.

DIFFERENTIATION
Give higher attaining children the freedom to think creatively and to organise the way they approach the activity for themselves. Support the lower attaining children by directing the way they organise the task, focusing on the adaptation of the questions into different formats rather than them having to think of how to approach the task themselves.

WHERE NEXT
Play the quiz to assess the children's knowledge and understanding of the unit of work.

ASSESSMENT
Use the quiz as an assessment to identify which children thought creatively to extend the ideas of the familiar format to devise an interesting quiz.

LEARNING OUTCOMES
All children will be involved in devising the quiz, thinking creatively and extending the ideas of quizzes with familiar formats.

FURTHER SCIENCE CHALLENGES
Blockbusters
Challenge the children to think creatively to devise a board in the Blockbuster format. The children should be given the freedom to decide for themselves how to approach the task to begin with, but those who need help should be encouraged to find the answers first, identify the first letter, select the number of questions needed to make the completed board

and write the questions on a list linked to each of the initial letters. Ask the children to work in small groups to devise several different boards and question sheets for each game.
Who Wants to be a Millionaire?
Devise a quiz to learn the facts about the Sun, Earth and Moon using the *Who Wants to be a Millionaire?* format.

EATING HABITS

SUBJECT: HISTORY. QCA UNIT: 13 HOW HAS LIFE IN BRITAIN CHANGED SINCE 1948?

LEARNING OBJECTIVE
To consider how people's eating habits have changed since World War II and to identify possible reasons for these changes.

THINKING OBJECTIVES
To collect and sort information; to plan research; to ask questions.

THINKING SKILLS
The children will think about how they can find out when, after World War II, people in Britain started to eat Italian foods such as pizza and pasta, and the range of Italian-style recipes that became available. They will identify questions to ask a visitor or elderly relative to find out what foods people ate after World War II and in the 1950s. Some will plan how they can find the information from recipe books and other sources of information. The children will then consider what changes in British society raised people's awareness of Italian foods.

WHAT YOU NEED
A large collection of recipe books and recipe cards, which show the date they were published, some of which contain a range of recipes from Italy and some older ones that do not; empty food cartons; large sheets of paper; writing materials.

WHAT TO DO
List all the food with which the children are familiar that are Italian recipes, including: ice cream, tiramisu, pasta, pizza and bolognaise sauce. Set this as a piece of research for homework. Collate the children's survey results onto one big piece of paper and add any further ideas. Discuss this range of foods and sort them according to the type of food they are, for example those that contain pasta, the range of pizza toppings, desserts and sauces. Use the sorted information to point out to the children the very wide range of Italian foods available today.

Tell the children that you want to find out whether people were aware of Italian recipes before, during and immediately after World War II. Plan the structure of the research together by identifying the sequence of questions to guide the process:

◉ *What do we need to know before we can start to plan our research?* (The range of different Italian-style recipes and foods available today, completed above.)

◉ *How can we begin to find out which foods were available when? What sources of evidence can we use?* (Ask a visitor, friend or relative; look in recipe books; search the internet; look in books about Italy.)

◉ *What questions do we need to ask these sources?* (Encourage the children to focus questions on what they already know.)

◉ *How can we find out which foods arrived in the country first?*

Identify possible answers to the questions to demonstrate how to approach the research and how to locate all the sources of evidence.

Organise the children into groups to plan how they can find the answer to their research query. Each group should take a different source of evidence to plan questions and suggest ways to approach the task. For example, one group should identify the questions they should ask visitors. They need to identify first of all how the visitor can be of help. Possible questions might be: *When did you first try spaghetti? Did you know it was Italian pasta? What about macaroni? How was this eaten?* Challenge this group to devise a questionnaire, using what they already know about Italian foods as starting points for their questions, and to try to put a date on when these foods first became available in Britain.

Ask another group to use the recipe books to plan research. Prompt them to locate the date the book was published to see if it gives a clue to the date the recipe first appeared. Challenge the children to sequence the foods by listing the date when they first appeared in the books.

Another group can try to use books and websites to find out when some of these foods were first introduced into British shops.

As a class, use the information to draw conclusions about when these foods first appeared on British menus and why. Ask the children to conclude, *What changes in British society widened our experience of foods from different countries?*

DIFFERENTIATION

Work with lower attaining children to plan research using the recipe books. Start with the most modern book and identify key questions to find out whether there are any Italian recipes in it. Note the date of

the book. Next look at the oldest book and note whether and how many Italian recipes are included in it. Challenge the children to think of the next question to structure the next step in their research, for example, *Are there Italian recipes in the other books and, if so, what date is given in the book?* Encourage the children to think about how they can record what they have found out to structure the information in date order. Higher attaining children should be encouraged to plan other ways of researching the query, such as writing to businesses and local supermarkets to ask when certain foods first appeared on their shelves or were manufactured.

WHERE NEXT

Prompt the children to plan research into other foods which are non-British in origin but which are now part of the British diet. Encourage them to build questions into the research plan to find possible reasons for the introduction of these foods, for example immigration, emigration, improved travel, holidays abroad and ever-widening communication links.

ASSESSMENT

Assess how well the children collect and sort information they already know to use as a starting point to plan their research. Note how well they structure their lines of enquiry and how they identify focused questions to ask visitors, or locate the information in books and other reference material.

LEARNING OUTCOMES

All children will learn how to structure research by identifying a planning process to find particular pieces of information. They will identify how to start with what they already know, how to identify the range of evidence sources and the focused questions they need to ask to find answers to their query. Many will draw conclusions independently from what they have found out to find reasons why British eating habits have changed.

FURTHER HISTORY CHALLENGES

Bolognaise sauce

Organise the children into groups to plan research into the origins of bolognaise sauce and why it became so popular in Britain. Prompt them to locate Bologna in atlases and ask them, *Is this where the sauce got its name? How can you find out?*

Pasta varieties

The pasta revolution is a recent phenomenon, but how recent? Challenge the children to plan research to find out how recently the current wide range of pasta became available. Plan where the children can look, for example in recipe books, to find out when more than spaghetti became popular. Ask the children to find out, *Did spaghetti become more popular after the war because more Italian people came to England to live? How did the changes in holiday habits raise people's awareness of Italian foods and recipes?*

BEACH LOCATION

SUBJECT: GEOGRAPHY. QCA UNIT: 24 PASSPORT TO THE WORLD.

LEARNING OBJECTIVE

To record and present information about Italian holiday resorts.

THINKING OBJECTIVES

To locate, collect and classify information; to ask questions.

THINKING SKILLS

The children will learn about the regions of Italy and use the information to locate beach resorts and cities. They will classify the resorts and cities in terms of whether they are situated on the east or west coast, to the north or south, in the middle of Italy, around the lakes or in a mountain environment. The children will then choose one city or resort location and identify a series of questions which will help them find facts about their chosen place to decide whether it would be a suitable holiday destination for a family.

WHAT YOU NEED

A large map of Italy; smaller maps of the different regions; tourist books and holiday brochures; internet access; labels; paper; writing materials.

WHAT TO DO

As a class, look at the large map of Italy and invite the children to name the country. It shoud be familiar because of the distinctive shape. Talk about the

island of Sicily at the bottom and ask the children, *Can you name a very famous feature of this island?* If they are unable to do so, tell them about Mount Etna and how it remains one of the few active volcanoes in the world. Link this to the fertility of the island and how it is a mainly agricultural island for this reason. Brainstorm with the children all the places they know that are in Italy. List the capital city of Rome and other famous cities, including Florence, Venice, Naples, Genoa, Milan, Pisa and Turin. Use map references to locate these cities on the large map with the children, describing their location in terms of the points of the compass and whether they are coastal, internal or island locations. Locate the seas around Italy and name these. Locate and name the Italian islands Sardinia, Sicily and Corsica.

Identify what each of the cities the children have found are famous for, for example the leaning tower of Pisa, the churches of Florence, the capital city of Rome, the floating city of Venice, and fashionable Milan. Talk about the unfamiliar cities and where the children could find more information.

Provide groups of children with maps of Italy and labels on which to write the names of the major cities and holiday resorts they find in the brochures and guide books. Ask them to locate these on a map and to classify them according to the particular region of Italy that they belong to. Ask pairs to identify a series of questions about one of the locations to help them identify some of the patterns and processes in weather statistics and tourist numbers. For example, *What are the average temperatures there in July? Is it hotter or colder than England? What are the average hours of sunshine? Is this more or less that in England? Why are the days shorter in Italy in the summer than in England? Why does it get darker earlier in the summer than in England? Is this the usual pattern of weather? How can we find out? How many people live there? Has the number increased? If so, why? Are there any famous buildings there? Is this place famous for anything? Does it have a famous football team? What crops are grown in this region?* and so on.

Ask the children to find answers to some of their questions and to present a news board to share with the rest of the class. From the information they have found out, ask the children if this would be an interesting place to visit with a family for a holiday. Prompt them to search for the place they are investigating on the internet and to find pictures to include on their news board.

DIFFERENTIATION

Locate the coast of Italy with lower attaining children and follow the coastline round. Stop when you locate a beach area, either from the symbol on the map or by matching the name with one found in a holiday brochure. Challenge higher attaining children to locate the different types of coastal regions in Italy using a range of information sources but primarily on a map. Challenge them to label these such as bays, estuaries, ports, shingle and sandy beaches and so on.

WHERE NEXT
Look for references to Italy on the news and in newspapers over the next few weeks to see if the children can find out any further information about their particular place. Identify a series of questions to ask which will help them to find any references, and to look for and locate the information. Locate and classify the regions in Italy according to what the region produces, the landscape and land use. Note where the major airports are and consider why these are placed where they are.

ASSESSMENT
Assess how quickly the children locate the different areas on a map and the skills they use to do this. Note the children who gather information and draw conclusions about an area or region from the symbols on maps.

LEARNING OUTCOMES
Most children will learn the names of major cities, features and regions of Italy using mapping skills to locate the different places on a map. They will consider how each place is known and for what, thus beginning to classify and record the significance of the information. Some will ask questions to identify the pattern and processes in weather statistics and tourist numbers to particular regions.

FURTHER GEOGRAPHY CHALLENGES
Italian Alps
Locate the Italian Alps on a map of Europe and look on the internet and in travel brochures for pictures of the area. Identify a series of questions to help the children plan research into this area which will help them decide when would be a suitable time of the year to visit for different activities. Challenge the children to ask questions which link cause with effect by posing questions such as, *What is the weather like in summer and winter? Which is the most dangerous time for avalanches and why?* (This activity links to QCA Unit: 15 The mountain environment.)
Mediterranean cruise
With the children, locate the major ports in Italy where cruise ships stop or could stop. Encourage the children to use a map to identify the places that

tourists from these ships could visit in a day and to plan the routes and time this is likely to take. Locate the nearest beach and consider whether a day on the beach is feasible. Put together a list of possible places to visit for each port of call.

ITALIAN BREAD

SUBJECT: DESIGN AND TECHNOLOGY. QCA UNIT: 5B BREAD.

LEARNING OBJECTIVE
To learn about the main ingredients of Italian bread and the way it is made.

THINKING OBJECTIVE
To collect and analyse information.

THINKING SKILLS
The children will collect Italian breads – ciabatta, focaccia, olive, tomato and herb – and analyse them for their ingredients, noting the similarities and differences with bread products from other countries. They will consider the herbs and vegetables included in some breads and consider how they can vary this to design and make new or improved Italian-style bread for others in the class to evaluate.

WHAT YOU NEED
Focaccia bread; pictures or actual examples of other Italian breads and a range of breads from other countries and cultures (a visit to the local supermarket where these are produced may be useful); recipes and ingredients for making Italian breads; breads made in an earlier session.

WHAT TO DO
Share some focaccia bread with the class and talk

about the taste and texture. Ask, *How do you think this bread is produced? Are the texture and taste due to the ingredients or the way it was cooked?*

Look at the general ingredients in Italian focaccia bread and note the similarities and differences between this and other breads made in an earlier lesson. Note the ingredients that are used in all bread production including flour and liquid, and which ingredients vary including oil, yeast, soda and sugar. Discuss the children's previous learning about the types and varieties of breads and how their taste and textures are determined by the types of flour and liquid, the raising agent, the amount of sugar, the quantity and variety of fat, the cooking process and additional ingredients including herbs and spices.

As a class, analyse the focaccia bread by the type of flour, raising agent, amount of water used in its production and any additional ingredients. Compare this with breads from other countries and cultures and note the ingredients it has in common with other breads. Ask, *Is focaccia bread similar to any other types of bread? Why is this?* For example, it is similar to English white breads because the same type of flour is used, plain white, although English bread is usually made using strong white plain flour. Discuss possible differences, for example absorbsion of more water rather than fat because of gluten content. Prompt the children to use this analysis to identify the type of bread focaccia is most like. Ask, *What makes it different? Is it the additional olive oil ingredient? Is it the way it is made?*

Ask the children to look at other Italian breads, including pizza bases, and to analyse the ingredients of these. They should note which ingredients are the same and which are different to the focaccia bread, and then compare the ingredients to other Italian breads and also to those from other countries. Refine the analysis by encouraging the children to

think about the narrow range of flours evident in the Italian breads, the types of fat, liquid and whether they are made and cooked in the same or in different ways. List the range and types of ingredients the children have identified. Ask, *If the ingredients are almost the same, why are the breads so different?*

Challenge the children to use the range of ingredients employed in the manufacture of the Italian breads to design, make and evaluate an improved recipe or new variety of bread.

DIFFERENTIATION

Analyse focaccia bread only with less able children and use this analysis to think about its taste and texture. Prompt this group to make changes to the type or amount of the ingredients and to evaluate subsequent tastes and textures. With higher attaining children, note the similar types of flours, liquid and fat used in a range of Italian breads and consider the cooking process and time in the manufacture of each one. Challenge them to change the cooking process and/or time to evaluate any improvements to the taste or texture as a result.

WHERE NEXT

Prompt the children to use their analysis to make a new flavour of pizza base to try out with a range of toppings.

ASSESSMENT

Note which children refine their analysis of the breads to types and amounts of individual ingredients, and relate this analysis to the taste and texture of each bread. Note those who consider this analysis when designing and making improved recipes or a new variety of bread.

LEARNING OUTCOMES

Most children will learn to identify what makes Italian bread taste the way it does through an analysis of the ingredients. Some will use this analysis to design and make an improved recipe or new variety of bread.

FURTHER DESIGN AND TECHNOLOGY CHALLENGES

What a pasta

Ask the children to collect a range of pastas available from the supermarket and analyse the ingredients of each one. They should note which ingredients are common to all the pastas, and which ingredients or cooking processes make them different to each other. Prompt them to think about the ingredients they found from their analysis of Italian breads, such as herbs and tomato, and to use this information to help them make a new variety of pasta for the rest of the class to evaluate.

Pepperoni pizza

SUBJECT: ICT. QCA UNIT: 6A MULTIMEDIA PRESENTATION.

LEARNING OBJECTIVE
To use a multimedia authoring program to organise, refine and present information in different forms for a specific audience.

THINKING OBJECTIVE
To generate ideas.

THINKING SKILLS
The children will analyse the way information is presented on pizza packaging and use the analysis to create their own design. They will use PowerPoint or another multimedia authoring program to design an advert for the pizza using sound, text and movement. They will then make the adverts and evaluate which is the most persuasive. (This activity will take at least two lessons, and links to literacy: persuasive texts.)

WHAT YOU NEED
A digital video camera; PowerPoint or similar program; adverts for pizzas from TV and magazines; empty pizza packaging.

WHAT TO DO
Together, look at a range of pizza packaging and analyse the contents. Note the range of pizzas available today to suit everyone's tastes. Ask the children, *How do the pizza manufacturers make sure that the public buy their pizza and not their competitors'? How do they make sure that everyone tries their pizza at least once so that if they like it they will buy it again? Is the name of the pizza snappy? How is this brought to our attention? If you were walking along a supermarket aisle, would it catch your attention? How much does the pizza cost? Is this relevant? Would you buy the cheapest pizza or go for a more expensive one because it looks mouthwatering?* Ask the children to recall pizza adverts they have seen in magazines and on the TV. Ask, *What was particularly good about them? How did they make you feel like buying a pizza for lunch or tea?*

Organise the children into groups and ask them to plan the type of pizza they intend to advertise, the title, flavours and size. They should think about the following questions: *Will it have a thin or crusty base? What variety will it be? How big?* The children should create a snappy name for the pizza and a catchy

slogan. Ask them to think about how they can present this to the public in a supermarket presentation and demonstration. Ask, *What pictures do you want to create in the mind of the shoppers? How will you entice the public to buy? Will you offer money-off vouchers? Will you rely on the quality of the product to sell it?*

Show the class how to produce a presentation on a series of screens, using different styles, and demonstrate how information is imported into the screen. Let the children spend the rest of the lesson time exploring the different ways they can organise the information and create ideas of their own. After the lesson, share some of the ideas and plan a series of screens for the children to develop in groups. Agree the title, slogan, selling price, type and flavour of pizza being sold, and who will present which part of the advert or presentation. Organise the children into fours and let them spend at least 20 minutes planning their own screen in two sets of pairs to sell the pizza. Each pair should evaluate screens in turn and agree any changes and improvements before choosing the final screen to present to the rest of the class.

Alternatively, let the children produce a group presentation with several screens, creating their own pizza product to sell to the rest of the class. This will mean they produce more than one screen per group and may need to work in two pairs on different screens.

DIFFERENTIATION
Organise the pairs and fours into mixed ability groups, ensuring that all the children contribute to the lesson.

WHERE NEXT
Allow the children to work independently to plan and produce a short class presentation to sell an Italian ice cream or dessert.

ASSESSMENT

Note how well the children work together in groups when planning their screens and generating ideas. Note whether they use a range of different options from the software to add variety to their presentation and whether they consider the needs of the shopper as an audience.

LEARNING OUTCOMES

The children will consider how products are 'sold' to the public and use the information to create their own ideas for selling pizza.

FURTHER ICT CHALLENGES

Holiday bonanza

Use the children's research from the beach location activity in this chapter to sell their resort to the rest of the class using a multimedia program.

Act it out

In groups of four, ask the children to create ideas for a short TV advert to sell the pizza. Ask two groups to work together to act out and video each other's advert to present to the rest of the class.

OPERATIC GENIUS

SUBJECT: MUSIC. QCA UNIT: 18 JOURNEY INTO SPACE.

LEARNING OBJECTIVE

To understand how musical styles create moods and effects.

THINKING OBJECTIVE

To think imaginatively.

THINKING SKILLS

The children will listen to different extracts from operas and imagine the story that each might tell. They will consider how well the music helps them to imagine what is happening or what is likely to happen in the opera as the story unfolds.

WHAT YOU NEED

Extracts from operas written in Italian with different styles, for example tapes by famous opera singers including Pavarotti and Lesley Garrett, the 'Anvil Chorus' from *Il Travatore* by Verdi, the overtures to Mozart's *Marriage of Figaro* and Rossini's *William Tell*; paper; writing materials.

WHAT TO DO

Listen to one of the songs performed by Pavarotti or Lesley Garrett and ask the children, *Do you like this music? What do you like? What don't you like? What sort of music is it?* Tell them that the songs come from operas – musical plays that tell stories through song. Listen to the overture from *William Tell* by Rossini, avoiding telling the children its title at this stage. Tell them, however, that it is the overture to a famous opera written by an Italian composer called Gioachino Rossini. Explain that an overture is the opening piece of music which sets the scene for the story that follows – it sets the mood for the whole opera. After listening to it once, work with the children to write a description using the correct musical terminology to describe the effects, mood and feeling that the music depicts. Ask, *What do you think this music is about?* Together, listen to the extract again and ask the children to imagine what might be happening at the beginning of the story. Explain that the opera tells a famous legend about a particular person. Invite them to say what this person may be like and who it may be.

Tell them that the opera is about William Tell. If necessary, outline the story for the children if it is unfamiliar to them. Allow the children to listen to the overture again, this time with the story in mind, and ask them to imagine the sort of person William Tell might be from the mood of Rossini's music. Ask, *Can you imagine what he looks like? Can you imagine the sort of person he is?* Collect the children's adjectives to describe William Tell's character.

Repeat the activity in the same way, listening together to the overture from Mozart's *Marriage of Figaro* and/or Verdi's 'Anvil Chorus' from *Il Travatore*. Ask the children to imagine what might be happening on stage during each piece of music, and gather their thoughts before telling them what the opera is actually about. Talk about how the composers use music to create these pictures.

DIFFERENTIATION

Talk about the events in the story of William Tell with the lower attaining children and then listen to the overture again. Encourage them to see how the musical elements are used to set the scene. Play a different piece to higher attaining children and ask them to imagine what it may be about.

WHERE NEXT

Challenge the children to find out the names of other famous Italian composers and singers who wrote or performed operas. Listen to some of these and prompt the children to imagine what the story might be about from the style of the music.

Help the children to compare Italian-style opera to the works of Wagner. They should note the similarities and differences between the style and the way musical elements are used, and relate this to the moods, feelings and emotions conveyed.

ASSESSMENT

If possible, ask another adult to record the different ideas the children imagine the music might be about. Alternatively, work with small groups of children listening to other pieces of music and note down the different ideas they generate, supported by the mood the music evokes.

LEARNING OUTCOMES

The children will all respond to the mood and effects in the music to imagine what the opera might be about, and suggest what story is being told.

FURTHER MUSIC CHALLENGES

Paint the picture

Listen to an extract from another opera and ask the children to write a poem or descriptive piece of writing, or to draw or paint the picture the music conjures up in their minds. Compare this to the actual content of the opera to see if the effects created by the music helped the children get close to the mood.

Saigon blues

Listen to the extract from *Madame Butterfly* by Puccini where she vows her undying love and then dies, and also to the similar extract from *Miss Saigon* by Claude-Michel Schonberg, Richard Maltby Jr, and Alain Boublil. Compare the two extracts and note how the composers create the same mood and effect but in different ways. Identify the features that are the same and those that are different in the extracts.

ROMAN CATHOLICS

SUBJECT: RE. QCA UNIT: 6E WHAT CAN WE LEARN FROM CHRISTIAN RELIGIOUS BUILDINGS?

LEARNING OBJECTIVE

To identify the range of artefacts and symbols in a Roman Catholic Church, and consider their different meanings to the people who worship there.

THINKING OBJECTIVE

To use the skills of inference and to give reasons.

THINKING SKILLS

Before the lesson, the children should visit a Roman Catholic church, watch a video or look at pictures and collect images of the artefacts that are found there. They will consider those artefacts found in most Christian churches before identifying items which are found only in Catholic churches, for instance the confessional boxes, holy water at the entrance and icons of the Virgin Mary. They will consider the importance of these items to Catholics in particular, and what they mean to this religious group. They will consider the Eucharist in detail and think about why it is so important to the Catholic religion.

WHAT YOU NEED

Extracts from the Bible, which tells the story of how Jesus was betrayed in the Garden of Gethsemane; copies of the Eucharist service and prayers for different services in the Roman Catholic church.

WHAT TO DO

Before the lesson, visit a Roman Catholic church with the class and identify all the artefacts and symbols it contains which are common to and different from other Christian churches. Tell the children that there are thousands of Christians all around the world. Ask them why they are called Christians and recall that it is because they believe that Jesus Christ is the Son of God. Identify with them all the Christian groups there are, including Church of England, Greek Orthodox and Roman Catholic. Explain that all of these people hold Jesus to be the Messiah and they include him in their prayers during worship.

Look together at the artefacts that are unique to the Roman Catholic church, such as the confessional box and the holy water at the entrance. Talk about the purpose of these. Remind the children how worshippers use the holy water to make the sign of the cross to recall the way Jesus died, and of the importance of confession in the Catholic church. Explain that although all Christians ask for forgiveness for their sins, Catholics think this practice so important that they have a special place and prayer for confession. Relate this practice to how Jesus died for our sins and explain that this is a way for Catholics to remember the reasons for his death. As a class, list the symbols and artefacts found in the Catholic church and for each one infer the meanings to practising worshippers.

Explain to the children that you want to look at one service in particular and this is called the Eucharist or Communion. Ask the children, *Do you know the purpose of this particular act of worship?*

Explain that it is a time when Christians confirm their beliefs in God and Jesus and life everlasting, revealed to Christians through the resurrection of Jesus. Quickly remind them of the story of how Judas betrayed Jesus and how the symbol of drinking wine and breaking bread reminds believers of Jesus and the reasons why he died. Look at the order of service in the Catholic church, and identify the elements included, such as prayer, blessing, taking of wine and bread and confessing the sins. Talk about how the breaking of bread and the drinking of wine are included in the Eucharist to remember the body and blood of Christ.

Organise a mind mapping or concept mapping activity where the children link the parts of the Eucharist service to its meaning to the people who attend. Give them or ask them to brainstorm all the words they can which are found in the service, and link these with a relevant meaning or feeling, identifying reasons for the link. For example, prayer can be linked to asking forgiveness, breaking bread with remembering why Jesus died.

DIFFERENTIATION
Ask higher attaining children to note the similarities and differences between the Eucharist and Communion services. Challenge them to list all the meanings these services have to the Christians who take part. Discuss what the children infer from these services.

WHERE NEXT
Prompt the children to look at other services and practices in the Roman Catholic church, and to draw out the inferred meaning, for example meeting the Pope, listening to his blessing at Christmas or the naming of new saints.

ASSESSMENT
Assess whether the children learn the facts of the services or whether they can infer the meaning and purpose behind the different parts of the Eucharist service. Note those who relate this to the symbols and artefacts found in the Catholic church.

LEARNING OUTCOMES
The children will all learn that there are similarities and differences between the different Christian groups, namely the Roman Catholics in this activity. Some will identify the similarities and differences in the meaning and purpose the Eucharist service infers.

FURTHER RE CHALLENGES
Prayers for the living
Together, list all the different services which take place in the Roman Catholic church and identify those that also take place in other Christian churches. Ask, *Which services are different?* Help the children to locate some of the prayers that are said during these services and practices in prayer books, and to think carefully about why they are said by inferring their meaning. For example, prayers are said to ask forgiveness, to confess, to ask for help or to say thank you for something. Prompt the children to find other prayers and to classify them.
Handel's Messiah
Think about the meaning of the word 'Messiah' and what this infers to Christians and Roman Catholics in

particular. Listen to the 'Hallelujah Chorus' by Handel and consider why he chose the words that he did. Ask, *How did he infer the meaning of the term 'Messiah' in his music?*

ITALIAN CALENDAR

SUBJECT: PE. QCA UNIT: DANCE ACTIVITIES UNIT 6.

LEARNING OBJECTIVE
To improvise a series of dance motifs to depict people, places and numbers.

THINKING OBJECTIVE
To generate ideas and to suggest improvements.

THINKING SKILLS
The children will create a series of dance motifs, phrases and sequences over a number of weeks to build a dance to depict the names of the months of the year. They will improvise freely their interpretation of the names of the months before using the full range of dance compositional principles to structure their dance and make improvements. They will think about where the names of the months came from and use these as a base for their ideas. They will learn to incorporate their motifs into phrases and then into sequences. They will build the basic structure of the dance before evaluating each other's performance. They will then make suggestions for improvement in terms of changing the way the sequences are performed, for example in canon, unison, introducing partner work for one repetition, performing in a line or circle and so on, as well as considering how the types of movement depict the subject of their particular month.

WHAT YOU NEED
Access to music from a range of sources; tape and/ or CD player; resources to research the origins of the names of the months; large space in which to practise the dance.

WHAT TO DO
Ask group to research the origins of the names of the months of the year. Share the research as a class,

and use this information to let the children consider in which dance 'month' they would like to be. Once the groups are organised into their chosen months, challenge them to work as a group to improvise different dance motifs to depict their month and what it is about. For example, think about a statue of Janus and how he looks in both directions. Ask, *What did he look like and what character did he have? How can this be depicted in a dance motif? Where did he stand? What did he see?* Prompt the children to build this into their dance by creating another motif. Use questions to help them develop suitable dance motifs for the other months.

In another session, ask the children to listen to a range of music and to evaluate which pieces would support their particular dance motifs. They should think about any characteristics they wish to portray, and any mood from the action or events they wish to include.

Allow the children to work in groups to fit their dance motifs to the music, extending these to build them into phrases and sequences. Encourage them to structure the sequences by placing the motifs and phrases in the same or different orders. For example, have two motifs for each phrase and develop two or three phrases. Give each phrase a letter and build them into a sequence. Make the first and last sequence the same structure, for example ABAA, with one in the middle ABCA.

When the groups have worked out their sequence they are ready to perform in front of the class. This will allow the class to evaluate the performance and to suggest improvements to increase the quality of the dance and to make it particularly interesting. For example, the January group might use partners working in symmetry to depict Janus looking in two directions, movement in canon could show April bringing in spring, while March could be a strong, lively dance. Encourage the children to think about their hand and facial expressions and whether to move in a line or a circle. Evaluate three months per lesson with the whole class working together to develop the dance and suggesting improvements.

After four weeks, when the sequences are developed in different ways for all the months, perform the dances as a whole to a compilation tape of each group's music.

DIFFERENTIATION
Ask higher attaining children to work in the groups depicting September through to December, as these months will require some imaginative thinking to generate ideas. Lower attaining children should work on months which tell a story or are named after particular people, such as February, March, April, July and August.

WHERE NEXT
Video the children's performance and, as a class, evaluate their work in terms of variety of structure and style. Discuss the range of dance traditions used and whether these reflect the subject of each month. Prompt the children to use this information to suggest final improvements to the dance.

ASSESSMENT
Watch each group as they create their ideas for a dance and note whether they take the story or character of the subject into account when using particular dance elements or choosing particular styles of music. Listen to the evaluations and note how well the children consider the range of dance traditions and elements to suggest ways of making the dance more dramatic or to depict the subjects more creatively.

LEARNING OUTCOMES
The children will use a wide context through which to create their ideas. They will consider the full range of dance traditions, structures and elements when making suggestions on how each group can improve their dance.

FURTHER PE CHALLENGES
Italian statues
Ask the children to look at pictures of the different statues found in Rome or other Italian cities, and to build up a dance to depict a minute in the life of this statue. Encourage them to generate ideas based on the expressions or subject of the statue, and to decide on the best dance style to depict this particular character. Each group should create their own one-minute dance routine before inviting the other groups to make suggestions on how this can be improved, taking into account the character of the statue being depicted. The children should focus on the dance elements of dynamics, levels and shape when suggesting improvements.

Trevi fountain
Show the children pictures of the Trevi Fountain and encourage them to build up dance motifs, phrases and sequences to depict the different people who come to the fountain to make a wish. Organise the children into groups and ask them to generate ideas to depict the wishes of the different people through dance. Encourage them to consider the range of dance elements and traditions they could include to evoke the desires and feelings of the people as well as the content of their wishes.

147

PLANNING A SCHOOL TRIP

Subject and QCA unit, NLS or NNS objective	Activity title	Thinking objective	Activity	Page
English NLS objectives: To evaluate a range of texts for persuasiveness, clarity and quality of information; to comment critically on the language, style, success of examples of non-fiction such as periodicals, reviews, reports and leaflets	Where shall we go?	To evaluate information (judging clarity, interest, persuasiveness and usefulness)	Evaluating a range of leaflets and deciding which is the most interesting, clearly presented and persuasive	149
Maths NNS objectives: To make decisions; to solve problems about real life using one or more steps; to begin to find simple percentages of small whole-number quantities	A trip to London	To use skills of deduction	Calculating the cost of a trip to London, France or the country and deciding on the best travel option in terms of cost	150
Science QCA unit: 6B Micro-organisms; 5D Changing state	Fresh milk	To anticipate consequences and to test conclusions	Finding the best way to keep milk fresh and stop it going sour. Using what they have found out to create a way of slowing down the melting process of ice cream and ice lollies	151
History QCA unit: 14 Who were the Ancient Greeks?; 16 How can we find out about the Indus Valley civilisation?	The British Museum	To collect information, to plan research and to evaluate information (judging value)	Finding out what exhibits museums have to offer and evaluating the value of each one in relation to a current topic (ICT link)	153
Geography QCA unit: 25 Geography and numbers	Map reading	To plan research and to locate information	Working out different routes, reading site maps and following a route to calculate how much further to travel	154
Design and technology QCA unit: 6A Shelters	Be prepared	To analyse	Designing and making umbrellas	155
ICT QCA unit: 6D Using the internet to search large databases and to interpret information	Arists and paintings	To evaluate information (judging usefulness)	Searching for a painting and artist using the internet and complex search	156
Art and design QCA unit: 6C A sense of place	Landscape photographs	To collect, match and analyse information	Collecting images by sketching or photography, matching and analysing how different features are painted by different artists	158
Music QCA unit: 18 Journey into space	Coach music	To evaluate information (judging quality)	Making a compilation tape of music to listen and/or sing along to on the coach going and coming home	159

Where shall we go?

SUBJECT: ENGLISH. NLS OBJECTIVES: TO EVALUATE A RANGE OF TEXTS FOR PERSUASIVENESS, CLARITY AND QUALITY OF INFORMATION; TO COMMENT CRITICALLY ON THE LANGUAGE, STYLE, SUCCESS OF EXAMPLES OF NON-FICTION SUCH AS PERIODICALS, REVIEWS, REPORTS AND LEAFLETS.

LEARNING OBJECTIVE

To comment critically on the clarity and quality of a range of literature promoting different places, and to decide which is the most persuasive.

THINKING OBJECTIVE

To evaluate information (judging clarity, interest, persuasiveness and usefulness).

THINKING SKILLS

The children will look at different leaflets promoting places of interest and comment critically about the clear and interesting way the information is conveyed, the quality of the information and how persuasive it is. They will list the criteria which informs the quality and usefulness of each leaflet, and consider how these persuade the reader to visit. From the information, the children will decide whether this would be a good place to visit to support a current topic.

WHAT YOU NEED

A range of leaflets about different places of interest, which are different in style, content and presentation; large sheets of paper; writing materials.

WHAT TO DO

Together, look at a leaflet of a place of interest, for example Disney World, and list the things that immediately capture the attention of the reader. As a class, list the range of information that the leaflet includes and discuss how the reader knows immediately where and how to find this. Ask the children, *How is the information presented? How does the leaflet make the information clear? Are there any symbols used to attract the eye? Does the information tell you what you want to know about opening times, where to eat, where to find the toilet or where to buy a drink? Does it give guidance on the possible length of the queues? How easily can you find the information?*

What is it that helps you do this?

Take one aspect of the leaflet and define more closely the quality in terms of interest, clarity and persuasiveness. For each aspect and defined quality, the children should evaluate what the strengths and the weaknesses are, building up 'For' and 'Against' lists against which to give the leaflet an overall judgement.

When the children have broken down the evaluation, they should reach an overall judgement about the clarity of information, and the interest and persuasiveness of each leaflet. Finally from the

Aspect	For	Against
Opening times	Easy-to-find information. Opening times broken down into clear days.	Would be more useful on the front of the leaflet. Not long enough time to have a good look round in one day.
Facilities	Wide range. Suitable for all ages. Clarity of map means they are easy to find.	Not enough toilets. Narrow range of food outlets.
Cost	Entrance cost given. Food costs given.	Expensive. Additional costs not given.

information collected, the children should decide whether it is a suitable place to visit to support a particular topic.

Organise the children into groups and, using a large sheet of paper to record their ideas, ask them to make 'For' and 'Against' lists for the different pieces of information each leaflet gives. They should list all the information the leaflet covers first, and then break down the evaluation of each item more closely in terms of its clarity, interest and persuasiveness. They should finally award the leaflet, not the venue, a mark out of ten based on this evaluation. Share the children's ideas at the end of the lesson, and agree on an overall evaluation.

DIFFERENTIATION

Collect leaflets of venues with which the lower attaining children are familiar, perhaps a local venue or one that they visited on a previous school trip. This will help them set the evaluation into context. Higher attaining children should be given a leaflet of a theme park which will make them think carefully about the objectivity of their judgements.

WHERE NEXT

Use the children's evaluation to decide on some practical and realistic places to organise for a school trip.

THINKING SKILLS: AGES 9–11

Assessment

Note how well the children evaluate the quality of the leaflet in terms of its clarity, interest and persuasiveness, and the usefulness of a visit with regard to a current topic, and how well they use this information to decide on a possible venue for a visit.

Learning outcomes

The children will learn to evaluate the quality of written information and to decide the importance of each component to its clarity, interest and persuasiveness, and usefulness in tempting people to visit.

Further English challenges

Theme parks

Challenge the children to evaluate which theme park offers the most persuasive leaflet and makes them want to visit.

Museums and art galleries

Prompt the children to evaluate the information that museums and art galleries provide about their interest and accessibility. The children should evaluate the information each venue provides in leaflets and on the internet, and judge whether it gives clear and interesting information which persuades them to visit. Add an extra criterion for evaluation: *Does the venue provide useful information for a current school project?*

A TRIP TO LONDON

SUBJECT: MATHS. NNS OBJECTIVES: TO MAKE DECISIONS; TO SOLVE PROBLEMS ABOUT REAL LIFE USING ONE OR MORE STEPS; TO BEGIN TO FIND SIMPLE PERCENTAGES OF SMALL WHOLE-NUMBER QUANTITIES.

Learning objective

To solve two-step problems using addition and division.

Thinking objective

To use skills of deduction.

Thinking skills

The children will be given different places to cost and to make decisions about the feasibility of organising a school trip. They will look at the different costs involved in, for example, a trip to London, to other parts of the country or to France, depending on where your school is situated, and deduce the total cost of the trip when using different travel options. They will then use the information to make decisions about the best travel options if this trip is organised. They will work out the cost per person if they travel by coach or train and add this to the admission price of any venues visited to work out an overall cost. They will evaluate each group's options to decide which place they would want to organise a trip to.

What you need

Prices of coach and train travel to London, to other parts of the country or France; the cost of admission to the chosen venue; the cost of train tickets and coach hire to the venue; paper; writing materials.

What to do

Talk to the children about the places they decided would be worth visiting, using the information from the previous activity. Tell them that now they need to decide whether they are cost effective. Talk about what this means and tell the children you want them to make a decision about whether these venues would be affordable or too expensive as a school trip. Decide together a maximum amount of money the children are prepared to pay for a school trip, taking into account the likely views of their parents on the subject.

Ask the children to imagine they are going to London for a day on a school trip (or another city if you already live in London), and together identify a plan of action to find out the cost for different travel options. Tell the children the cost of a train ticket, the cost to hire a coach and the cost of admission to the different venues they might like to visit. First, invite the children to suggest how they can deduce the cost of the trip for each child if they travel by train. Agree that they need to add the cost of the train ticket to the cost of admission to each of the venues. Do this together to consolidate the skills and strategies used in the addition of money. Next, deduce how much the trip would cost each child if they travel by coach. Agree that the total cost of hiring the coach needs to be divided by the number of children travelling. Calculate this together and add on the costs of admission of one attraction. Compare the two prices and agree which is the best option. Ask the children, *Are there any additional costs to think about, such as insurance and spending money? Would these amounts be the same or*

different for the different travel options? Agree that these costs would probably be the same. Add these costs on to the total and check the option that was agreed on earlier is still the cheapest.

Organise the children into groups and provide each group with the cost of admission for other attractions to add into the cost of the trip so far. Encourage them to work out a total cost per child per trip.

Share the information at the end of the session, and decide which is the most cost-effective way to travel. Ask the children, *Looking back to the amount of money you were prepared to pay, is this trip affordable or too expensive? If it is too expensive, how could we reduce the costs? By how much do we need to reduce the cost? Are some atttractions better value for money than others?*

DIFFERENTIATION
Challenge higher attaining children to cost a trip to Disneyland Paris so that they can consider more variables, including travelling by coach, train, ferry, through the tunnel or by air. They can use the internet to cost and evaluate different options offered by tour companies. Ask them to imagine that certain companies will provide a ten per cent reduction or a free place for every ten people who travel. Ask, *How does this change your calculations?* Lower attaining children should be given totals for the complete trip which can be divided by the number of children exactly.

WHERE NEXT
If at all possible, the class should use the information they have above to decide where to go on a school trip and organise this with your help.

ASSESSMENT
Use the children's working out to demonstrate whether they understand which strategies to use to

deduce the total cost of the different travel options, and whether they use the information to make decisions about the cost effectiveness of each type of travel and the value for money offered by the attractions.

LEARNING OUTCOMES
All the children will learn to compare two totals to make decisions about the cost effectiveness of different travel options, and decide which attractions provide value for money for a school trip. Most will learn how to deduce the total cost of the trip using addition and division to solve two-step problems.

FURTHER MATHS CHALLENGES
How long?
Provide each group with a different destination, and ask them to work out the length of the journey, and how long it would take to get there if they travelled at an average of 30 or 40 mph. Ask, *Is there a way of speeding up the journey, for example by using the motorway?* Prompt the children to use this information to work out and decide what time they need to leave school in the morning, and what time parents should come to collect them at the end of the day.

Gift shop
Organise groups to use the internet to look up the gift shops at one of the places you plan to visit (or write to the attraction for a price list or catalogue). Using the price list of gifts available ask the children to work out what items they could buy with a set amount of money. For example, ask, *If you have £2, what items could you buy for this amount?* Ask the children to use the information to decide what they are likely to want to buy from the gift shop when you go on the school trip.

FRESH MILK

SUBJECT: SCIENCE. QCA UNIT: 6B MICRO-ORGANISMS; 5D CHANGING STATE.

LEARNING OBJECTIVE
To learn that micro-organisms can cause food to decay.

THINKING OBJECTIVE
To anticipate consequences and to test conclusions.

THINKING SKILLS
The children will use their knowledge and understanding of what happens when milk is not kept cool by anticipating that it will go sour if kept warm for too long a period. They will predict that if they

can find a way of keeping the milk cool, it will not go sour. They will test out their conclusions by devising different ways to keep the milk fresh, and then use this information to make a cool box.

WHAT YOU NEED
Ice; water; buckets; thermometers; paper; writing materials.

WHAT TO DO
Tell the children that you want to take milk with you on the school trip so you can have a cup of coffee in the afternoon. Invite their suggestions about how you can take the milk. Ask, *What container could we use? Why is it best not to put the milk in an ordinary cup with a lid?* Discuss with the children what happens to the milk if it is not kept cold enough, and agree that it will go sour. Discuss the different states between fresh and sour milk, noting the changes in texture, taste and smell. Discuss how micro-organisms grow in the milk because of the heat and this is what causes the milk to go sour. It is not necessary to take sour milk into the classroom because most children will be familiar with its smell and appearance.

Invite the children's suggestions about how you could take milk on the trip and keep it as fresh as possible. Tell the children how, in the 1950s, most people did not own a fridge. Ask, *Why do you think they did not go to the supermarket every day to buy more milk? How did they get their milk?* Explain that there were no supermarkets at the time and that many people did not have cars so could not easily go to the shop every day. Explain that they had to find a way to keep their milk fresh and to stop it from going sour. Ask, *What do you think people did to keep the milk fresh?*

Collect the children's suggestions and use these to help them set up a fair test to investigate their ideas. Provide them with any equipment they need, or encourage them to bring in what they need from home. Once the test has been set up, they need to measure the freshness of the milk by taking the temperature after an hour and finding which place/container/method kept the milk cooler. Ask each group to record and interpret the results and to draw conclusions about the best way to keep milk fresh in the absence of a fridge. Ask the children to agree the conclusions in writing and to evaluate these to see if the test is secure and whether there is any need to make improvements on the way the temperature was tested.

DIFFERENTIATION
Organise the children into mixed ability groups, monitoring closely how much lower attaining children are involved in the measurement and recording of results.

WHERE NEXT
Prompt the children to research, using secondary sources, the micro-organisms that send milk sour. They should note the usefulness of some of these in food production.

ASSESSMENT
Record the children's suggestions and note who anticipates that the milk will go sour and why. It is important that the children understand that this process is caused by micro-organisms but it's not necessary for them to know any further detail at this stage.

Watch the children as they carry out the investigation and note those who remain focused on the question in order to solve the problem.

LEARNING OUTCOMES
Most children will learn to anticipate that food items will go bad, rotten or sour if exposed to heat for too long. They will learn how to plan and carry out a fair test to test their conclusions.

FURTHER SCIENCE CHALLENGES
Ice cream treats
Anticipate with the children what happens to ice

cream on a hot day, and challenge them to find a way to stop it melting. Ask, *How long do you think it will take for ice cream to melt? Can you find a way to slow this down?*

Choose ice lollies

Challenge the children to find out if ice lollies are better to buy than ice cream. Ask, *Will they melt slower? Why does it take longer for ice lollies to melt than ice cream?* Test the children's ideas and find out whether ice cream or ice lollies melt quicker, or whether they melt at the same rate. Prompt them to make decisions about whether to buy ice lollies or ice cream if the weather is hot on the trip.

THE BRITISH MUSEUM

SUBJECT: HISTORY. QCA UNIT: 14 WHO WERE THE ANCIENT GREEKS?; 16 HOW CAN WE FIND OUT ABOUT THE INDUS VALLEY CIVILISATION?

LEARNING OBJECTIVE

To use the internet to find information on museums.

THINKING OBJECTIVE

To collect information, to plan research and to evaluate information (judging value).

THINKING SKILLS

The children will log on to the internet and find the website for the British Museum, or another chosen museum. They will collect information about the range of exhibits on show before planning research into which ones to visit to support a particular topic, for example the Ancient Greeks or the Indus Valley civilisation. They will judge the value of the site in terms of how well it helped them to make a decision about whether to visit this museum or not.

WHAT YOU NEED

Internet access; reference books and CD-ROMs on the Ancient Greeks or the Indus Valley civilisations; paper; writing materials.

WHAT TO DO

Together, search for the website for the British Museum (www.thebritishmuseum.ac.uk) and look at the layout of the front page. Prompt the children to note what information this page offers about the museum. Note the categories and how clearly

the information is presented. Ask, *What kind of information does it provide? Does it list the types of exhibits available? Where can we find this information?* As a class, look through the menu and discuss all the information headings, noting what each one includes to give the children an idea of the information available on the site.

Next, help the children to plan research to find out whether this museum would help them with their current topic. Ask, *What do you need to know to find out whether the site will be useful, or a visit valuable, to your research?* Prompt the children to identify key questions to help define their plan:
⊙ What do we need to find out (about the particular topic in school we are researching)?
⊙ Where on the website can I find information about this topic?
⊙ Does the museum contain the information I need?
⊙ Are there useful exhibits to help with our research?
⊙ Would a visit to the museum help our studies?
The children should then follow their research plan to find answers to their questions and evaluate whether a visit would be helpful.

During a plenary, ask the children to report back on the useful parts of the website and why this is the case.

WHERE NEXT

Ask the children to decide whether the visit to the museum could be conducted online or whether an actual visit would be better.

Prompt the children to look at the websites of other museums and to evaluate their usefulness in presenting information clearly, and how valuable the information is in helping them decide whether a visit would be useful to support their studies and research. The children could plan research to find out what their nearest museum has to offer in terms of local history.

DIFFERENTIATION

Help less able children identify the questions they will need to plan research into the chosen topic. Higher attaining children should be encouraged to evaluate each piece of information carefully and note how useful it is when making decisions about the value of a visit to their research.

ASSESSMENT

Assess the questions the children ask and whether these define the research process. Note how well they use the information to evaluate whether a visit is worthwhile.

LEARNING OUTCOMES

The children will plan research to find out what a museum has to offer in terms of information to help them research a particular topic. They will evaluate the information to reach a decision about how worthwhile the visit is likely to be.

FURTHER HISTORY CHALLENGES

Information leaflet

Prompt the children to collect information from the website about their chosen museum or art gallery and to download some pictures and text to use in an information leaflet. They should plan research on how they can use other ICT sources of information for the leaflet. Encourage them to present their plan as a list of key questions to help them search CD-ROMs and the website to collect suitable information. They should evaluate whether to use this information on their leaflets in terms of usefulness (either to give information about the venue, or value offered in terms of whether it would be a good place to visit). The children could also consider postcards and pictures of exhibits from brochures and books, and scan these into the computer for inclusion in the leaflet.

MAP READING

SUBJECT: GEOGRAPHY. QCA UNIT: 25 GEOGRAPHY AND NUMBERS.

LEARNING OBJECTIVE

To interpret the information on maps to work out distance travelled and to plan a route between two points.

THINKING OBJECTIVE

To plan research and to locate information.

THINKING SKILLS

The children will plan how they can find out the best route to a particular venue. They will work out the distance between the venue and the school, and calculate what time they need to leave at the end of the visit to return to school. They will use grid references to locate the two points on a map, and then plan possible routes by road, train or ferry, depending on the venue. They will use the scale, or map symbols, to calculate how far and how long the journey will take.

WHAT YOU NEED

Road maps containing indicators of mileage distances between two points and/or a mileage scale; leaflets of different places of interest to visit.

WHAT TO DO

Tell the children that you want to work out what time you need to leave the venue they have chosen to visit to make sure you get back to school before hometime. Ask the children to think of a way to deduce this. Collect their suggestions and let them follow these ideas if they are feasible. Alternatively, explain that you need to work out how far away the venue is from the school so that you can deduce how long the journey is likely to take. Ask, *What do we need to do first?* Agree that you need to locate the school and the venue on the map. Ask, *How are we going to do this?* Look on the leaflet for the address and ask the children to suggest how you can go about locating this on the map. Ask, *How can we find out on which page this venue is? How can we find a map reference?* Demonstrate how to use the index and locate the page on which the venue is found. Show the children how to use the grid reference to locate the venue on the map, and mark its position with a piece of Blu-Tak or similar. Next, ask the children to say whether they can still see the school. If they can, mark this in a similar way.

Discuss with the children all the possible routes they could take to the venue. Next, ask them to suggest how they could work out the distance between the two places. Note the distance on the map and look to see if there is a scale. Help the children to calculate the distance using the scale. Alternatively, they could look for the map symbols which mark the differences between two places and the mileage number. This is usually a blue triangle with the distance in miles written in blue somewhere between the two points. Invite a child to locate the symbols and mileage numbers, and then together calculate the distance for each of the routes and say, therefore, which is the most direct route.

Tell the children that the coach is likely to travel about 30 mph. The children should use this information to deduce how long the journey is likely to take and, therefore, the time to leave the venue to return to school.

Organise the children into groups and, providing each group with a leaflet on a different place of interest, ask them to follow the plan: locating the two points of travel, working out possible routes and calculating the distance and time the journey is likely to take. The children should consider the different venues and eliminate those that will take too long, note those which will allow them to arrive back in school later than the usual finishing time or which will fit nicely into the school day.

DIFFERENTIATION

Provide higher attaining children with a venue which is not on the same page of the road map. Some very able children should be asked to evaluate whether a train journey would be better and to compare the distance by road and time taken to go by train. They should consider how the class would get from the train to their chosen venue. Give lower attaining children the research plan to follow and act as a model to help them locate the position of their venue. They should work on a more local venue so that the distance is easier to calculate. For example, choose a venue which is 30 miles away so they can locate its position on a map of an area with which they are familiar and calculate easily that it will take an hour to get there.

WHERE NEXT

Prompt the children to plan research to find out how long it will take to walk to, for example, the nearest swimming pool from school or, if the school is too far away, to walk to some other point in the locality, such as the bus station. Note the key questions the children identify to structure the research process and how they use the scale to work out the distance. Ask, *What did you include in your plan to find out how long it would take to walk this distance?*

ASSESSMENT

Assess how quickly the children use the grid references to locate the venues on the map and note how they deduce the distance between these and school. Note those who use the scale and those who use the map symbols to calculate the distance.

LEARNING OUTCOMES

The children will locate two specific locations on a map, plan possible routes and use a scale or map symbols to deduce the distance travelled by road.

FURTHER GEOGRAPHY CHALLENGES

How much further?
Whether the children are on an actual journey or a virtual journey, prompt them to locate where they are on a road map. They should locate their destination and deduce how much further there is to travel, either by using the blue triangular arrows or the scale.

Grid references
Ask the children to locate the different venues they looked at in the activity 'Where shall we go?'. They should give the grid references of the venues for others to locate, plan possible journeys and deduce the distance each journey covers. Challenge them to plot the venues on a large map and to attach the leaflets in the correct places.

BE PREPARED

SUBJECT: DESIGN AND TECHNOLOGY. QCA UNIT: 6A SHELTERS.

LEARNING OBJECTIVE

To learn how to make a stable structure to act as a frame for an umbrella.

THINKING OBJECTIVE

To analyse.

THINKING SKILLS

The children will look at a simple mechanism for making an umbrella and use the information to create a structure for their own umbrellas or parasols to take on their school trip.

WHAT YOU NEED

A collection of umbrellas and/or parasols; strong plastic straws; pipe cleaners; tubing of different thickness; fabric and polythene; paper; cocktail umbrellas; wooden cocktail sticks; sticky tape.

WHAT TO DO

Together, look at the structure of the umbrella frame. Talk about how the spokes are joined to make a collapsible mechanism. Open and close the umbrella very slowly and encourage the children to describe what is happening to each of the components: to the fabric, the spokes attached to the fabric, the spokes attached to the frame and the way the tube with these attached slides up and down the handle. Note with the children the way the tube slides up the handle, pushing the frame upwards and stretching the fabric out.

Allow the children to work in pairs to make a prototype structure for an umbrella which can be put up and let down. They should make a frame by gluing strong plastic straws to the top of a piece of tubing which will act as a handle. Then they need to glue smaller lengths of straws onto a piece of plastic tubing placed over the handle, and attach the other end to the middle of those which make the frame with sticky tape. Finally, they should attach a piece of plastic over the frame to complete the umbrellas.

DIFFERENTIATION

With higher attaining children, note the way the spokes are joined in a telescopic umbrella to make the mechanism which pushes them in different directions, and analyse the way the umbrella opens and closes. Place an open umbrella in the middle of the tables as the children make their prototypes so that they can copy the designs and positions of the spokes if necessary.

WHERE NEXT

Ask the children to make parasols in the same way to protect them from the sun.

ASSESSMENT

Listen to the children's explanations and note whether they analyse the way one component makes the other parts move to make the umbrella open and close. Note the children who internalise this analysis to make a prototype structure from memory.

LEARNING OUTCOMES

The children will analyse how a mechanism makes an umbrella open and close and use this information to make their own prototype umbrella frame.

FURTHER DESIGN AND TECHNOLOGY CHALLENGES

Umbrella hats

The children could design and possibly make prototypes for hats which also act as umbrellas or parasols. Ask them to analyse the structure needed and to think about how they can attach this to the hats in a suitable way.

ARTISTS AND PAINTINGS

SUBJECT: ICT. QCA UNIT: 6D USING THE INTERNET TO SEARCH LARGE DATABASES AND TO INTERPRET INFORMATION.

LEARNING OBJECTIVES

To learn to use complex searches to locate information and to work with others to interpret information.

THINKING OBJECTIVE

To evaluate information (judging usefulness).

THINKING SKILLS

The children will set up a complex search to find a particular painting by a particular artist to support their work in art and design. This could be linked to their work on landscapes, or to the previous cross-curricular activity to find Italian artists who painted pictures of a particular type, or sculpted statues of a religious nature. The children will identify key words and set up a research plan to note the different ways the search can be carried out, before trying out their ideas and evaluating which is the most useful.

WHAT YOU NEED

Internet access; paper; writing materials; a list of suitable paintings.

WHAT TO DO

Before the lesson, check that the data described below is available.

Tell the children that you want them to learn how to set up an advanced search on an internet site to find information about particular paintings by famous artists.

Explain that you want them to find a painting by Picasso, called *Child with a Dove*, to find out when it was painted and whether it is a watercolour or an oil painting. Together, compose a research plan for finding this information using an internet search facility. In the plan, include possible key words to use in the search, for example 'Picasso', or 'Child with a Dove'. Gather the children's suggestions about possible websites for finding the information. If the class have a favourite search engine, note that. Keep the plan handy for the children to refer to during the independent task.

Alternatively, go to nationalgallery.org.uk and show the children how to set up a search to find Picasso's *Child with a Dove*. This can be done by entering the name of the artist or the name of the painting. Note with the class how quickly the painting is found from the gallery's database. Ask, *Why was it so easy to find this painting? Was it because it is the only painting in this gallery by this artist?* Ask the children to suggest how they could find a different painting by Picasso that they are familiar with and try this. Finally, enter the name of an artist which the gallery does not include in its database, such as Lowry. Note that the computer does not find a match.

Ask the children how they might be able to find a painting by Lowry called *Coming out of School*. Go to 'Search tips' and note the links to the Tate gallery and the EuroGallery. Go to the Tate website. Set up an advanced search by typing in all words, including 'Lowry', as a match. Explain to the children how this refines the search so that the website does not show too many matches. Note how quickly the painting appears!

Finally, go to EuroGallery and set up a simple search for information about Monet's *The Water-Lily Pond*. Type in the artist's name, 'Monet', and note the number of matches (158) that the gallery holds for this artist. Decide with the children whether this would be a good way of finding a particular painting and agree that it could be. Ask, *Could we use a different key word such as the title of the painting?* Agree with the children that an advanced search which uses both the artist's name *and* the title of the painting may be more productive and quicker. Set up an advanced search on the site to find the painting. Note the speed with which it sends us back to the National Gallery website when locating the painting. Organise the children into pairs and provide each pair with a different search engine to find the same painting. Ask them to time how long it takes, and note whether they are able to locate what they want from the website, and how easy it was to find what they wanted.

Share the children's evaluations at the end of the lesson and note together the most useful way to find the information – by setting up an advanced or complex search using any search engine.

DIFFERENTIATION
Work alongside lower attaining children, helping them to identify and enter the key words accurately. Higher attaining children should use www.yahooligans.com or a similar search engine for children, to locate the information and note the list of useful websites it finds.

WHERE NEXT
Challenge the children to locate information to help their research into other topics in the same way.

ASSESSMENT
Note the children's evaluations of the websites they found. Note whether they used the criteria discussed in the lesson about the speed of locating the information, the usefulness of the information found and whether the complex or simple search was the most useful.

LEARNING OUTCOMES
The children will learn to evaluate the usefulness of websites to their research and note how more efficient an advanced or complex search is to find precise information quickly.

FURTHER ICT CHALLENGES
Find a poster
Challenge the children to use Yahoo (it should take them to postershop.com), or a similar search engine,

to set up a search into where they could buy a poster of one of the paintings. They should think about which key words to use in the advanced search, and evaluate how quickly the matches are found. Ask, *How many matches are there? Can you refine the search to reduce this number?*

Book club

Prompt the children to set up an advanced search to find where they can buy a copy of the latest Harry Potter book.

LANDSCAPE PHOTOGRAPHS

SUBJECT: ART AND DESIGN. QCA UNIT: 6C A SENSE OF PLACE.

LEARNING OBJECTIVE

To collect visual information to help develop ideas about capturing images in the environment.

THINKING OBJECTIVE

To collect, match and analyse information.

THINKING SKILLS

The children will collect interesting images from their visit using a camera and through sketching. They will talk about why they chose to sketch or photograph the items they did before looking for matching features in paintings by famous artists. This match could be in terms of similar objects amd compositions, style, use of colour and light. The children will analyse how the artist has created these effects and consider these when matching them to their own sketches or photographs.

WHAT YOU NEED

A camera; sketchbooks or paper; clipboards; sketching materials; postcards and prints of paintings of landscapes and buildings by different artists, for example *Une Baignade, Asnières* by Seurat, suitable paintings by Dali, *Paris Street, Rainy Day* by Gustave Caillebotte.

WHAT TO DO

When you go on your visit, take snaps of interesting parts of the landscape or buildings. Let the children share the camera so that they take ownership of the collection. At times during the visit, ask them to make quick sketches of those features they find particularly interesting, such as a cloud formation, a chimney, a door knocker or other small feature in the landscape, such as a tree or stream.

Look at the photographs on return to the classroom and talk about why the children thought the item was particularly interesting. Ask, *Was it the colour, shape, size, pattern or some other reason, such as the light falling through the trees or the shadow of the tree on the ground?* Look at one of the paintings of a landscape which contains an item which matches a feature the children have collected, such as where the light falls through the trees, or a building which has the same interesting chimney. Talk with the children about the other items in the painting, and analyse how the artist has created certain effects, such as the contrasts of colour, the way he creates light and dark patches, how he shows perspective by making the items in the background smaller. Match the photograph to this particular painting.

Look at one of the children's sketches and ask them to say why they chose to sketch this particular item. Ask, *Did they like the colour, shape, form or pattern? Was there some other reason?* Invite them to find a painting which has something in common with their sketch.

Organise the children into pairs within groups and, giving each group postcards and prints from which to choose, ask them to select one of their sketches and to tell each other why they chose to sketch this particular item. The pairs should then find a painting that they think matches the sketch in some way, perhaps because it is the same study, the same colour or has a similar interesting shape. Then ask them to choose a photograph from their collections and to talk about what makes it interesting. Again, they should match it to a painting.

As a class, talk about some of the pairings. Invite the children to say why they sketched the particular item and why they think it matches the painting they have chosen.

DIFFERENTIATION
Provide higher attaining children with more obscure paintings to match with their own sketches and photographs, such as a work by Seurat or a piece of abstract art by Picasso. With less able children use prints of paintings which contain similar items to match, such as paintings containing the same type of buildings, or landscape features such as trees and streams.

this analysis to match certain aspects of this painting to their own sketches or photographs.

LEARNING OUTCOMES
The children will consider different colours, shapes and patterns in the landscape or buildings around them and collect these as sketches and/or photographs to use in their own paintings. They will analyse how famous artists have used the same items and effects to create certain images, moods and feelings.

FURTHER ART AND DESIGN CHALLENGES
The Industrial Revolution
Challenge the children to analyse how different artists represent the machine age in their landscape paintings. Paintings to use include *Les Constructeurs* by Leger, *States of Mind* by Boccioni, and many paintings by Lowry.

Colour spread
Prompt the children to analyse how different artists use colour in landscape paintings to create certain effects and moods. Paintings to use include *Rain, Steam and Speed* by Turner which uses yellows to create an effect of the train rushing towards you at speed; *Collioure* by Derain who uses reds and oranges to depict the heat in his landscapes of the south of France; *Nocturne in Black and Gold: The Falling Rocket* by Whistler which uses splashes of gold to light up the dusk.

WHERE NEXT
Prompt the children to use the collection to plan and paint a landscape picture to reflect the school visit.

ASSESSMENT
Assess the children's collections and note whether they can say why they chose to sketch or photograph those particular items. Listen as the children talk to their partner, and note how well they analyse the different techniques that have been used in each painting to create perspectives, light and shade and certain moods and effects. Note whether they use

COACH MUSIC

SUBJECT: MUSIC. QCA UNIT: 18 JOURNEY INTO SPACE.

LEARNING OBJECTIVE
To consider the feelings evoked by different music.

THINKING OBJECTIVE
To evaluate information (judging quality).

THINKING SKILLS
The children will think about the feelings they are likely to have when going to and returning from their visit. They will consider the styles of music to include on a compilation tape which will contrast some of these feelings, for example calming effects for the

journey there, and a sing-along followed by quieter music to listen to on their return. They will evaluate the quality of the different pieces of music suggested in terms of the feelings they evoke, and choose pieces to include on the tape to suit the wishes of everyone in the class.

WHAT YOU NEED
Large sheets of paper; writing materials; CDs, tapes and stereos on which to play and record these.

WHAT TO DO
Explain to the children that you want to make a compilation tape to play on the way to the venue and another to play on the return journey. Ask the children to suggest how you can go about this task. Collect their ideas for the process of research.

Talk about how the children might feel on the way and on the return journey. List these down the left-hand side of the large sheet of paper. Down the right-hand side, list the kind of music the children need to find that *contrasts* with the feelings. For example, link excited feelings with calming music, and boredom with sing-along music. Allow the children time to work in groups to research and evaluate the pieces of music they want to include. When each group has compiled a list of suggested music for each journey, share the lists and compile the different pieces into one list. As a class, agree which pieces are most suitable to evoke a calming effect for the journey to the venue and mark these with a red dot. Note those that should be included on the return journey and mark these with a green dot. Split the children into two groups and ask them to agree the order in which the music should be recorded.

DIFFERENTIATION
Invite lower attaining children to concentrate on one type of music only. For example, ask them to make a list of their favourite songs and music and to identify those which will have a calming effect to listen to on the journey to the venue. Alternatively, ask them to think of suitable sing-along songs to sing on the first part of the return journey. Higher attaining children can be asked to evaluate the quality of the music in terms of being fun to sing-along to but that will still have a calming effect to prevent the children from getting too excited!

WHERE NEXT
Challenge the children to locate the pieces of music on CDs and tapes, and to record them onto a compilation tape. They should evaluate the quality of each piece of music in terms of whether it has the required effect.

ASSESSMENT
Listen to the children as they link the pieces of music to the feelings each one evokes and evaluate its quality in terms of whether it has a calming effect, stops the boredom or lets the children listen quietly.

LEARNING OUTCOMES
The children will learn to evaluate the quality of music in terms of the feelings it evokes as they listen. They will judge this quality by noting the feelings it needs to contrast.

FURTHER MUSIC CHALLENGES
Emotional music
Play extracts of music and ask the children to evaluate the quality in terms of how it evokes feelings. Note whether each extract makes them feel lively, excited, happy, sad, frightened and so on. Ask them to suggest suitable times to play this music, for example to cheer them up or take their minds off something.

Film scores
Listen to pieces of music from films and ask the children to evaluate their quality in terms of setting the mood of the film. Challenge them to identify the kind of film the music is depicting, for example mystery, horror, science fiction, adventure, love, comedy or cartoon, before telling them the name of the film and the genre.